Into His Presence

Other Books by Charles Stanley from Thomas Nelson Publishers

Into His Presence

AN IN TOUCH® DEVOTIONAL

CHARLES STANLEY

OLIVER NELSON

THOMAS NELSON PUBLISHERS
Nashville

ISBN 0-7852-6854-5

Printed in the United States of America
1 2 3 4 5 6 BVG 05 04 03 02 01 00

Contents

Introduction

THE MOUNTAINTOP EXPERIENCE

The biblical record is filled with stories of men and women who encountered God's presence in the solitude of the mountains. It was on Mt. Moriah that Abraham was established as the father of nations. During Moses' time alone on Mt. Sinai, God revealed His glory; and Jesus often retreated to the quiet of the mountainside to pray to the Father.

This devotional focuses on mountaintop experiences revealed in the Scriptures. But whether your daily times with God take place in the solitude of a garden or a restful retreat in the mountains, you are invited to journey through the pages of this devotional and discover a new level of intimate encounters with God.

During the coming months we will learn about the journey to the mountains. In January, we will ascend the mountain of the Lord described in Psalm 15 to fellowship in holiness with God. In February, we will tarry at Mount Zion, where the prophet predicted the word of the Law would flow to the nations. March will find us climbing the mountain with Jesus to learn to pray (Matt. 14:23). During the month of April, we will cross into the promised land to survey "our mountain of inheritance" as we discover who we are in Christ.

The month of May will allow us to follow in the footsteps of Abraham as he ascended Mt. Moriah to worship God. We will travel with Jesus to the mount of temptation during the month of June, learning strategies for overcoming the snares of the enemy. July will allow us to grow in faith as we learn the principles of moving mountains of difficulty (Matt. 17:20). In August we will travel to Mount Carmel with Elijah to learn the strategies of spiritual warfare that will defeat the enemy.

September spotlights God and His relationship with us as we study Jesus' teachings on the mount of the Beatitudes. During October, we will join with Elijah as we come to know the voice of God. During November, we will learn from Caleb that a mountain of difficult challenges often results in the ecstasy of victory. Finally, in December, we will climb the mount of ascension with Jesus and His disciples and we will hear the promise of His return and focus on the hope that inspires.

The spiritual status quo is common ground for too many Christians. Many of us settle down to live at a level that is far below God's will for us. All the while, God longs to take us to new heights, to reveal His glory, and draw us into His presence. Our life in Christ can be an exciting adventure of faith where we can move out of the mundane valleys of this world to explore new realms.

Listen carefully, and you can hear the voice of the Father calling you to the safety and quiet of the mountains . . . "For behold, He who forms mountains, and creates the wind, who declares to man what His thought is, and makes the morning darkness, who treads the high places of the earth—the LORD God of Hosts is His name" (Amos 4:13).

Into His Presence

JANUARY

Holiness

MOUNTAIN: Mountain of the Lord's holiness

KEY VERSES: Psalm 15:1–5

LORD, who may abide in Your tabernacle?
Who may dwell in Your holy hill?
He who walks uprightly,
And works righteousness,
And speaks the truth in his heart;
He who does not backbite with his tongue,
Nor does evil to his neighbor,
Nor does he take up a reproach against his friend;
In whose eyes a vile person is despised,
But he honors those who fear the LORD;
He who swears to his own hurt and does not change;
He who does not put out his money at usury,
Nor does he take a bribe against the innocent.
He who does these things shall never be moved.

Intimacy with God

SCRIPTURE READING: Matthew 17:1–9   KEY VERSE: Psalm 15:1

LORD, who may abide in Your tabernacle?
Who may dwell in Your holy hill?

Matthew 17:1–9 is a dramatic example of how God pulls us aside to reveal Himself to us. The Lord had been with His disciples more than two years, and it was time for three of them to rise to a higher spiritual level. Warren Wiersbe explains,

> Peter could not understand why the Son of God would submit to evil men and willingly suffer. The Transfiguration was God's way of teaching Peter that Jesus is glorified when we deny ourselves, take up our cross, and follow Him.
>
> The world's philosophy is "Save yourself" but the Christian's philosophy is "Yield yourself to God!" As He stood there in glory, Jesus proved to the three disciples that surrender always leads to glory. First the suffering, then the glory; first the cross, then the crown.
>
> Each of the three disciples would have a need for this important truth. James would be the first of the disciples to die (Acts 12:1–2). John would be the last of the disciples to die, but he would go through severe persecution on the Isle of Patmos (Revelation 1:9). Peter would experience many occasions of suffering and would, in the end, give his life for Christ (John 21:15–19).

Intimacy, when cultivated, yields an inner strength that is not shaken by trial or tragedy. As you seek to experience God, seek to know His intimate side, the part of Him that longs to experience your closeness.

Having increased intimacy with You, dear Lord. That is my prayer today. My heart and soul cry out for it.

Living Clean in a Dirty World

SCRIPTURE READING: 2 Corinthians 6:14–18   KEY VERSE: John 8:12

Jesus spoke to them again, saying, "I am the light of the world. He who follows Me shall not walk in darkness, but have the light of life."

How do you live clean in a dirty world? One of the first steps toward discovering this comes when you realize that God has given you a different nature from that of the world.

In 2 Corinthians 6:14, Paul asked, "What communion has light with darkness?" If you are a believer, the light of God's salvation burns within you. Jesus is the Light of the World. He told His followers, "He who follows Me shall not walk in the darkness, but have the light of life" (John 8:12).

While you remain physically in the world, your eternal place of residence is in heaven. Through Jesus Christ, God has purified your life. Binding association with the world only darkens the light of Christ's presence within you.

God instructed the nation of Israel to keep the lamps in the temple lit throughout the day and night. Only the very best olive oil was to be burned in the lamps. However, the people became complacent in their devotion to the Lord and began burning cheaper oil. As a result, smoke filled the temple, blackening its walls.

This is what happens to us when we fail to keep ourselves pure before the Lord. We think our association with the world will not harm us, but it blackens our lives. Then the clarity and brightness of God's life within us are dimmed. Ask Him to reveal to you any impurity in your life so you can remove it and live clean in a dirty world.

Dear Lord, reveal any impurities in my life so that I can seek Your forgiveness and live clean in a dirty world.

Holy in Behavior

SCRIPTURE READING: 1 Peter 1:14–16   KEY VERSE: Leviticus 11:44

I am the LORD your God. You shall therefore consecrate yourselves, and you shall be holy; for I am holy.

God commanded Israel to be holy because He is holy. He also admonished them to remain clean spiritually by not becoming involved in any impurity—greed, lust, idolatry, or wrongful attitudes. In other words, they had to abstain from compromising the sincerity of their faith, love, and devotion to the Lord.

Why was doing that so important, and is this commandment relative to us today? God gave Israel this instruction because He loved them and wanted them to experience the goodness of His blessing. God cannot bless disobedience.

Satan has one goal in mind for the lost man: keep him spiritually lost and estranged from God. The enemy's goal for the believer is to discourage him and cause him to compromise his faith by yielding to temptation.

The enemy accomplishes this by tempting us to sin and then by accusing us before the Father. When we yield to temptation, we stifle the flow of God's grace in our lives, and our spiritual insight becomes fuzzier.

There is only one way to live, and that is in purity and devotion to Christ. The apostle Peter wrote, "As obedient children, not conforming yourselves to the former lusts, as in your ignorance; but as He who called you is holy, you also, be holy in all your conduct" (1 Peter 1:14–15).

Heavenly Father, keep me from temptation. Don't let me stifle the flow of Your grace in my life.

Transparency Before God

SCRIPTURE READING: Matthew 26:36–46   KEY VERSE: Matthew 26:38

He said to them, "My soul is exceedingly sorrowful, even to death. Stay here and watch with Me."

Transparency is an oft-overlooked element in our growing closer to Jesus Christ. Intimacy with the Lord requires our full, humble, and honest openness before Him.

Jesus Himself was a wonderful model of openness as He dealt with His disciples. For instance, we discover in today's reading that in the Garden of Gethsemane, Jesus shared with the disciples His anguish over His upcoming crucifixion and brief separation from God the Father.

Knowing that the sins of the entire world were about to be cast upon Him, Jesus grieved, even to the point of near death. God, clothed in human flesh, was being completely honest, open, and forthright about His emotions. That is how Christ would have us react to Him.

A proud, arrogant, egotistical, self-sufficient Christianity bristles at the thought of such transparency: "Why should I burden God with this when I can handle it myself? I'm just not going to deal with God about this." Such thinking and behavior go against everything for which God created us.

However, God cherishes and honors a humble, contrite spirit from someone trying to be himself before the Lord. Confess sin, worry, doubt, and fear. He already knows all, but your willingness to intimately share with Him all the details speaks volumes about the bent of your heart.

Father, I confess my worry, doubts, and fears. Cleanse me from sin and let me be transparent before You.

Intimacy with Jesus

SCRIPTURE READING: Luke 10:18–20   KEY VERSE: John 14:9

Jesus said to him, "Have I been with you so long, and yet you have not known Me, Philip? He who has seen Me has seen the Father; so how can you say, 'Show us the Father'?"

Concerning John 14:9, Oswald Chambers commented,

These words were not spoken as a rebuke, nor even with surprise; Jesus was encouraging Philip to draw closer. Yet the last person we get intimate with is Jesus. Before Pentecost the disciples knew Jesus as the One who gave them power to conquer demons and to bring about a revival (Luke 10:18–20). It was a wonderful intimacy, but there was a much closer intimacy to come: "I have called you friends" (John 15:15). True friendship is rare on earth. It means identifying with someone in thought, heart, and spirit. The whole experience of life is designed to enable us to enter into this closest relationship with Jesus Christ. We receive His blessings and know His Word, but do we really know Him?

It is a joy to Jesus when a disciple takes time to walk more intimately with Him. The bearing of fruit is always shown in Scripture to be the visible result of an intimate relationship with Jesus Christ (John 15:1–4).

Once we get intimate with Jesus we are never lonely and we never lack for understanding or compassion. We can continually pour out our hearts to Him without being perceived as overly emotional or pitiful. The Christian who is truly intimate with Jesus will never draw attention to himself but will only show the evidence of a life where Jesus is completely in control.

I want to be truly intimate with You, Jesus. Let my life demonstrate that You are in complete control.

The Initiator of Love

SCRIPTURE READING: Psalm 18:1–6   KEY VERSE: 1 John 4:10

In this is love, not that we loved God, but that He loved us and sent His Son to be the propitiation for our sins.

From the beginning of time, God has been the Initiator of love (1 John 4:10). In his book *Lectures in Systematic Theology*, Henry Thiessen writes, "He is unlike the gods of the heathen, who hate and are angry, and the god of the philosopher, who is cold and indifferent." God loves us with a personal and intimate love.

Those who have yet to discover the intimacy of God often view Him as being cool and demanding toward His creation. But nothing is farther from the truth. Even in the Old Testament, we find God constantly moving toward mankind in an effort to reveal more of Himself on an intimate basis. Love motivates Him to do this.

In fact, love is the motivating factor of every true relationship. It motivated the heart of God not to destroy man in the Garden of Eden. And it was the one thing that motivated Him to deliver Israel from the Egyptians.

Love brought down the walls of Jericho, and love was the motivation behind the coming of Christ. Love took our place on Calvary's cross and later rose from the grave. And love reaches out to us each day with freshness and hope.

You were created by love to live within its embrace. Many wonder how God could love them so deeply. But He does. He is love, and He loves you and me.

Heavenly Father, I thank You that You are not a cold, indifferent God. Thank You for reaching out to me in love.

At the Feet of Jesus

SCRIPTURE READING: Luke 10:38–42   KEY VERSE: Luke 10:42

One thing is needed, and Mary has chosen that good part, which will not be taken away from her.

Can you imagine what it was like to sit at the feet of Jesus? Mary of Bethany knew. So did Peter and James and John. They all knew what it was like to be in the presence of Eternal Love. Yet even though Jesus was with them, they still did not have the fullness of God that we enjoy today through the presence of the Holy Spirit.

You may be thinking: *That was fine for Mary and the others, but I am so easily drawn away by temptation. I love God, but there are so many other things that grab my attention. What does He think of me, and how can I be sure He will accept me when I come to Him?*

God will never turn you away. Those who followed the Savior knew this because they witnessed His love and acceptance each day. Mary was at the Savior's feet because she chose to be there. God's love drew her, but she decided to go to Him. The same was true for John and Peter and the others.

There always will be temptations vying for our hearts, but we must decide who or what we love the most. When it comes to God and the things of this world, there is only one choice.

Those who find themselves at the Savior's feet choose humble devotion over worldly prestige, power, and fame. Love is never complex when it comes to God. He loves us without hesitation, and this is what He longs from us in return.

Thank You for Your love and acceptance, Father. I am grateful that You never turn me away.

The Source of Lasting Love

SCRIPTURE READING: Luke 15:11–24   KEY VERSE: Psalm 5:11

Let all those rejoice who put their trust in You;
Let them ever shout for joy,
because You defend them;
Let those also who love Your name
Be joyful in You.

When was the last time you heard the words *I love you?* Many have the opportunity to hear them every day. Countless others go weeks, even months, never hearing these words.

In *The Friendship Factor,* Alan Loy McGinnnis reports,

> In 1925 a tiny sanitarium for mental patients was established on a farm outside Topeka, Kansas. At a time when the "rest cure" was in vogue in psychiatry, a team of physicians were determined to create a family atmosphere among their patients.
>
> The nurses were given specific directions on how they were to behave toward specific patients: "Let him know that you value and like him." "Be kind but firm with this woman—don't let her become worse . . ."
>
> Menninger Clinic, using such "revolutionary" methods, has become world famous. Karl Menninger, summing up, said: "Love is the medicine for the sickness of mankind. We can live if we have love."

God told us from the very beginning that in love—His love—we find the answer to all our needs as well as healing for our broken souls.

When your heart is anchored to the heart of Jesus Christ, you will find Him near and always eager to confirm His personal love for you. The love of the world will pass away, but God's love is guaranteed never to fade. He is the Source of all true, lasting love.

Dear God, I thank You that in Your love I find the answer to all my needs
and healing for my broken soul.

Your Greatest Desire

SCRIPTURE READING: Matthew 16:13–19   KEY VERSE: John 6:48

I am the bread of life.

Part of the disciples' training was practical application. Jesus would teach, then He would bring the lesson to life through a parable or a real-life experience. By walking on water, He demonstrated supernatural abilities. Withdrawing to be alone with His heavenly Father, He portrayed His devotion and set an example for His disciples to do the same.

A good example was the feeding of the four thousand; they were hungry and Jesus fed them. It was His way of teaching that He was the "bread of life" (John 6:48). Peter was so overwhelmed by all he had witnessed, he made the following confession, "You are the Christ, the Son of the living God" (Matt. 16:16).

Jesus came to point men to God. He also came to identify personally with each one of us. The people prayed that Jesus was the One who would set Israel free from years of Roman oppression. They didn't understand His greatest desire was to restore the love for God that man had lost.

What is your greatest desire? Is it to know God's love and affection? During the Transfiguration, Peter was so overcome with emotion, he could only whisper his heart's desire: "Rabbi, it is good for us to be here; and let us make three tabernacles" (Mark 9:5). Jesus was much more than flesh and bone; He was God, and all Peter wanted was to be found hidden in His love.

Dear God, my greatest desire is to know Your love and affection. Reveal Yourself to me in a new and greater dimension.

Difficult Lessons

SCRIPTURE READING: Matthew 16:21–28   KEY VERSE: Matthew 16:22

Peter took Him aside and began to rebuke Him, saying, "Far be it from You, Lord; this shall not happen to You!"

Often the lessons surrounding love are difficult to learn. Peter and the others discovered this one afternoon as they listened to Jesus teach God's truth. For the first time, Christ's words tore at their minds, filling them with anguish and fear.

The Lord explained how He had to go to Jerusalem where He would suffer and die. Up until that point, the disciples had not fully heard what Jesus was saying to them. But now they did, and their hearts were wild with fear. Peter immediately tried to rebuke the Lord by saying, "This shall not happen to You!" (Matt 16:22).

But Jesus stood firm. Like the others, Peter could not yet see the strength of eternal love supporting and protecting the Son of man.

Perhaps you are going through a difficult season, and you don't understand why God has allowed you to suffer. Be assured that God loves you and that He has a plan for your life. Even when darkness seems to surround you, God is at work. His love never stops, never gives up, and never gives in to devastating circumstances.

Jesus understood how painful it would be for His disciples to hear of His impending death. He administered comfort when it was needed and eternal hope when the emotional darkness became too much for them to bear—and He will do the same for you.

Father, thank You for Your comforting presence in the dark times. I am so glad that You love me and have a wonderful plan for my life.

Unconditional Love

SCRIPTURE READING: 1 John 4:13–21   KEY VERSE: Romans 5:8

God demonstrates His own love toward us, in that while we were still sinners, Christ died for us.

God is not afraid to love us just the way we are, with all our flaws and short-comings. He is secure in who He is. Therefore, He loves us unconditionally and without regard to our failures.

He created us not to live apart from His love but to be partakers of His holiness. However, He knows that there will be times when we look and act unholy. Our misguided actions do not erase or stop the love of God. Sin can separate us from His blessings and intimate fellowship, but there is never a time when God withholds His love.

In loving us, God knows that we can never give back to Him what He has given to us, but He does require us to love one another with the same love that He has demonstrated toward us.

In his book *Mighty Is Your Hand,* David Hazard paraphrases the words of Andrew Murray,

> In our life with people, the one thing on which everything depends is love. The spirit of forgiveness is the spirit of love. Because God is love, He forgives. Consequently, it is only as we are dwelling in the love of God that we can forgive as God forgives.
>
> Our love for others is the evidence of our love for God. It is our grounds for confidence before God in prayer. It is our assurance that our prayer will be heard (1 John 4:20).

Let your love for God be a symbol of love and forgiveness to all you meet.

Lord, let Your presence shine through my life as a symbol of Your unconditional love and forgiveness.

The Power of God's Love

SCRIPTURE READING: 1 Cor. 13:1–13   KEY VERSE: 1 Cor. 13:7

Love . . . bears all things, believes all things, hopes all things, endures all things.

The house was in the pathway of the storm. As the winds blew, the telephone and electrical lines were blown and stretched to the point of separation. Finally, the few lines connecting to the electrical transformer gave way, and darkness fell across the city.

God created us to live in the light of His love. He never meant for the storms of life to separate us from Him. However, many times this is exactly what happens. Without thinking, we overlook the approaching storm clouds of temptation and yield to their confusion and fury. Only Christ has the ability to restore the power of love—His love—to our lives once it has been severed. In repentance we find that He forgives our sins and also restores and refreshes our weary, storm-driven lives.

Stop counting the number of times you have failed the Lord. Look up into the eyes of His eternal love where you can find unconditional acceptance. Many wonder what God wants from them. He desires for each of us to experience the goodness of His intimate love and personal care.

His love frees you from the bondage of guilt and shame. And His love encourages you to try once more whenever you fall. This is the power of God's love: love believes all good things (1 Cor. 13:7).

Dear Lord, please forgive my sin, restore me, and refresh my weary, storm-driven life.

The Strength to Say No

SCRIPTURE READING: 1 Timothy 4:6–8   KEY VERSE: Romans 6:19

I speak in human terms because of the weakness of your flesh. For just as you presented your members as slaves of uncleanness, and of lawlessness leading to more lawlessness, so now present your members as slaves of righteousness for holiness.

An inevitable result of walking with the Lord in daily relationship is an increased desire to see your character shaped according to His will. In his book *The Pursuit of Holiness,* Jerry Bridges explains,

As unbelievers, we formerly gave ourselves to developing habits of unholiness—what Paul called "ever increasing wickedness" (Romans 6:19). Every time we sinned . . . we were developing habits of ever-increasing wickedness . . .

But now, Paul declared, just as we formerly gave ourselves to these wicked habits, so we are to give ourselves to developing habits of holiness . . . We are to put off our old self—our sinful disposition and habits—and put on the new self, with its character and habits of holiness. To train ourselves in godliness (1 Timothy 4:7) is to discipline and structure our lives so that we develop godly habits . . .

Though we are to deal with these habits of unholiness, we must not try to do it in our own strength. Breaking sinful habits must be done in cooperation with the Holy Spirit and in dependence upon Him . . .

Therefore, in dependence on the Holy Spirit, we must systematically work at acquiring the habit of saying no to the sins that so easily entangle us . . . The more we succeed in saying no to our sinful desires, the easier it becomes to say no.

Dear God, break the bondage of sinful habits and desires in my life. Give me the strength to say no!

Spiritual Hunger and Thirst

SCRIPTURE READING: John 7:37–39   KEY VERSE: Psalm 11:7

For the LORD is righteous,
He loves righteousness;
His countenance beholds the upright.

The more you learn about the Lord, the more you want to know Him. That's what happens when you get just a taste of His goodness—you can't get enough of His fellowship. In her book *Lord, Only You Can Change Me*, Kay Arthur observes:

> God's righteousness begins with a dissatisfaction, a yearning. When sin's presence is finally realized, an inner longing is kindled and begins to burn with a slow, steady flame. A longing to be righteous! With every glimpse of God's shining holiness and purity comes an accompanying awareness of self.
>
> Finally the realization comes: "God, You alone are righteous." A hunger and thirst for righteousness—His righteousness—awakens and grows. But how is that hunger and thirst to be satisfied?
>
> We know we cannot quench it in ourselves, so we run to the fountain of living waters and receive the gift of the indwelling Holy Spirit. He alone can lead us into a life of righteousness, by leading us into the truth . . .
>
> Jesus is the fountainhead of God's righteousness. Oh Beloved, do you see it? You can be as righteous as you want to be! How?
>
> By totally depending upon God. By yearning for Him more and more. Ours is to be an ever-increasing hunger and thirst.

Satisfy my spiritual hunger and thirst for You, O God. Lead me into a life of righteousness through the continuing revelation of Your truth.

The Lover of Your Soul

SCRIPTURE READING: Hosea 11:1–9 KEY VERSES: Lamentations 3:22–23

Through the LORD's mercies we are not consumed,
Because His compassions fail not.
They are new every morning;
Great is Your faithfulness.

The nation of Israel grieved God's heart continually by chasing after other gods and withholding their devotion and adoration from Him. To provide the errant nation with a living illustration of His righteous grief and anger, God gave the prophet Hosea an unusual command.

He told him to wed a harlot and begin a family with her. Without questioning, Hosea obeyed and took the prostitute Gomer to be his wife. Though she wandered and continued in an unfaithful lifestyle, Hosea obeyed the Lord and did not cast her away. The book of Hosea contains God's words to the people of Israel as revealed through Hosea's dramatic example of steadfast love.

The moving poetry of this book also reveals the longing of God for uninterrupted intimacy with His people. Can you feel the agony of separation in these words?

How can I give you up, Ephraim?
How can I hand you over, Israel? . . .
My heart churns within Me,
My sympathy is stirred.
I will not execute the fierceness of My anger. (Hos. 11:8–9)

God longs for the same intimate relationship with you. He would do anything to get your love—and He did. In the most radical display of all time, He provided His Son, Jesus Christ, as the means to make such fellowship possible. God is the passionate and faithful Lover of your soul.

Dear God, thank You for displaying Your love by giving Your Son, Jesus Christ, to restore my fellowship with You.

Your Best Friend

SCRIPTURE READING: John 15:12–17   KEY VERSE: Proverbs 18:24

A man who has friends must himself be friendly,
But there is a friend who sticks closer than a brother.

Do you remember having a best friend as a child? This person went every-where with you, from recess in the schoolyard to adventures around the neighborhood. You had small fights and squabbles occasionally, but you stuck by each other when a difficulty came along.

As an adult, you may have a friend like this today, but you are certainly aware that such friends are rare indeed. The blessing of a friend who under-stands your deepest thoughts and needs and loves you through the hard times is a gift from the Lord. It is important to recognize, however, that the best friend in the whole world can still let you down at times. It is not a cliché to state that Jesus is your only true Friend.

Joseph Scriven, an Irishman born in 1819, discovered this truth in a pow-erful way. The night before he was to be married, his beloved fiancée drowned. Grieving deeply, Scriven decided to move to Canada and begin a new life, ded-icated entirely to letting the Lord use him in others' lives. Out of this experi-ence and several others, he penned the words to the favorite hymn "What a Friend We Have in Jesus."

Can you imagine writing this poetry after going through such pain? Scriven saw the Lord's faithfulness. He knew firsthand that when all earthly supports and emotional props disappear, Jesus is there to love and comfort eternally.

Jesus, You are the best Friend I will ever have. Thank You for Your faithful-ness and this wonderful relationship we share.

A True Friend

SCRIPTURE READING: John 14:1–18   KEY VERSE: Proverbs 17:17

A friend loves at all times,
And a brother is born for adversity.

Have you ever had a friend who liked you because you were fun to be with and put on a good appearance? However, the moment your life took a turn for the worse, you found him distancing himself from you. If you have experienced such rejection, you're not alone. Jesus experienced all kinds of rejection.

And in some ways that rejection continues. Perhaps He asks something of us that we think is too harsh or requires something we don't want to give up. We back off in hopes that He will leave us alone. Once Jesus began talking about a deeper life commitment, many of His followers left.

The disciples told Him that His words were too severe. But Jesus was not persuaded by human opinion, and He held fast to the message the Father had given Him. His words were meant to convict while separating those who would remain with Him from those who would leave.

What kind of Friend is Jesus? He is the kind who willingly laid down His life as payment for your sins—past, present, and future. Without complaint He bore all your sorrows and suffering, while pledging never to leave or forsake you (John 14:18).

He is a Friend who sticks closer than a brother. And before you whisper your most intimate prayer, He knows your heart and rushes to your side.

Jesus, thank You for laying down Your life for my sin and bearing my sorrow and suffering. Thank You that You will never leave me or forsake me.

A Passion to Know Him

SCRIPTURE READING: John 4:1–42   KEY VERSE: James 4:8

Draw near to God and He will draw near to you. Cleanse your hands, you sinners; and purify your hearts, you double-minded.

If you have ever had a best friend, you know what it feels like not to be able to get enough time with him. When you thoroughly enjoy someone's company, it is no trouble at all to arrange ways to spend time with that person. Going a season of time without seeing your friend can be a real emotional letdown.

The same is true of your relationship with the Lord. Jesus is your most intimate Friend, the One who loves you with agape love. If you go a period of time without fellowshipping with Him, you will experience the effects of separation from your very lifeline—an inner sadness and loneliness that can be satisfied only by drawing near to Him again (James 4:8).

The more time you spend with the Lord and in meditation on His truth, the greater your passion to know Him. The Samaritan woman at the well discovered this principle in the short amount of time she spent talking with Jesus.

When Jesus offered her living water, her curiosity was piqued. She was flooded with many emotions, including surprise and wonder. The woman was so excited about this new relationship that she left her water pot and ran to tell others in town (John 4:1–42).

That is what happens when you know the Lord; your excitement grows and, with it, your fervor for sharing His good news with others.

Give me a passion to know You better, dear Lord. Then give me a fervor for sharing the good news of the gospel with others.

Knowing God

SCRIPTURE READING: Psalm 34:1–22   KEY VERSE: Psalm 34:8

Oh, taste and see that the LORD is good;
Blessed is the man who trusts in Him!

K nowing God is not simply an intellectual proposition. You "know" God in a manner much similar to the process of getting to know a human companion.

J. I. Packer explains in his book *Knowing God*:

> Knowing God is a matter of personal involvement—mind, will, and feeling. It would not, indeed, be a fully personal relationship otherwise. To get to know another person, you have to commit yourself to his company and interests, and be ready to identify yourself with his concerns. Without this, your relationship with him can only be superficial and flavorless.
>
> "Taste and see that the Lord is good," says the psalmist (Psalm 34:8). To "taste" is, as we say, to "try" a mouthful of something, with a view to appreciating its flavor. A dish may look good, and be well recommended by the cook, but we do not know its real quality till we have tasted it.
>
> Similarly, we do not know another person's real quality till we have "tasted" the experience of friendship. Friends are, so to speak, communicating flavors to each other all the time, by sharing their attitudes both toward each other (think of people in love) and toward everything else that is of common concern . . .
>
> The same applies to the Christian's knowledge of God, which, as we have seen, is itself a relationship between friends.

Dear heavenly Father, strengthen the bonds of our relationship. I really want to know You better.

Spiritual Pride

SCRIPTURE READING: 1 Corinthians 10:1–13   KEY VERSE: Luke 18:11

The Pharisee stood and prayed thus with himself, "God, I thank You that I am not like other men—extortioners, unjust, adulterers, or even as this tax collector."

Most believers would balk at the idea of being labeled as having a "holier than thou" attitude. We think of classic examples of spiritual arrogance, such as the Pharisee in Jesus' story who got on his knees to thank God that he was not as bad as some other people (Luke 18:11).

What creeps into our hearts more often is a subtle spiritual pride, a smug security that we are not vulnerable to certain kinds of sins anymore. Joni Eareckson Tada illustrates this issue in her devotional *Diamonds in the Dust*.

"You'll never catch me doing that!" one might say. Oh yeah?

Upright and obedient, Noah stood alone against a carousing, lustful world that drank itself silly. Who would have thought that Noah would end up drunk?

Bold and courageous David was brave enough to go up against Goliath, the warrior giant of the Philistines; later on he made believe that he was a madman for fear of his enemies.

And consider Elijah. We take him to be a rather brave man, wielding the sword of God's vengeance against tens of thousands. But the threat of one woman sends him into suicidal despair . . .

Just when you think you know yourself, you do or say something that seems so out of character. But it's not . . . Don't be surprised. Just be careful that you, too, don't fall.

Keep me from spiritual pride, dear Lord. Let me walk in true holiness.

A Man After God's Heart

SCRIPTURE READING: 2 Samuel 23:13–17   KEY VERSE: Acts 13:22

When He had removed him, He raised up for them David as king, to whom also He gave testimony and said, "I have found David the son of Jesse, a man after My own heart, who will do all My will."

Hidden within the text of 2 Samuel 23:13–17 is a revealing detail of King David's life. The Philistines had captured Bethlehem, David's birthplace, and established a garrison there. The city was shut up: no one could go in and no one could leave. David was in his stronghold in the nearby cave of Adullam. There with selected members of his mighty men, David plotted the next attack against the enemy.

There he longingly expressed a desire for a drink of water from the well of Bethlehem. As his men listened to his words, their devotion for their commander was stirred. Three of the men risked their lives by crossing enemy lines to bring a single cup of Bethlehem's water to David. When he saw what they had done, David's heart was humbled. He refused to drink the water, choosing instead to pour it out as a drink offering to God.

David recognized the valor of his men, but he also understood that only God was worthy of such devotion. The other aspect to the story is that David refused to elevate himself above the others.

The entirety of David's heart was humbly committed to God. That is why God said of David: "He is a man after My own heart." In God's eyes, humility is a sign of greatness and obedience a characteristic of those who intimately walk with God.

Dear God, help me walk humbly and obediently with You. Make me a person after Your own heart.

Enjoying God

SCRIPTURE READING: Jeremiah 32:39–41   KEY VERSE: Deuteronomy 30:9

The LORD your God will make you abound in all the work of your hand, in the fruit of your body, in the increase of your livestock, and in the produce of your land for good. For the LORD will again rejoice over you for good as He rejoiced over your fathers.

The *Shorter Catechism* encapsulates the Christian's purpose in this terse statement: "The chief end of man is to glorify God and to enjoy Him forever."

Most committed followers of Christ passionately seek to honor Him. Fewer, however, really know how to enjoy God. Perhaps this is due in part to the misunderstanding of how God feels about you. He takes great pleasure in you.

John Piper writes in *The Pleasure of God:* "God is rejoicing over my good with all His heart and with all His soul. He virtually breaks forth into song when He hits upon a new way to do me good."

Piper continues:

> But the promise is greater yet. Not only does God promise not to run away from doing good to us, He says, "I will rejoice in doing them good" (Jeremiah 32:41). "The Lord will again take delight in prospering you" (Deuteronomy 30:9). There is a kind of eagerness about the beneficence of God. He does not wait for us to come to Him. He seeks us out, because it is His pleasure to do us good.
>
> God is not waiting for us, He is pursuing us . . . I have never forgotten how a great teacher once explained it to me. He said God is like a highway patrolman pursuing you down the interstate with lights flashing and siren blaring to get you to stop—not to give you a ticket, but to give you a message so good it couldn't wait till you get home.

Set me free to enjoy You, dear Lord. Thank You for Your goodness and the blessings You bestow upon me each day.

Experiencing God's Presence

SCRIPTURE READING: Philippians 1:1–30   KEY VERSE: Philippians 2:13

It is God who works in you both to will and to do for His good pleasure.

In the award-winning movie *Chariots of Fire*, Eric Liddell remarked that he felt God's pleasure when he ran. Enjoying our relationship with Christ, or feeling His pleasure while we work and live, is not simple, but certainly possible.

You can enjoy God as you watch Him work through your circumstances (Phil. 1:12; 2:13). Troubling situations can overwhelm us for short or extended seasons. Handling them with an optimistic perspective that God is somehow at work for good is the way to live above difficulties. Trust Him to use your situations for eventual good, as foreboding as they may appear.

Enjoy God as you live under His grace, not law. You don't have to perform to please God. You already are pleasing to Him. Living under grace severs the legalistic mesh of "I must do this" or "I should do that" to gain God's acceptance. You are accepted by grace, and His favor is extended to you freely. God has forgiven you. Forgive yourself.

Enjoy God by learning to live one day at a time. Worrying about the future is a great thief and one that Scripture urges you to avoid by trusting God for your daily needs. Don't get ahead of Him. Accept His provision and daily challenges. Living under a load of anxiety rapidly depletes your joy and peace.

Christ came to give not only eternal life but abundant life as well. That is life to the fullest, and you can experience it!

Father, help me learn to live one day at a time, enjoy You, and experience Your pleasure.

Keeping in Step with God

SCRIPTURE READING: Galatians 5:16–26   KEY VERSE: Galatians 5:25

If we live in the Spirit, let us also walk in the Spirit.

Have you ever held someone's hand as you walked along together? You surely noticed how important it is to maintain the same stride. You can't walk too slowly and you can't walk too fast, at least not without pulling your hand away.

That is what Galatians 5:25 is talking about when it says "walk in the Spirit." The *New International Version* captures the original Greek flavor of the word *walk* here: "Since we live by the Spirit, let us keep in step with the Spirit." The word picture is one of "walking in line with."

When you are not following your fleshly urges to walk at your own pace, you feel the direct guidance of the Holy Spirit step by step along the way. When you are walking in harmony with the Spirit, the fruit of this relationship is evident. It makes sense that the fruit of the Spirit is the subject of the remaining verses of Galatians 5.

How many of these fruits do you see in your attitudes and behavior—love, joy, peace, patience, kindness, goodness, faithfulness, gentleness, and self-control? It is truly an awesome list. As you think through these attributes, remember that they are not the products of a decision to try harder. The fruits of the Spirit are products of a walk with God, a personal relationship with Him. When you keep in step with Him, He keeps your feet on His good path.

Let me keep in step with You, O Lord. Manifest the fruits of Your Spirit in my life.

Worthy Of Praise

SCRIPTURE READING: Philippians 4:5–23   KEY VERSE: Psalm 147:1

Praise the LORD!
For it is good to sing praises to our God;
For it is pleasant, and praise is beautiful.

Whenever you read a passage of Scripture concerning suffering, you almost always find an exhortation to praise God.

It seems an odd mix—the moment when you are enduring the greatest internal stress is the time when you least feel like offering praise and thanksgiving. In her book *31 Days of Praise*, Ruth Myers explains the connection:

> Why do I at times feel reluctant to praise in the midst of everyday trials: when I hear news that makes me anxious about someone I love, or when I face a major disappointment, or when I'm angry or under a lot of pressure?
>
> Could it be that one of Satan's major strategies is to divert us from praise? After all, he knows that God delights in our praise, and that doesn't exactly make him happy. He also detests the rich benefits praise brings to us and others. Or is it simply that our flesh prevails over our spirits, dampening our desire to glorify God? Might it be some of both? . . .
>
> Praise flourishes as you weed and water and fertilize your spiritual garden in which it grows. It becomes more constant as you nurture your soul on God's Word and walk in His ways, depending upon the Holy Spirit. It gets richer and more spontaneous as you grow in your knowledge of how worthy the Lord is to receive honor and glory and praise.

You are worthy to receive praise, O Lord. I praise You today with my whole heart.

The Sin Revealer

SCRIPTURE READING: Hebrews 4:12–16   KEY VERSE: Psalm 77:12

I will also meditate on all Your work,
And talk of Your deeds.

Oscar Wilde's classic novel *The Picture of Dorian Gray* is a chilling exploration of what happens when a person refuses to deal with the sin inside his heart.

In this fantasy tale, the handsome character Dorian commissions a portrait of himself that will capture his good looks. He is so captivated by this picture that he makes a wish—he wants to stay young forever and let the picture "grow old" in his place.

Dorian gets his wish and then uses his youth and attractiveness to fulfill his desires. His motives are self-seeking, vain, and greedy in everything he does. As the years pass, Dorian periodically checks the picture in his back room.

Not only is his face growing old; it becomes gnarled and vicious. Dorian is so ashamed that he covers the picture and refuses to let anyone look at it. The picture has become a horrifying portrait of his soul!

Even though Oscar Wilde did not profess to be a Christian, he understood the effects of sin run rampant. Dorian's picture was his sin revealer, even as God's Word is the instrument of conviction in your life.

When you meditate on Scripture and feel the tug of His Word on your heart, pay attention. God is urging you to confess your sin and experience the renewing power of forgiveness in Christ.

Reveal my sins, O Lord, so I can deal with them. Show me what is really in my heart.

On the Team

SCRIPTURE READING: Colossians 3:1–25   KEY VERSE: Colossians 3:3–4

For you died, and your life is hidden with Christ in God. When Christ who is our life appears, then you also will appear with Him in glory.

In *Living Free in Christ*, Neil Anderson writes:

> While I was pastor, my son, Karl, had established quite a reputation as a soccer player . . . When I accepted an invitation to teach at Talbot School of Theology, it necessitated a move that was very unsettling for Karl. He had to leave behind a team, friends, awards, and recognition.
>
> However, his reputation preceded him to our new location. There, I was called by a soccer club inquiring whether Karl would care to be a part of their team. After the first practice, the coach expressed to me his delight at having Karl as a player, saying what a vital member of the team he was going to be.
>
> Karl practiced with reckless abandonment and afterward approached me with a long look on his face and a profound sense of insecurity that was baffling to me. Finally, he broke the silence: "Well, am I on this team?"
>
> I replied, "Karl, you were already on the team before we came. The coach had already made the necessary provisions, the roster had already been filled out, and your name was on it" . . .
>
> Dear Christian, you, too, are already on the team. Your name is on the roster: it's called the Lamb's Book of Life. "Your life is now hidden with Christ in God. When Christ, who is your life, appears, then you also will appear with him in glory" (Colossians 3:3–4).

Dear heavenly Father, I am so glad that my name is written in the Lamb's Book of Life and that my life is hidden with Christ in You. I'm on Your team!

Freedom from Pride

SCRIPTURE READING: Romans 8:6–9   KEY VERSE: Proverbs 16:18

Pride goes before destruction,
And a haughty spirit before a fall.

C. S. Lewis spoke of pride:

In God you come up against something which is in every respect immeasurably superior to yourself. Unless you know God as that—and, therefore, know yourself as nothing in comparison—you do not know God at all. As long as you are proud you cannot know God. A proud man is always looking down on things and people and, of course, as long as you are looking down, you cannot see something that is above you.

The virtue opposite to it, in Christian morals, is called humility . . . The utmost evil is pride. Unchastity, anger, greed, drunkenness, and all that are mere fleabites in comparison. It was through pride that the devil became the devil. Pride leads to every other vice. It is the complete anti-God state of mind . . .

If you want to find out how proud you are, the easiest way is to ask yourself, "How much do I dislike it when other people snub me, or refuse to take any notice of me, or patronize me, or show off? . . . Is it because I wanted to be the big noise at the party that I am so annoyed at someone else being the big noise?" . . . Pride gets no pleasure out of having something, only out of having more of it than the next man.

The greatest struggle of a believer is with pride. All other sins flow from this one polluted stream. Ask God to free you from pride's grasp. Boundless freedom awaits those who make the journey.

Dear God, free me from pride's grasp. I want to walk humbly with You.

God's Greatest Provision

SCRIPTURE READING: Romans 7:14–25   KEY VERSE: Joshua 24:15

If it seems evil to you to serve the LORD, choose for yourselves this day whom you will serve, whether the gods which your fathers served that were on the other side of the River, or the gods of the Amorites, in whose land you dwell. But as for me and my house, we will serve the LORD.

Paul wrote about the conflict between the believer's new nature and the power of sin. Our sin is rooted in Adam, while our new nature is founded in Jesus Christ. The part of us that is tempted to sin is the part belonging to Adam.

When you accepted Jesus Christ as your Savior, you were given a new nature that is eternally rooted in God's Son. The difficult part is that while you are spiritually a new creature, you live in a fallen world with all kinds of trials and temptations.

God created you with a free will. Therefore, you must choose between right and wrong. Obvious sins such as adultery and murder are easily detected, but what about sins such as envy, jealousy, lying, pride, gossip, and lust? Are you as quick to walk away from them?

Many people toy with sin because their perspective of God is inadequate. They have yet to grasp the full extent of God's love for them. When they do, sin is no longer an option.

Genuine repentance results in changed desires. Allowing your new nature to outshine your old nature is a matter of submitting your life to Jesus Christ on a daily basis. If you keep tripping over the same sin, ask God to reveal the reason why you are struggling. God's greatest provision is His eternal forgiveness.

Dear God, please reveal the reason why I am struggling so that I can deal with my sin and allow my new nature to outshine my old nature.

Fellowship with Jesus

SCRIPTURE READING: John 1:9–14   KEY VERSE: John 1:14

The Word became flesh and dwelt among us, and we beheld His glory,
the glory as of the only begotten of the Father, full of grace and truth.

Before sin entered the world, man enjoyed unbroken fellowship with the Lord. In Genesis, we read that God would come to Adam, walking in the cool of the day. There was a natural flow of fellowship between God and man. No hint of discontentment or pressure emerged—just loving fellowship. However, that came to an abrupt end when man disobeyed God by eating of the tree of knowledge.

God loves you with an everlasting love. He does not have evil in mind for your life but is constantly seeking to bring blessing and hope to encourage you along the way. Man's sin struck the first hurtful blow to the heart of God. For that, man suffered a grave consequence—separation from the abiding presence of God.

The eternal love of God did not burn dim, and God was motivated to send His Son as an atonement for our sins. The birth of Jesus Christ brought restoration to a lost world. God in His grace once again reached out to mankind.

Now we can enjoy what the Old Testament patriarchs could only envision—continual fellowship with almighty God. Just as God walked in the Garden with Adam and Eve, He walks with you. No detail in life is too small for Him, and nothing is too difficult for Him to handle. When you come to Him, He listens and brings hope to whatever you face.

Father, I thank You that there is no detail in my life that is too small for You
to handle. There is no problem too large for You.

Sin Is a Choice

SCRIPTURE READING: James 1:13–16   KEY VERSE: 1 Corinthians 1:29

That no flesh should glory in His presence.

Of all who have ever lived, Eve was the one who could come the closest to using legitimately the phrase "the devil made me do it." And God did not accept this excuse even from Eve, who had the serpent speaking directly to her (Gen. 3). We cannot pass the buck for sinning to anyone else. God wants us to understand the true source of sin so that we can come to terms with it honestly before Him.

Patrick Morley describes our blame passing in his book *Walking with Christ in the Details of Life:*

> We give Satan too much credit. Satan is fallen. He cannot foretell the future. He is limited in space and time—he can only be one place at a time. He is not eternal . . .
>
> It is impossible for Satan to make you sin. Sin is a choice. Satan can tempt us, but we decide to sin. "By his own evil desire, he is dragged away and enticed" (James 1:14). Since the devil is unable to make us sin, we need to reconsider blaming him for our wrong choices . . .
>
> The bigger enemy is our flesh. To square off against Satan is easy by comparison. The flesh must be battled daily, even momentarily. That's why the Scriptures say, "For the . . . Spirit desires what is contrary to the sinful nature." . . . The battle against Satan is already won. The ongoing battle is with the flesh.

If you want to ascend the mountain of His holiness and dwell in the presence of God, then you must recognize that sin is a choice. Reject it.

Father, I realize now that sin is a choice. Help me choose the paths of righteousness that will lead to new spiritual heights with You in the mountain of Your holiness.

FEBRUARY

The Word of God

MOUNTAIN: Mount Zion

KEY VERSES: Isaiah 2:2–3

Now it shall come to pass in the latter days
That the mountain of the LORD's house
Shall be established on the top of the mountains,
And shall be exalted above the hills;
And all nations shall flow to it.
Many people shall come and say,
"Come, and let us go up to the mountain of the LORD,
To the house of the God of Jacob;
He will teach us His ways,
And we shall walk in His paths."
For out of Zion shall go forth the law,
And the word of the LORD from Jerusalem.

The Light of God's Word

SCRIPTURE READING: Hebrews 4:12–16   KEY VERSE: Hebrews 4:12

The word of God is living and powerful, and sharper than any two-edged sword, piercing even to the division of soul and spirit, and of joints and marrow, and is a discerner of the thoughts and intents of the heart.

Many Christians' lives are like the proverbial VCR clock. They have a power source from which to draw, but like the unset blinking clock that flashes 12:00—12:00—12:00, their Christian walk is stuck in neutral. They feel no real sense of purpose.

Whether you are operating a VCR or traversing the difficult terrain of life, your most essential obligation is to read the instructions. The only way to know the proper course of action is to see what the expert designer says about each step in the process.

God gave us one instruction manual: the Holy Bible. There is no way to navigate life in a way that glorifies God or edifies yourself and others unless you know what God has to say. If you have cyclically gotten away from His Word throughout your life only to come back later, ask yourself why you keep returning. It's because it's much easier with the instruction manual.

There are two reasons why people wander from God's Word. They may be ignorant of its precious truths and overwhelmed by its magnitude and complexities (as with many new believers), or they simply lay it aside and endeavor to make it in life in their own wisdom.

This start-and-stop approach stymies proper growth and, as with the VCR clock, leaves Christians emitting only an intermittent light.

Keep my light brightly shining, Lord, as it is illumined by Your truth. I want to live my life with Your divine instruction manual as my guide.

A Lamp and a Light

SCRIPTURE READING: Psalm 119:105–112   KEY VERSE: Psalm 119:105

Your word is a lamp to my feet and a light to my path.

Have you ever hidden God's Word in your heart? If you have memorized a particular verse or passage because it spoke to you in a special way or helped you deal with a certain burden or sin, then you have hidden God's Word in your heart, just as the psalmist did.

Many Christians struggle with staying motivated to read the Bible. In their workaday world, wedging a quiet time into a manic schedule can be difficult. And once you've missed a day or two, the enemy will whisper his discouragement to keep you from your daily soul nourishment.

The Bible is your blueprint for life. The Bible can guide you through all circumstances. It can even keep you from the ravages of sin:

> Your word I have hidden in my heart,
> That I may not sin against You. (Ps. 119:11)

In the same chapter, Psalm 119:105 tells us that God's Word is a lamp to our feet and a light to our path. This isn't just a literary device for pretty writing. Why do you need a lamp or a light? Because the evil world system is full of darkness, and its temporary overseer is the Prince of Darkness. The only way you can see the right path and avoid the enemy's pitfalls is to consistently carry a lamp.

Psalm 119 is the longest chapter in the Bible. There is a reason. Its main purpose is to hail the importance of God's Word.

Thank You for Your Word, dear Lord. It is a lamp to my feet and a light to my path.

The Helmet of the Word

SCRIPTURE READING: Psalm 119:97–104   KEY VERSE: Proverbs 13:13

He who despises the word will be destroyed,
But he who fears the commandment will be rewarded.

In *The Tender Commandments,* pastor Ron Mehl uses a word picture to remind us of the importance of obeying God's Word:

> My friend Larry told me about one of the first bike rides (sans training wheels) he attempted with his young son Matthew. Going down a hill near their home . . . little Matt lost control of his bike. When the bike crashed, Matt went over the handlebars, landed on his head, and scooted along the asphalt for several feet . . . on the top of his helmet.
>
> When Matthew got up off the ground okay, just a little shaken, Larry looked at the helmet and saw that its top—and not the top of his little son's head—had been badly scraped and scored by the rough asphalt.
>
> How do you think Larry felt about that helmet? He loved that helmet. He kissed that helmet. He valued and honored that helmet, and used it as an object lesson for his boy.
>
> Proverbs 13:13 says: "He who despises the word will be destroyed, but he who fears the commandment will be rewarded."
>
> A person who resists, scorns, and rejects God's Word will meet with destruction. I wish I could say it in a nicer way, but I know it to be true and no overstatement . . . That person's life will come to disaster in one way or another, and God's Word is not shy about saying so.

Protect me with the "helmet" of Your Word, O Lord. I honor, respect, and value the truths it contains. Help me apply it to my life today.

God's Word at Work

SCRIPTURE READING: Romans 7:15–8:17   KEY VERSE: Romans 7:22

For I delight in the law of God according to the inward man.

Nothing anyone told him made him feel any better. He felt like a failure. He asked Jesus Christ to be his Savior three years ago, and for a while his life seemed to change. Some of his private, bad sin habits went away, and others were diminishing as he began to understand more of God's Word. But lately, some of those old habits were starting to come back, and even worse, on some days he didn't even mind.

"Maybe I'm not really a believer," he worried. "Or maybe God has given up on me. After all, I was pretty poor material to start with." The more he told himself these lies, the more he believed them, and the more he felt like a failure.

Does this story sound uncomfortably familiar? This man struggles with guilt over the issue of unresolved sin patterns. Listen to what Paul wrote, "For the good that I will to do, I do not do; but the evil I will not to do, that I practice . . . O wretched man that I am! Who will deliver me from this body of death? I thank God—through Jesus Christ our Lord!" (Rom. 7:19, 24–25).

That was the apostle Paul talking, the one God used to send His Word to countless people. His "secret" was that he understood Jesus was in the process of rescuing him and would never give up on him. Always remember that you have "the Spirit of adoption by whom we cry out, 'Abba, Father'" (Rom. 8:15). God's Word is at work in you today!

Father, thank You for the Spirit of adoption at work in me today. I am so grateful that You will never give up on me!

The Basis for Belief

SCRIPTURE READING: Psalm 119:89–96   KEY VERSE: Isaiah 51:1

Listen to Me, you who follow after righteousness,
You who seek the LORD:
Look to the rock from which you were hewn,
And to the hole of the pit from which you were dug.

What is the basis for what you believe? If you say the way you were raised or what you were taught in school, then your belief system could be faulty. God needs to be the basis for the principles you hold dear. His Word is a sure guide through the difficult circumstances of life. In fact, God prepares you to face the future as you read and study His Word.

When you are tuned in to the Word of God, you are tapping in to the infinite mind of Christ. The temptation to think that God is not personal or interested in what you are facing quickly fades. God's Word teaches us that He is actively involved in every aspect of our lives. Knowing that God eternally cares for you is a good place to start as you seek to build a strong spiritual foundation. Pastors and clergymen can teach you about the Lord and how to worship Him, but the Holy Spirit living within you illuminates the truth of God to your heart.

When you understand the principles of God's Word and apply them to your life, your vision changes. You see things from God's perspective and are more willing to trust Him with the entirety of your life.

Some say the Bible is difficult to understand. However, if you will begin to read through its contents, God will help you understand His truth and principles.

Heavenly Father, through Your Word enable me to see things from Your perspective and become more willing to trust You with my life. Illuminate Your truth to my heart.

Responding to God's Word

SCRIPTURE READING: Nehemiah 9:1–3   KEY VERSES: John 4:13–14

Jesus answered and said to her, "Whoever drinks of this water will thirst again, but whoever drinks of the water that I shall give him will never thirst. But the water that I shall give him will become in him a fountain of water springing up into everlasting life."

As Nehemiah was rebuilding the walls of Jerusalem, the Book of the Law was found and brought out to be read. Those who resided in the city had experienced both war and captivity. God's Word had been lost to them. Although they understood the significance of being descendants of Israel, they had not lived under the protective spiritual covenant of God.

When Ezra stepped out into the light and began reading God's Word, the response of the people was overwhelming. They immediately confessed their sins. The Lord has not removed His love from Israel, but He has certainly allowed them to go their own way. Israel's sin and rebellion against God had led to a spiritual, emotional, and physical wandering.

Not all the trouble that touches your life will occur as a result of sin. Some hardships come as the result of our fallen world. Don't look at the accidents of life and think God is trying to harm you. His only goal in allowing adversity is to teach you to trust Him.

And while there are consequences to sin, there are also hope and forgiveness for all who return to the Lord and seek His face. Let His Word become a lamp to your path. Set the affections of your heart on Him, and know that whatever burden you are carrying, He will bear it for you the moment you turn to Him.

Dear Lord, help me respond to the truth of Your Word today in the midst of the adversities of my life.

Faithful to the Word

SCRIPTURE READING: 1 Peter 1:22–25   KEY VERSES: 2 Cor. 11:13–15

*For such are false apostles, deceitful workers, transforming them-
selves into apostles of Christ. And no wonder! For Satan himself
transforms himself into an angel of light. Therefore it is no great
thing if his ministers also transform themselves into ministers of
righteousness, whose end will be according to their works.*

One of the major concerns of the New Testament was false teachings that
contradicted the message of the gospel. Early church leaders such as Peter,
James, and John wrote strong appeals to young believers to remain true to the
way of Christ and not to compromise their faith by being drawn away in error.

Satan is the master of deception. He mixes just enough truth within his lies
to catch the attention of weak and undiscerning people. Complacency and a
heart divided by sin are breeding grounds for apostasy.

You may think this was a problem faced only by the early church, and surely, it is not our problem today. Nothing could be farther from the truth. Today
Islam makes up nearly 20 percent of the world's population. It is the fastest
growing religion, second in size only to Christianity.

Shocked? Our tolerance and lack of godly conviction have led us to weather courtroom battle after battle where we have witnessed the Word of God
being confined—and many times banned from use—within our society. We
are a world no longer interested in the sole purpose and passion of God.

However, God is not changed by our rebellion. His faithfulness remains.
His Word and holiness are the standards by which all things will be judged.
May your sincere love for Him keep you faithful to His Word.

*Keep me faithful to Your Word, O Lord. Don't let me be drawn away by
error.*

Disciples of the Word

SCRIPTURE READING: John 5:24–38   KEY VERSE: Galatians 5:1

Stand fast therefore in the liberty by which Christ has made us free, and do not be entangled again with a yoke of bondage.

Oswald Chambers wrote,

A spiritually minded man or woman will never come to you with the demand, "Believe this and that," but with the demand that you square your life with the standards of Jesus.

We are not asked to believe the Bible, but to believe the One whom the Bible reveals (John 5:39–40). We are called to present liberty of conscience, not liberty of view. If we are free with the liberty of Christ, others will be brought into that same liberty—the liberty of realizing the dominance of Jesus Christ.

Always keep your life measured by the standards of Jesus. Bow your neck to His yoke alone, and to no other yoke whatever; and be careful to see that you never bind a yoke on others that is not placed by Jesus Christ. It takes God a long time to get us out of the way of thinking that unless everyone sees as we do, they must be wrong. That is never God's view. There is only one liberty, the liberty of Jesus at work in our conscience enabling us to do what is right.

Don't get impatient, remember how God dealt with you with patience and with gentleness; but never water down the truth of God. Let it have its way and never apologize for it.

Jesus said, "Go and make disciples," not "make converts to your opinions."

Dear Lord, help me make disciples to Your Word rather than converts to my opinions. Set me free through Your Word and then empower me to share that freedom with others.

The Inspired Word of God

SCRIPTURE READING: 2 Timothy 3:16–17   KEY VERSE: 1 Timothy 4:15

Meditate on these things; give yourself entirely to them, that your progress may be evident to all.

As we read through Paul's letters to his young protégé, Timothy, we find that their content is written just as much for us. Every man, woman, and young person who studies God's Word comes face to face with truth inspired by God. Henry Thiessen commented on inspiration:

> God has revealed himself in nature, history, and conscience. He has also revealed himself in his Son and in his Word. The Holy Spirit so guided and superintended the writers of the sacred text, making use of their own unique personalities, that they wrote all that he wanted them to write, without excess or error.
>
> Several things must be noted. (1) Inspiration is inexplicable. It is the operation of the Holy Spirit. (2) Inspiration is limited to the authors of Scripture. Other books are not inspired in the same sense. (3) Inspiration is essentially guidance. That is, the Holy Spirit supervised the selection of the materials to be used and the words to be employed in writing. (4) The Holy Spirit preserved the authors from all error and from all omission. (5) Inspiration extends to the words of the Bible, not merely to the thoughts and concepts.

Although these concepts may seem difficult to grasp, they show us one thing: God has taken great care to preserve His Word. It is His gift to you and me for our instruction and encouragement as we grow in our love for Him.

Thank You for preserving Your Word for me, Lord. Help me build my life and ministry upon its eternal, unchanging truths.

A Love for God's Word

SCRIPTURE READING: Psalm 119:57–64   KEY VERSE: 2 Timothy 2:15

Be diligent to present yourself approved to God, a worker who does not need to be ashamed, rightly dividing the word of truth.

Paul's final words to his understudy Timothy were words that God wants us to apply to our lives: "Be diligent to present yourself approved to God."

A part of becoming approved is learning how to flee from the temptations that keep you from becoming all that God has planned for you to be.

Immersing yourself in the study of His Word prepares you not only for the trials of life but also for the blessings that come your way. And God has many blessings stored up for those who walk in the light of His truth.

His Word is a road map, a framework, and a blueprint to life. Paul knew that regardless of what Timothy faced, as long as God's Word was hidden within his heart, he could meet all challenges victoriously.

Becoming approved of God is not a work you perform. It requires the guidance of the Holy Spirit. Time spent in the study of God's Word teaches you more about Christ's personal love and desire for you. While He wants you to attend church, His greater joy comes in watching you study His Word and then apply it to your life.

Through the power of the Holy Spirit, God will teach you how to accurately handle His Word. If you are ready for a true adventure, pick up the Bible and ask God to breathe fresh life into your love for His Word.

Father, through the power of Your Holy Spirit, teach me how to handle Your Word. Breathe fresh life into my love for Your Word this day.

The Ultimate Escape Artist

SCRIPTURE READING: John 8:31–36   KEY VERSE: John 8:36

If the Son makes you free, you shall be free indeed.

Have you ever felt uncomfortable during church? Even in an age in which quaint hand fans have been replaced by powerful air-conditioning systems and wooden pews have been exchanged for upholstered ones, people can still feel terribly uncomfortable during a worship service. This discomfort has nothing to do with a church building's amenities. Often, it has everything to do with the Holy Spirit's conviction.

Sometimes God will use a statement by your pastor or a reading of Scripture to burn a truth into your heart. Often, the message can be uplifting. At other times, it can be a sobering reminder that you still have an issue with which you must obey and trust God.

If God has pricked your heart, deep down you will know the truth. And the longer you delay in dealing with the issue on God's terms, the more difficult it will be to finally submit to God's will.

There is an escape to the trap that the enemy has laid for you. Jesus said, "If you abide in My word, you are My disciples indeed. And you shall know the truth, and the truth shall make you free" (John 8:31–32).

When you accepted Christ as your Savior, His Holy Spirit fully equipped you for freedom. Chains of bondage are a needless hazard for the believer. The truth can make you the ultimate escape artist.

Equip me for freedom through Your Word, O Lord. Break the chains that bind me so I can escape from captivity to sin.

The Word of Truth

SCRIPTURE READING: Colossians 3:1–8   KEY VERSE: John 14:6

Jesus said to him, "I am the way, the truth, and the life. No one comes to the Father except through Me."

Everyone must eventually answer three questions: (1) Where did we come from? (2) Why are we here? and (3) Where are we going?

Philosophers, sages, and prophets have sought to provide solutions, all usually with unsatisfactory conclusions. The Bible claims to have the only adequate response to each of these questions because it provides God's omniscient perspective in contrast to the futile reasoning of man, who is limited by time, education, observation, culture, and prejudice.

First, we come from God. He created us in His image. We were placed on earth by God and for God. We are not the products of impersonal time or chance. Our origins are rooted in the eternal mind of God.

Second, we are here on earth to know and glorify God in our relationships and through our works.

Third, we shall return to God—for judgment if we have ignored or rejected His terms for knowing Him (reconciliation through the Cross) or for everlasting joy if we have embraced His purposes and presence through the person of Jesus Christ.

All of these answers are revealed in the Word of truth—the Bible—which alone can answer the perplexing problems that confront each generation.

O Lord, thank You for the Word of truth, which answers all my questions.

God gets joy from us wanting to communicate with him. He has created us to be like him. He hurts when we go our way & don't talk to him. He finds pleasure in helping, listing, providing for us who ask him with thanks

The Universal Standard

SCRIPTURE READING: 1 Timothy 2:4–6   KEY VERSE: 2 Timothy 2:25

In humility correcting those who are in opposition, if God perhaps will grant them repentance, so that they may know the truth.

Each age has no end of philosophies, reasoning, and belief systems that are presented as truth. To be substantiated, truth must meet three unyielding criteria:

First, truth must be universal in that it must apply to everyone: African, European, American, and Asian. There can be no cultural distinctions if it is unalterable truth.

Second, it must be uniform in that it must apply to everyone in the same manner. The criteria for applying ultimate truth cannot be differentiated to any degree. Truth must work equally for children and adults, for the well-educated and the unschooled.

Third, truth must be unending in that it must be eternally valid. What was truth for the fifth-century man must also be truth for the twentieth-first-century man.

Using those guidelines, only one body of truth can suffice—the Word of truth, the Bible. It applies to everyone, in the same manner, for every age.

Whether one is a conquistador or a computer operator, rich or poor, black or white, the Bible is the truth upon which everyone can build a lasting life. It is the wisdom for salvation, liberated living, and eternal security.

Are you building your life on the unalterable, all-sufficient truth of the Bible, or are you following the vain reasoning of man?

Lord, I reject the philosophy, reasoning, and belief systems of this world. Please apply the universal standard of Your Word of truth to my life.

Holding Fast to the Faithful Word

SCRIPTURE READING: Psalm 119:41–48   KEY VERSE: John 17:17

Sanctify them by Your truth. Your word is truth.

Think for a moment about how many books, magazines, newspapers, and other materials you have read in the last year. What we read and see is not the sort of material that gives meaning and purpose to our existence.

For that, we must always turn to the Bible, which is the revelation of God to man concerning His unchanging plan for mankind. God's Word is the foundation upon which you and I can establish an enduring life.

"For whatever things were written before were written for our learning instruction, that we through the patience and comfort of the Scriptures might have hope" (Rom. 15:4). The Holy Scriptures unfold the plan of salvation, unveil the Lord's plan for abundant living, and share what life after death will be like.

The Word of God is faithful: "Your word is truth" (John 17:17). You can count on its truth and power to deal with every aspect of life.

God's Word will never lead you astray because the God who cannot lie is its Author and Guarantor: "All Scripture is given by inspiration of God, and is profitable for doctrine, for reproof, for correction, for instruction in righteousness, that the man of God may be complete, thoroughly equipped for every good work" (2 Tim. 3:16–17).

Equip me for every good work, O Lord, as I build my life on Your unchanging Word.

Drifting from the Word

SCRIPTURE READING: Hebrews 2:1–4   KEY VERSE: Titus 1:9

Holding fast the faithful word as he has been taught, that he may be able, by sound doctrine, both to exhort and convict those who contradict.

A Christian song tells of a friendship shared between two people. In the beginning both had a deep, burning desire to serve the Lord. Yet two years later, one had drifted away from God's fellowship.

The writer of Hebrews admonishes us to "give the more earnest heed to the things we have heard, lest we drift away" (Heb. 2:1). Drifting begins subtly and usually includes compromising the principles found in God's Word. The movies you attend, the way you dress, the friends you associate with, or any number of other things could be a source of compromise.

Once we take the first step, Satan urges us to do it again. "After all," he reasons, "nothing happened the first time." Before we know it, our attitude has changed and our lifestyle reflects the shift in our commitment to Christ.

No one is immune to drifting. All of us have felt the temptation to let our devotion slide so as not to become too serious. However, Jesus gave up everything to come to earth and die in our place. We have eternal life because He took the principles of His Father seriously. By His grace, we are saved and set free from sin. Once realized, this should be enough to curb any notion of drifting.

Anchor your life to the Word of God and you will never drift.

Heavenly Father, anchor my life in Your Word. Keep me from compromise that will cause me to drift away from You.

An Eyewitness Account

SCRIPTURE READING: John 9:1–38   KEY VERSE: John 9:25

He answered and said, "Whether He is a sinner or not I do not know.
One thing I know: that though I was blind, now I see."

The blind beggar would not be dissuaded. Even when the rich and influential Pharisees harassed him, trying to make him go back on his story, he refused to give in. He had been blind; now he could see, and he knew Jesus Christ was the One who had healed him. Nothing the Pharisees did made him say otherwise.

Few things are more compelling than an eyewitness account. An eyewitness knows the truth. He does not depend upon someone else's interpretation of events because he was there.

Like the blind beggar, the apostle John had an eyewitness, life-changing encounter with Jesus. John knew from one-on-one personal experience that Jesus is the Messiah. John was there when Jesus healed this beggar. He stood at the foot of the cross when Jesus hung there in agony. John staked his life, his very being, on the truth that Jesus is God's Son. Eventually, the hostile Roman emperor Domitian left John on the Isle of Patmos to die because he wouldn't recant.

Through the Gospels, you also meet Jesus face to face. Have you staked your life on the truth of God's Word? As you obey, you become an eyewitness to the reliability and power of Scripture.

Lord, I stake my life on Your Word. I thank You that I am an eyewitness to the reliability and power of its truths through what it has accomplished in my life.

A Firm Foundation

SCRIPTURE READING: 1 Corinthians 2:1–5   KEY VERSE: 1 Corinthians 2:7

We speak the wisdom of God in a mystery, the hidden wisdom which God ordained before the ages for our glory.

The people of Corinth were proud intellectuals. They loved to debate, philosophize, and speculate, depending on their human reasoning to work through problems and understand their world. It wasn't long before this cultural emphasis carried over into the church.

Paul didn't waste any time using the human arguments they were used to hearing. Instead, he said, "[I] did not come with excellence of speech or of wisdom . . . For I determined not to know anything among you except Jesus Christ and Him crucified" (1 Cor. 2:1–2).

Jesus is the foundation of our faith. He is the one foundation. Through Jesus alone, we are cleansed from sin, reconciled to and adopted by God. The Word of God is the foundation of our beliefs.

Have you been sidetracked by minor issues? Are your relationship with Jesus and conformity to His Word your top priorities? Faith that relies solely on Christ and His Word makes you stable, secure, discerning.

Make me stable, secure, and discerning, Lord, as I rely solely upon Your Word. I want to know nothing except Jesus Christ and Him crucified.

The Good News

SCRIPTURE READING: Luke 24:44–49   KEY VERSE: John 3:16

For God so loved the world that He gave His only begotten Son, that whoever believes in Him should not perish but have everlasting life.

The concept of news in our culture is overwhelmingly pessimistic. Murder, extortion, political corruption, disease, poverty, war—these are the staple elements in the majority of influential news periodicals and television programming.

Perhaps that is why the good news (the translation of the Greek word for "gospel") is viewed with skepticism and cynicism.

"There must be a catch somewhere," modern man sneers. "I do not know of anything today that is completely good."

What he fails to understand is that this gospel, this good news, is about the perfect God-man, the Lord Jesus Christ, whose offer of salvation is untainted and unblemished. The startling good news of the gospel is that Jesus Christ has dealt with the bad news about sin, which infects all men, receiving its death blow on our behalf. Now, man can receive the fantastic free gift of salvation by simple faith in Christ, believing that He died for our sins and rose again on our behalf.

The good news of the gospel is for the asking. It is free. It is permanent. It is for every age, every temperament, every color, and every creed. No prejudice. No strings. No gimmicks.

The gospel is this: God loves you, died for your sins, and offers you His eternal friendship—all that's needed is your personal response of faith.

Father, thank You for the good news of the gospel, which is revealed in Your Word. Thank You that Your offer of salvation is free. I humbly receive it!

Remembering the Word

SCRIPTURE READING: Psalm 119:33–40   KEY VERSE: Isaiah 40:8

The grass withers, the flower fades,
But the word of our God stands forever.

In the book *The Light and the Glory,* Peter Marshall Jr. tells how Isaac Potts, George Washington's temporary landlord, once discovered the future president in prayer. Potts, a Quaker and a pacifist, came upon Washington's horse tethered by a secluded grove of trees . . . Hearing a voice, he approached quietly and saw the General on his knees at prayer. Not wanting to be discovered, he stood motionless until Washington had finished and returned to his headquarters.

Potts then hurried to tell his wife Sarah, "If George Washington be not a man of God, I am greatly deceived, and still more shall I be deceived, if God does not, through him, work out a great salvation for America."

Washington once said, "It is impossible to rightly govern . . . without God and the Bible." This tremendous truth was one he would carry with him through the years of the American Revolution and then into the office of the presidency.

Joining Washington was Benjamin Franklin who wrote, "If a sparrow cannot fall to the ground without God's notice, is it probable that an empire can rise without His aid?"

The question is not, Has God forgotten America? but, Has America forgotten God and His Word?

Write Your Word upon the tables of my heart, dear Lord. I don't want to forget You!

The Power of the Gospel

SCRIPTURE READING: Psalm 119:9–16   KEY VERSE: Acts 26:18

To open their eyes, in order to turn them from darkness to light, and from the power of Satan to God, that they may receive forgiveness of sins and an inheritance among those who are sanctified by faith in Me.

Two powerful dynamics about the good news of Jesus Christ make it exceedingly attractive to man.

First, the good news of the gospel is divinely powerful. When the wonderful news about Jesus Christ's offer of salvation is heard and received, it comes with unequaled and unbridled power.

Embraced, the good news transfers a man from the kingdom of Satan (living under the dominion of sin) into the kingdom of God. It ushers him into the presence of God from whom he was alienated.

We are no longer helpless to deal with our habits. God is with us. We are no longer prisoners of circumstance or passion. God is for us and in us, sovereignly orchestrating our lives.

Second, once we partake of the good news, we possess a message to share with others. We have truth, hope, encouragement, comfort, and joy to share with others. We have something to give that everyone needs.

The good news is hope for the hopeless, strength for the weary, peace for the striving, freedom for the oppressed—and it is available to anyone who will receive it.

Have you experienced the power of the gospel that is revealed in the Word of God? If so, are you spreading the message about the good news of salvation through Christ?

Thank You for the power of the gospel that has transformed my life, dear Lord. Empower me to spread its message of salvation through Christ to a lost and dying world.

The Grid of the Word

SCRIPTURE READING: Colossians 1:3–13   KEY VERSES: Psalm 119:167–68

My soul keeps Your testimonies,
And I love them exceedingly.
I keep Your precepts and Your testimonies,
For all my ways are before You.

The apostle Paul was in prison when he learned that the church in Colosse was in danger of falling into heresy. Doctrines were being taught that refuted the truth of the gospel message.

A combination of Eastern philosophy, Jewish legalism, and elements of Gnosticism was spreading rapidly. Gnostics, emphasizing knowledge rather than faith, believed they had special knowledge when it came to spiritual matters. The doctrine introduced to the Colossians was based on this man-made philosophy, not on the divine truth of God's Word.

The heretics in Colosse denounced the person and work of Jesus Christ. They believed God responded only to perfection. In their eyes the human body was evil. Because Jesus came as a man, they were convinced He was only an emanation from God, not the Son of God in the flesh. Anytime we add or take away from the gospel message, we deviate from its foundational truth.

Similar problems face us today through the New Age movement and a number of religious cults. Therefore, it is extremely important that you run everything you hear through God's grid system—His Word. If something does not bear witness to God's Word, then it is not of Him, and you need to let it go.

Dear Lord, let me filter everything today through the grid system of Your
Word. If it is not of You, then help me let it go.

God's Dependent

SCRIPTURE READING: Luke 15:11–32   KEY VERSE: Luke 15:18

I will arise and go to my father, and will say to him, "Father, I have sinned against heaven and before you."

As we grow up, we long for more autonomy, the freedom to make our own choices and function as adults. Can you remember waiting for certain "milestone" ages? The day you could go to school, the day you could drive a car—these are important steps in becoming mature.

If parents are wise, they help their children learn how to make the right choices for themselves. In fact, from a social perspective, a person is often not looked upon as being a complete adult until he is able to support himself and be responsible for his decisions. That is why it is difficult for many to understand the principle of dependence when it comes to abiding in Christ.

The prodigal son in Jesus' parable, in one way, represents all believers when we choose to go in our own direction with complete disregard for our Father. God does not want you to live as a child in the sense of being irresponsible as you function in daily life. However, He does want you to live as a spiritual child, humbly acknowledging your complete dependence upon Him and His Word.

When you order your life on the principles of God's Word, you can relax in His care, rest in His love, and know beyond doubt that He is leading you in a good direction. He is the perfect Father, and He longs for you to return home again to Him if you are wandering in your own selfish ways. It's never too late to be God's dependent.

Make me Your dependent, Father. I want to relax in Your care, rest in Your love, and follow the path You have ordained for me.

Pruning the Branches

SCRIPTURE READING: John 15:1–6   KEY VERSE: John 15:16

You did not choose Me, but I chose you and appointed you that you should go and bear fruit, and that your fruit should remain, that whatever you ask the Father in My name He may give you.

The late Francis Schaeffer observed that the average Christian's objective in life appeared to be personal peace and affluence. Whether we agree with his assessment, we must at least admit that subconsciously, if not overtly, we prefer the pleasant over the painful, the comfortable over the distressful.

Despite this decidedly normal human disposition, you will stumble badly through the Christian journey if you adopt these longings as your chief aims. Christ's goal for your life transcends this limited perspective. He has something far more sublime in mind for you—to make you productive in the work of His kingdom. This involves a process Christ termed *pruning,* a continual trimming of character and habits that are unproductive for your personal growth as a believer, conforming you to the image of God and the standard of His Word.

Unfortunately, this can be painful at times, even severe when the pruning lops off sensitive areas. But whatever God sees as detrimental to your fruitfulness and well-being, He will seek to sever. The tools of Providence may be sharp, but they are held by loving hands.

Perhaps you can identify an area that God's Spirit has surfaced as deleterious to your spiritual health. Cooperate with the Husbandman. Though it may be trying for a time, God's goal is to grow you into the image of Christ. In this kind of pain, there is godly gain.

Dear Lord, conform me to the image of Your Son and the standard of Your Word. Prune out everything that is detrimental to my fruitfulness and well-being.

Trusting Your Conscience

SCRIPTURE READING: John 16:7–15   KEY VERSE: John 16:13

However, when He, the Spirit of truth, has come, He will guide you into all truth; for He will not speak on His own authority, but whatever He hears He will speak; and He will tell you things to come.

At the most fundamental level, your conscience gives you the capacity to distinguish between right and wrong. It is like a personal alarm system that works for your protection. You have probably had this experience: just as you were about to participate in or initiate something questionable, warning bells went off in your mind: *Are you sure you should do this?* If you went ahead and did it, you surely had a bad feeling in the pit of your stomach that did not go away until you made things right.

By itself, the conscience is a built-in monitor that signals you when a thought or action may violate your personal moral program, whatever that may be. The conscience cannot force you into a certain choice, and it does not necessarily point you to the option that is in line with God's truth. This is a vital principle to understand in order to avoid misdirection.

Only when you accept Christ as your Savior does the conscience function as God planned. The Holy Spirit dwells within you the moment you place your faith in Jesus, and in His hands the conscience becomes a tool to assist you in making decisions according to God's Word.

The Holy Spirit correctly interprets the messages your conscience sends. The Spirit then brings appropriate biblical principles to mind and urges you to live in line with their direction.

Father, I choose to trust Your Word rather than my conscience. Help me bring my life into alignment with the truths of Scripture.

A Cure for the Conscience

SCRIPTURE READING: 1 Timothy 4:1–12   KEY VERSE: Acts 24:16

This being so, I myself always strive to have a conscience without offense toward God and men.

Sometimes a subtle problem with the conscience develops. If you experience feelings of condemnation but cannot identify the source, you may be the victim of a struggling conscience. This is essentially a conscience in overdrive, excessively critical and hypersensitive.

For some, the cause is legalism or allegiance to man-made rules. Others take on responsibilities that are not really theirs, and they feel blame when things go wrong. In any case, false guilt is the culprit.

Is there a cure for a conscience that is out of condition? In Acts 24:16, Paul wrote: "I myself always strive to have a conscience without offense toward God and men." He made himself transparent before God by confessing his sin, repenting, and recognizing the forgiveness and purity he had in Christ.

Ask the Lord to show you the truth about what is occurring inside your heart. He will point out areas of concern. When He reveals the problems to you, you must move immediately into repentance. Remember that you can repent from sins only that you yourself have committed. False guilt tries to burden you with others' transgressions.

The more your conscience is programmed according to God's standards, the more accurately it detects discrepancies. With your conscience in God's control, He guides you in righteousness.

Dear heavenly Father, please program my conscience according to Your standards. Show me the truth about what is occurring inside my heart.

Benefits of Obedience

SCRIPTURE READING: Psalm 119:1–8   KEY VERSE: 1 Samuel 15:22

Then Samuel said:
"Has the LORD as great delight in burnt offerings and sacrifices,
As in obeying the voice of the LORD?
Behold, to obey is better than sacrifice,
And to heed than the fat of rams."

Have you ever considered the benefits of obedience? Being accountable to authority is a topic that is usually spoken of in terms of negative consequences, but obeying the Lord brings a wealth of blessing:

A growing faith. Obedience is a step-by-step process, beginning with the little things. When you say yes to God in personal, daily matters, you see how He takes care of the issues and consequences that arise. Obedience in more difficult situations becomes easier and less of a struggle because you already have a foundation of faith on which to build.

A positive impact on others. Others are watching your behavior, whether you realize it or not. They want to see a difference in your life; they are eager to see the results of living for the Lord. The fruit of the Spirit that God produces in you brings a rich harvest for His kingdom as it blesses others.

A sense of security. Your reasons for worry and anxiety are rendered null and void. When you trust God to take care of you, you do not have to worry about negative response or failure or lack of support.

Then you will say with the psalmist:

> Give me understanding, and I shall keep Your law;
> Indeed, I shall obey it with my whole heart.
> Make me walk in the path of Your commandments,
> For I delight in it. (Ps. 119:34–35)

Lord, give me understanding, and I will keep Your law and obey it with my whole heart. Make me walk in the path of Your commandments, for there I find delight.

The Standards of the Word

SCRIPTURE READING: Ephesians 5:1–21   KEY VERSES: Ephesians 5:26–27

That He might sanctify and cleanse her with the washing of water by the word, that He might present her to Himself a glorious church, not having spot or wrinkle or any such thing, but that she should be holy and without blemish.

In his book *Love for All Seasons,* John Trent tells a story he heard Billy Graham relate at a crusade:

> Graham recalled being on a cross country flight, when a man in the seat ahead of him began to create a disturbance. This particular individual had been drinking heavily before he got on the plane and continued to drink as much as they would serve him on the flight.
>
> Not only was he getting more drunk, but he was becoming louder and more abusive to the flight attendants. When they finally refused to serve him any more alcohol, his anger climaxed in a torrent of foul language.
>
> In total frustration, one of the flight attendants told him, "Sir, do you know that Billy Graham is sitting right behind you?"
>
> The man whirled around and said, "Oh, Mr. Graham! I'm so glad to meet you. I went to one of your crusades, and it changed my life!"

It doesn't take a telephoto lens to zoom in on that man's problem. Any inner "cleansing" that might have taken place at a crusade had been totally covered up by the mud and dirt of shameful actions.

It doesn't take much to be lulled into thinking that a particular sin isn't so bad. The conscience becomes so muddied that it is no longer a sensitive instrument in God's hands. You cannot trust your conscience. You must evaluate your life on the standards of God's Word.

Lord, help me always evaluate my life on the standards of Your Word.

The Foundation of Your Faith

SCRIPTURE READING: 2 Corinthians 3:1–11   KEY VERSES: James 1:6–7

Let him ask in faith, with no doubting, for he who doubts is like a wave of the sea driven and tossed by the wind. For let not that man suppose that he will receive anything from the Lord.

It was 1866 in England, and pastor Samuel J. Stone's congregation was in an uproar. In fact, the entire Church of England was in a state of upheaval. A certain bishop had just written a book concerning the authenticity of the first five books of the Bible.

In his "intellectual" examination of these books, the bishop called their accuracy into question. Liberals in the church sided with this bishop, while the conservative group continued to assert the inerrancy of all Scripture. The debate raged. Samuel Stone was concerned for the health and stability of his congregation. Controversy was tearing them apart, and surely, severe consequences would follow.

To combat this growing division, Stone composed a series of hymns that focused on church unity. With stirring words he celebrated Christ's eternal position as Head of the church in his most famous hymn, "The Church's One Foundation."

Seeing Christ as the Cornerstone of the body of believers puts peripheral church issues into perspective. You are not swayed by every wind of philosophy and every controversy because you measure them by the Lord (James 1:6–7). On the steadfast mountain of Christ and His Word, you stand prepared for every issue.

Father, help me build my life on the foundation of Your Word, prepared to face every issue on the basis of its life-changing truths.

MARCH

Prayer

MOUNTAIN: Mountain where Jesus prayed

KEY VERSES:

Matthew 14:23

When He had sent the multitudes away, He went up on the mountain by Himself to pray. Now when evening came, He was alone there.

Luke 6:12

Now it came to pass in those days that He went out to the mountain to pray, and continued all night in prayer to God.

Pray Without Ceasing

SCRIPTURE READING: Psalm 5:1–3   KEY VERSE: 1 Thessalonians 5:17

Pray without ceasing.

What did the apostle Paul mean when he wrote, "Pray without ceasing"? For one, he was indicating that we can live in an attitude of prayer even though we are engaged in everyday activity. That does not mean we walk around mumbling prayers to God, though there will be days when we pray much more than others.

Instead, the indication here leans to one of opportunity. We can have a natural attitude of prayer surrounding our lives. Prayer is a sign that we are dependent on the Lord and not on ourselves. Should you pray about trivial matters? Yes. God listens to every prayer. A prayer to find lost glasses or to mentally retrieve forgotten information is a worthy request.

God has called us to be people of prayer. Communication on this level is one of intimate fellowship with the Savior. Through prayer, we discover the goodness and personal devotion of God. Though taking time to be alone with God is the ideal, we don't have to limit ourselves. God hears our prayers no matter where we pray.

Oswald Chambers spoke to this issue: "So many of us limit our praying because we are not reckless in our confidence in God. In the eyes of those who do not know God, it is madness to trust Him. But when we pray through the power of the Holy Spirit we realize the resources of God. He is our perfect heavenly Father, and we are His children."

Dear Lord, give me reckless confidence in You as my loving heavenly Father, one who is concerned about my every need.

Praying to Your Father

SCRIPTURE READING: Matthew 6:9–13   KEY VERSE: Matthew 6:6

You, when you pray, go into your room, and when you have shut your door, pray to your Father who is in the secret place; and your Father who sees in secret will reward you openly.

On the subject of prayer, A. B. Simpson writes,

> The first view given of God in the Lord's Prayer is not His majesty but His paternal love. To the listening disciples this must have been a strange expression from the lips of their Lord as a pattern for them. Never had Jewish ears heard God so named, at least in His relation to the individual . . . No sinful man had ever dared to call God his Father.
>
> They, doubtless, had heard their Master use this delightful name of God . . . but that they should call Jehovah by such a name had never dawned upon their legal and unillumined minds. And yet it really means that we may and should recognize that God is our Father.

The entire idea of Jesus addressing God as Father is one of personal love and devotion. You cannot know a person unless you love him. And you certainly cannot love God unless you know Him and realize He is intimately in love with you.

The idea of God as your Father is one of extreme love. Regardless of what your earthly father was like, God is a Father of love, and He cares for you. His parental love offers security, encouragement, and nurturing. Therefore, know that He has the ability to step aside from the occupation of the world's demands to listen to your heart. For the believer, prayer is a lifeline of eternal love and hope.

Listen to my heart today, Father. You are my lifeline in the midst of the storms of life.

The Deepest Form of Intimacy

SCRIPTURE READING: Luke 11:1–4   KEY VERSES: Matthew 6:14–15

If you forgive men their trespasses, your heavenly Father will also forgive you. But if you do not forgive men their trespasses, neither will your Father forgive your trespasses.

In Luke 11, Jesus provided a rich pattern for prayer. Yet we know He never prayed this prayer because He was sinless and, therefore, did not have to ask forgiveness. However, He used these words to teach us how to pray.

Jesus was specific about the need for forgiveness. Even though God has provided a way through His Son for your eternal forgiveness, there is still a need for you to acknowledge your sinfulness whenever you yield to temptation.

Forgiveness is crucial to your spiritual growth. Remember the words of Jesus on the cross, "Father, forgive them, for they do not know what they do" (Luke 23:34).

Prayer that comes from the heart involves responsibility: "Father, I love You, and I choose to do Your will even when it seems difficult and unbearable." It always honors God for who He is. Jesus taught us to pray: "Hallowed be Your name." He went on to show us how to present our requests to the Father by praying, "Give us day by day our daily bread" (Luke 11:2–3).

Recognize that God is your sovereign Provider. He loves you unconditionally and wants you to experience His goodness, no matter what comes your way. His daily bread for you is His Word, and He gives it as a source of encouragement and hope.

Prayer changes you and leads you into the deepest form of intimacy, time spent with your loving heavenly Father.

Father, give me a heart to do Your will even when it seems difficult and unbearable. Change me as I wait before You today.

The Priority of Prayer

SCRIPTURE READING: Daniel 6:1–28   KEY VERSE: Daniel 6:10

When Daniel knew that the writing was signed, he went home. And in his upper room, with his windows open toward Jerusalem, he knelt down on his knees three times that day, and prayed and gave thanks before his God, as was his custom since early days.

Sometimes it doesn't take much to throw you off track when it comes to spending time in prayer. You finally get by yourself and bow your head, and the phone rings. You suddenly remember another obligation. One of the children runs in with a question or a problem that cannot wait. Or maybe you can't concentrate, and you decide to give up and try again later.

For Daniel, not even the threat of becoming lunch for lions deterred him from his daily habit of prayer. The edict to worship the king was handed down, and the rulers waited with delight to catch Daniel in the act of defiance. Of course, they did not have to wait long. Daniel continued to pray before God three times a day, as he always did.

What gave Daniel his determination and resolve? He believed without a shadow of a doubt that God would honor his commitment to prayer and take care of any trouble. Daniel did not concern himself with who might see or what others would think; he focused on the Lord alone.

In the end, Daniel was saved, the king was awed, and the rulers got to meet the lions. And here is the good news: God protects and uplifts you, too, when you trust Him to handle the consequences of obedience in prayer.

Dear Lord, give me the determination and resolve to make prayer a priority. Make it the consuming passion of my life.

A Safe House

SCRIPTURE READING: Philippians 4:4–7   KEY VERSE: Psalm 31:3

You are my rock and my fortress
Therefore, for Your name's sake,
Lead me and guide me.

In her book *Seeking God,* Joni Eareckson Tada explains what turning to God as a refuge means to her:

> I know something about fortresses. I have happy childhood memories of my sister Kathy and me constructing a tree house on the farm. Our little fortress was some distance from the farmhouse, so it was private and far away from adults . . .
>
> To my childlike way of thinking, that tree house was a fortress. Not just a shelter or a place to hide, but a safe house that would protect us from the rain beating on the tin roof and the wind shaking the branches of the tree. We were safe. We felt secure . . .
>
> There's a lot more safety and security in the Lord than in safe houses of our own making and design . . . Now that I'm an adult, I put childish activities behind me and go . . . to a place, a Person, who is the Everlasting Rock.

Where do you go when you feel burned out, used up, overcommitted? Do you run to the Lord or to your own devices? All other sources of relief—friends, hobbies, sports, vacations—are ultimately disappointing. Once they're out of the picture, the pressures return.

Take your tensions and troubles to Jesus in prayer. He gives lasting peace that is beyond your comprehension.

You are my safe house, O God. Help me turn to You in prayer for strength in difficult times.

Where Do You Go?

SCRIPTURE READING: 2 Corinthians 1:8–11   KEY VERSE: 2 Corinthians 1:8

We do not want you to be ignorant, brethren, of our trouble which came to us in Asia: that we were burdened beyond measure, above strength, so that we despaired even of life.

When the world feels as if it is caving in around you and there is nothing you can do to change your circumstances, where do you go to find strength and hope?

In 2 Corinthians 1:8, Paul told of being "burdened beyond measure, above strength, so that we despaired even of life." Whatever he was facing, the thought of impending death was on his mind. Yet his hope did not rest in his human ability.

The Person he turned to was the only One who could administer peace to his heart and truth to his mind. Even though he despaired, he did not give up or give in to fears. He ran to Jesus: "In whom we trust that He will still deliver us" (2 Cor. 1:10).

From the world's perspective, there are many places you can go to find comfort. But there is only one place you will find a hand to catch your tears and a heart to listen to your every longing. True peace comes only from God. Nothing is so great that God is not greater still.

Is there an urgency in your heart? Something that threatens your emotional well-being as well as your ability to perform in life? Take it to Jesus. Run to Him. He is your solid, unshakable Source of strength in cruel and hurtful times, One who is faithful and One who is true.

Heavenly Father, I run to You today. You are the One who is faithful and true. You are my unshakable Source of strength in difficult times.

Bearing Burdens

SCRIPTURE READING: Galatians 6:1–5   KEY VERSE: Galatians 6:2

Bear one another's burdens, and so fulfill the law of Christ.

The casual chat over the fence turns serious. The routine conversation about teenage dilemmas leads into an emotional admission by your neighbor.

"My son is about to be suspended from school for something he said to his teacher. I am going to talk with the principal today and would appreciate your prayers. I'm pretty upset about the possible consequences."

You wince. You are not sure what to say. Since you both attend the same church, you assure him that you will pray for his son. He is grateful.

The next weekend you notice your neighbor working in his yard. You would like to walk over and inquire about his son's status, but you are apprehensive about how to approach the subject.

Bearing the burdens of a fellow Christian is a ticklish issue. We do not want to appear nosy and certainly don't desire to say something that could be misconstrued. For the most part, we keep at arm's length, opting for our basic generic prayer. This approach is far removed from the biblical notion of bearing one another's burdens, which entails a significant sharing of the spiritual and emotional weight.

Have you entered into this kind of burden bearing? Aren't there episodes when you desperately need this kind of assistance? God has a way to make it happen.

Dear Lord, make me sensitive to the needs of others. I want to be a burden bearer.

The Ultimate Burden Bearer

SCRIPTURE READING: Philippians 2:19–30   KEY VERSE: Psalm 55:22

Cast your burden on the LORD,
And He shall sustain you;
He shall never permit the righteous to be moved.

Shouldering the load of a fellow Christian's troubles is both hard and easy. It's hard because often we are consumed with our own problems and have little time for another's pain. It's easy because once we see Christ's power and wisdom unleashed to solve another's strait, we develop a taste for the spiritual adventure of burden bearing.

It begins with a commitment to cultivate relationships with a few friends. This is the right context for authentic sharing and caring. We can't handle everyone's assortment of woes, but as we see in our Scripture reading for today, we can help bear the hurts of some, especially those friends with whom we have developed accountability and a track record of trust.

Most people are reluctant to unload their burdens for fear of rejection. Actually, many are not sure we really want to hear about their problems. A phone call, a letter, a lunch, a walk around the block are practical means to provide the opportunity for effective burden bearing. Take the initiative. Be sensitive and timely, but don't wait for the hurting person to knock on your door.

Lean on God, and don't try to solve the problem alone. Beneath the obvious issue can be a maze of root causes that only God can deal with through the Holy Spirit. Trust Christ to guide, comfort, and provide. Remember, He is the ultimate Burden Bearer.

Father, thank You for the privilege of extending Your love by bearing the burdens of others to You in prayer. Work through me to lighten their heavy load.

A Personal Invitation

SCRIPTURE READING: Matthew 11:28–30   KEY VERSE: Psalm 116:7

Return to your rest, O my soul,
For the LORD has dealt bountifully with you.

It marked a turning point in Jesus' ministry. He preached to great crowds, His words convicting and startling. He healed many, to their wonder and amazement. Yet up to that point, only the disciples had experienced personal intimacy with the Savior. Following a stinging rebuke to those who refused His message, Jesus issued a compassionate invitation: "Come to Me, all you who labor and are heavy laden, and I will give you rest" (Matt. 11:28).

"I'm here," Jesus in essence said to His listeners, "to lift the burdens of life from your shoulders. I'll take them on Me if you will let Me."

If you are oppressed and bent under the accumulation of too many demands and concerns, Jesus stands ready to lighten your load. If you are exhausted from juggling bills, kids, work, and other pressing problems, Jesus can restore your weary spirit.

He invites you to come to Him. There are no strings attached, no restrictions, no fine print. He won't condemn you for past failures. His arms are open wide to take you as you are and give you the help you need.

What a relief! What a Savior! Accept His personal invitation, and get out of the pressure cooker and into His rest. In the shadow of His wings you will find unconditional love and acceptance. Whatever you are facing, let the Savior face it with you.

I accept Your invitation, Lord. I enter into Your rest and hide myself in the shadow of Your wings.

Open Your Heart to God

SCRIPTURE READING: Luke 2:25–40   KEY VERSES: Luke 2:36–38

There was one, Anna, a prophetess, the daughter of Phanuel, of the tribe of Asher. She was of a great age, and had lived with a husband seven years from her virginity; and this woman was a widow of about eighty-four years, who did not depart from the temple, but served God with fastings and prayers night and day. And coming in that instant she gave thanks to the Lord, and spoke of Him to all those who looked for redemption in Jerusalem.

Anna's husband died when she was quite young. They had been married only seven years before death took his life. Alone she took up the mantle of prayer and devoted herself to seeking God for the coming of the Messiah (Luke 2:37).

How many of us would have done this? There's no mention of worrying about her state of widowhood or how her needs would be provided. No record of anger over being left without her husband, her friend, and her beloved at such an early age. These elements are especially important when we look at her life in the context of Judaism.

Most women were married and had children. To be barren was a disgrace, but not for Anna. Her devotion was solely to the Lord. Day and night, her heart's desire was to seek audience with almighty God through prayer. Times of fasting gave her a spiritual sensitivity that few experience.

When Christ came to earth, one of the first places He went was to the temple. Even as a baby, Jesus was God. He had heard this woman's fervent petition, and with His birth God answered her call.

Prayer transports us into the presence of God. Anna did not concern herself with the talk and gossip of her day. She was focused on the coming of the Messiah. Have you made the decision to open your heart only to God?

Lord, I focus my attention upon You right now as I kneel in Your presence. I open my heart to You.

Requirements of Biblical Meditation

SCRIPTURE READING: Matthew 14:22–23　　　KEY VERSE: Psalm 27:11

Teach me Your way, O LORD,
And lead me in a smooth path, because of my enemies.

In her book *Discipline: The Glad Surrender,* Elisabeth Elliot writes about the requirements of biblical meditation:

> We have been discussing making an offering of the body, which is an act of worship . . . offered by mind and heart. The next thing we are to do is to let our minds be remade and our whole nature transformed.
>
> We cannot do this by ourselves. It is the Holy Spirit who must do the work. But we must open our minds to that work, submit to His control, think on the things that matter rather than on the things that come to nothing in the end. Here again we see both the necessity of a sovereign God working in and through us and the responsibility of the disciple himself to adapt to what God wants to do . . .
>
> In times of prayer and meditation, do not try to "think about nothing." "Set your mind," Paul says, not, "Empty your mind." Set it on Christ, not on earthly things. One phrase from God's Word can be taken and repeated quietly, asking that we may be given . . . the spiritual power of wisdom and vision, by which there comes the knowledge of Him.

Make sure the place you select for your quiet time is relatively distraction free. Avoid putting God in a spiritual box. Instead, be open to the newness and joy He brings each day as you enter His throne room with praise.

Lord, keep me open to the newness and joy You bring each day as I enter Your throne room with praise!

Seeking God

SCRIPTURE READING: 1 Peter 1:13–19   KEY VERSE: Matthew 6:33

Seek first the kingdom of God and His righteousness, and all these things shall be added to you.

Do you long to have a close relationship with God, but getting there seems a distant dream? In her book *His Imprint, My Expression,* Kay Arthur helps you over some common hurdles to intimacy with the Lord:

> Seeking God—intimacy with God—must be your priority.
>
> Maybe knowing God intimately has not been a priority . . . or maybe you're so overwhelmed by simply trying to meet the demands of daily living that you don't see how knowing God intimately at this stage in life could be a priority. That may be why you feel like you're treading water. You're not alone! . . .
>
> Seeking God doesn't mean that you are to stop earning your living, but it does mean that you may have to be satisfied with less, rather than working harder and longer hours in order to have more!
>
> Seeking God may mean you will have to lay aside some of your time-consuming activities. Television, sports, hobbies . . . may have to go and maybe some of your ambitions. But not your work. God says that if you don't work, you shouldn't eat. Besides, He promises that if you seek His Kingdom and His righteousness, the basics of life will be provided (Matthew 6:33).
>
> Of course you'll never see the fulfillment of this promise until you do what God says. But when you begin seeking Him, God in His grace will move on your behalf . . . God keeps His promises!

Father, sometimes I'm overwhelmed by the daily demands of life, but I really do want to make seeking You in prayer a priority.

Pouring Forth Your Heart

SCRIPTURE READING: 2 Chronicles 20:1–12   KEY VERSE: 2 Chronicles 20:3

Jehoshaphat feared, and set himself to seek the LORD, and proclaimed a fast throughout all Judah.

Jehoshaphat had a huge problem. This good king of Judah had just received some bad news. The armies of the Moabites and Ammonites were about to march on them. It was a time of national emergency, and most leaders would have called their advisors or mustered the army, but not King Jehoshaphat.

Jehoshaphat was afraid and sought the Lord. He didn't falter, complain, or waste time in pessimistic thinking. Instead, he immediately called the people together for a time of prayer with fasting.

Notice the attributes of God he named at the beginning of his prayer: "O LORD God of our fathers, are You not God in heaven and do You not rule over all the kingdoms of the nations, and in Your hand is there not power and might, so that no one is able to withstand You?" (2 Chron. 20:6).

The king recognized God's ultimate power and authority; therefore, he was not afraid of what mere men might do to him. Furthermore, he showed that he was willing to be involved in the process of God's answer. The king didn't mouth a halfhearted, unemotional statement; he prayed with passion and sincerity.

Have you ever poured forth your heart to the Lord? He wants you to cry out to Him and actively seek His deliverance.

Lord, I pour out my heart before You right now. Hear my cry. Deliver me!

A God-Centered Prayer

SCRIPTURE READING: 2 Chronicles 20:13–30   KEY VERSE: 2 Chronicles 20:17

You will not need to fight in this battle. Position yourselves, stand still and see the salvation of the LORD, who is with you, O Judah and Jerusalem! Do not fear or be dismayed; tomorrow go out against them, for the LORD is with you.

Jehoshaphat's prayer was God centered. He did not indulge in negativism by dwelling on the details of the difficulty. God wants you to be specific about a problem, His desire is to move your focus onto His power. Name your concern and begin with praise for His action and blessing in the past; then express the truth of His omnipotence.

The king was no novice in rulership, and that wasn't the first kingdom problem. He had learned the value of coming to God in absolute humility, acknowledging his utter dependence. So complete was his trust that he never lapsed into self-reliance.

In other words, he could have quickly thanked God and then spread out the battle maps to make plans with his commanders. In your situation, the temptation to figure it out yourself may be the same, but God wants you to let Him handle the strategy.

What is even more awesome is that while the king prayed, God already had their deliverance under way. By the time the army of Judah arrived on the scene, what they beheld was a field of corpses. Not one foe was left standing. God provided what they needed, and He supplied them with gracious abundance.

Trusting Him to provide the resources for every demand makes you a God-centered person.

Lord, thank You for Your faithfulness in the past. I praise You for what You will do in the future. I lay my problems, plans, and issues before You right now.

Praying in Jesus' Name

SCRIPTURE READING: John 14:12–14   KEY VERSE: John 15:16

You did not choose Me, but I chose you and appointed you that you should go and bear fruit, and that your fruit should remain, that whatever you ask the Father in My name He may give you.

Have you ever paused to think about the significance of saying "in Jesus' name" at the end of your prayers? Maybe you've said it since you were a child and never questioned the meaning of the phrase, but in those three words is a world of truth about prayer.

"In the name of" means "by the power and authority of." For example, in certain legal contracts, you can be given special authority to act in the name of someone else or on that person's behalf. You are allowed to make decisions and take actions as though you were that person.

In prayer, by saying "in Jesus' name," you acknowledge that what you're asking is through the power, authority, and permission of Jesus. Jesus explained in John 14:13–14: "Whatever you ask in My name, that I will do, so that the Father may be glorified in the Son. If you ask anything in My name, I will do it."

Some have greatly misunderstood this verse, interpreting it as a license to ask God for anything in Jesus' name and believing that God is then somehow bound to give them their desires. What Jesus is really saying, however, is that praying in His name means praying according to His character and His will.

Praying in Jesus' name is a serious matter and a matchless blessing. His name is your assurance that He will shape your prayers in His image.

Heavenly Father, I pray today in the name of Jesus. Thank You for the assurance that You will shape my prayers in Your image.

In the Presence of God

SCRIPTURE READING: Psalm 141:1–9   KEY VERSE: James 1:5

If any of you lacks wisdom, let him ask of God, who gives to all liberally and without reproach, and it will be given to him.

Through prayer, you come in contact with the tremendous power of God. In prayer, you acknowledge your inability while professing your trust in Someone who will provide for your every need. If there is a need for wisdom, God's Word tells you to ask (James 1:5). If there is a need for relief from stress, financial ruin, or some other trial, God is your answer and prayer is your connecting point.

Many Bible teachers have said that for a Christian, the distance between success and failure is the distance that it takes for him to drop to his knees in faith and prayer. We are not talking about naming and claiming something. We are talking about placing our trust and hope in God who commands us to seek His face. He may not always answer your prayers the way you want Him to, but He will answer them in love, according to His plan for your life.

Prayer allows you to step into the holy presence of God. It also gives you a spiritual opportunity to know and experience an intimate love that cannot be duplicated by the world. Make prayer a continuing goal in your life. The Lord hears you when you call to Him (Ps. 141). Also, study His Word for insight into the prayers of His saints. Many books have been written on prayer; however, the greatest manual on this subject remains God's holy Word.

Father, thank You for the privilege of coming into Your presence. I am grateful for the opportunity to know and experience intimacy that cannot be duplicated by the world.

The Fabric of Your Life

SCRIPTURE READING: Psalm 119:169–76   KEY VERSE: Hebrews 4:12

The word of God is living and powerful, and sharper than any two-edged sword, piercing even to the division of soul and spirit, and of joints and marrow, and is a discerner of the thoughts and intents of the heart.

Amy Carmichael made a habit of collecting short prayers written throughout the Bible. When a need arose, she would pray God's Word to Him. One of her favorites is found in Psalm 119:175: "Let my soul live, and it shall praise You; and let Your judgments help me."

Two things immediately happen when you use God's Word as a prayer source. First, you are strengthened within your soul. God's Word is powerful (Heb. 4:12). It reveals the message of His heart written just for you. If you are weary from the battles of life, the Word of God is a minister of hope and truth. It is God breathed; therefore, it has the ability to refresh and renew the downtrodden.

Second, you experience intimate fellowship with the Lord by reading His Word. In picking it up, you are telling Him that you want to know more about Him, your life, and the situation at hand. He honors your devotion just as He honors the promises in His Word.

Too many people wait until desperation hits before they turn to God for guidance. But you don't have to wait until the alarm sounds. God's Word is a standard of truth. When you weave it into the fabric of your life through prayer, your trust level rises, and you can see clearly the hope that is given to you by a faithful, loving God.

Lord, help me weave the fabric of my life with prayer. Lift the level of my trust so I can see clearly the hope that You have given me.

Praying for Others

SCRIPTURE READING: Colossians 1:9–14   KEY VERSE: Colossians 1:9

For this reason we also, since the day we heard it, do not cease to pray for you, and to ask that you may be filled with the knowledge of His will in all wisdom and spiritual understanding.

Perhaps you are driving your car and a friend comes to mind. It may be someone you have not seen in years. Or you could be reading through your devotions and God places a burden on your heart to pray for a family member. His Spirit is calling out to you to be sensitive and pray for that person.

You don't need to know what the other person is going through in order to pray for him. God will show you what is necessary. One of the greatest blessings comes when you recognize the moving of the Holy Spirit and follow Him in prayer.

Paul encouraged the Colossians by telling how he prayed for them. Imagine what it was like to have Paul pray for you!

Prayer is the greatest gift you can give another person. When you approach the throne of God on behalf of another, you are doing exactly what Jesus has done for you.

Paul prayed that these early believers would have "all wisdom and spiritual understanding, that you may walk worthy of the Lord" (Col. 1:9–10).

Prayer reveals new dimensions of God's love. It keeps us from becoming self-focused. Instead we become others focused. God takes our prayers and uses them to unlock doors of blessing in the lives of others.

Father, use my prayers to unlock doors of blessing in the lives of others. Help me to be sensitive to the prompting of Your Spirit to pray for those in need.

The Value of Prayer

SCRIPTURE READING: Joshua 1:1–9   KEY VERSE: Joshua 1:8

This Book of the Law shall not depart from your mouth, but you shall meditate in it day and night, that you may observe to do according to all that is written in it. For then you will make your way prosperous, and then you will have good success.

The value of spending time alone with God in prayer cannot be underestimated. It's more than a spiritual exercise to be checked off as you move through your schedule for the day. It's a vital part of your growing relationship with Jesus Christ.

You learn to develop a quiet spirit. When you stop the rush and bustle of the moment and sit before Him, the harried feelings begin to melt away. If you've done a good job of putting aside all possible distractions, you can focus on Him alone and feel His peace settle over you.

Your heart will be purified. Your motives will be sifted, clarifying your purpose and helping you view your life and circumstances from the perspective of God's Word. He gives you this promise: "This Book of the Law shall not depart from your mouth, but you shall meditate in it day and night, that you may observe to do according to all that is written in it. For then you will make your way prosperous, and then you will have good success" (Joshua 1:8).

You can confirm outside counsel. If something others are telling you doesn't square with what God says in prayer and the Word, then you know to reject others' advice. The Holy Spirit interprets Scripture to you as you read, reminding you of what you know and adding to your learning with further dimensions of truth.

Lord, as I wait before You in prayer today, speak to me through Your Word. Purify my heart, sift my motives, clarify my purpose, and help me view my circumstances from Your perspective.

A Matter of the Heart

SCRIPTURE READING: Psalm 105:1–4   KEY VERSE: James 4:8

Draw near to God and He will draw near to you. Cleanse your hands, you sinners; and purify your hearts, you double-minded.

The Lord tells us in His Word that when we seek Him, we will find Him (1 Chron. 28:9; Jer. 29:13). But have you ever thought about what is actually involved in seeking God? It is not a matter of just attending church or following a certain religious tradition.

Seeking God is a matter of the heart. This one activity leads you to cross over being a "churchgoer" to becoming a follower of "the way of Christ." You seek Him, not in a mysterious mythical sense, but through intimate devotion. In your seeking, you thirst after God much like the psalmist who wrote: "As the deer pants for the water brooks, so pants my soul for You, O God" (Ps. 42:1). A longing to your seeking ushers you into the presence of God where you experience the fullness of His love and undivided care for your soul.

Jesus was quick to ask those who followed Him, "Why do you seek Me?" Was it the miracles He performed, or was it the closeness of His presence that drew them? Why do you seek the Lord? Is He an emergency switch you push in times of crisis, or do you truly long to experience His presence on an intimate level?

God desires your love and devotion. By itself, memorizing amounts of Scripture will not draw you closer to Him. What grabs God's heart is the humble, abiding love of someone who seeks Him above everything else.

Give me a heart to seek You above all else, Lord. I want to experience Your presence on an intimate level.

A Season of Waiting

SCRIPTURE READING: Psalm 25:1–22   KEY VERSE: Matthew 7:7

Ask, and it will be given to you; seek, and you will find; knock, and it will be opened to you.

Is there some prayer that you have been longing for God to answer? Maybe your longing for this one prayer to be answered has continued for months or even years. Temptation comes and you feel like giving up. You think, *Where are You, God? And how will I ever get beyond this point of need?*

God operates along a perfectly designed time line. He knows what you need and when to provide it. But He wants you to learn how to trust Him for the blessings He has planned. "Delight yourself also in the LORD; and He shall give you the desires of your heart," declared the psalmist. "Commit your way to the LORD, trust also in Him, and He shall bring it to pass" (Ps. 37:4–5). Seeking God involves delighting yourself in His faithfulness, praising Him for His goodness, and loving Him because He cares for you.

At times, God requires a season of waiting before He sends His blessing. Then trust becomes your greatest asset. If you don't trust God with your need, you will cry out in fear and panic. At one point during a storm on the Sea of Galilee, the disciples thought they would perish. But Jesus commanded the wind and waves to be still. He taught those men how to trust Him even in the most tempestuous of circumstances, and He is teaching you to watch and wait for His outstretched arm. As you wait in His presence today, receive peace—for He is with you.

Father, I delight in Your faithfulness. As I wait in Your presence, I praise You for Your goodness and what You have planned for me in the future.

Praying for Leaders

SCRIPTURE READING: 1 Timothy 2:1–4   KEY VERSE: Luke 18:1

Then He spoke a parable to them, that men always ought to pray and not lose heart.

Whether or not the man who leads your country is one you have personally chosen is not the issue. Once a leader is elected or placed in a position of authority, each of us has a responsibility to pray for that individual.

You need to be committed to pray for his personal relationship with Christ and his willingness to seek God's wisdom for every decision. Pray that your leader would learn to hate evil and love righteousness. Only then can true justice be administered in the maze of government and politics.

Be committed to pray that your leader's convictions will be based on God's Word and not preferences founded on the unstable ground of political consensus. Ask God to protect his family, and pray that each family member would be given the opportunity to know Jesus Christ as Savior and Lord.

Rulers often think they are in control of their country's circumstances, but God is quick to point out that He is Lord over all. Men and nations are under the control of God and not the House of Representatives, the Senate, Parliament, or any superior court.

You may feel as though your prayers are insignificant, but they are vital links to God's throne room where eternal decisions are made on a daily basis.

O God, rulers are under Your authority—every politician, every law enforcement officer, every judge. You are Lord over all. I pray for blessings upon these leaders today.

Praying Specifically

SCRIPTURE READING: Ephesians 1:15–23   KEY VERSE: Ephesians 1:18

The eyes of your understanding being enlightened; that you may know what is the hope of His calling, what are the riches of the glory of His inheritance in the saints.

Do you ever struggle sometimes with knowing what to pray for? Do you ever have trouble coming up with the words to say? Maybe you can think of certain requests, but when it is time to voice them to God, you resort to using such vague phrases as, "Bless this person, Lord."

You don't need to feel guilty about this concern. God wants you to pray and communicate with Him, whatever words you use. You don't have to be eloquent or polished to talk to your intimate Friend.

But you do need to realize that by not praying specifically about what is on your heart, you're missing out on a whole level of blessing in talking to God. Notice how Paul prayed in Ephesians 1:18, as just one example: "The eyes of your understanding being enlightened; that you may know what is the hope of His calling, what are the riches of the glory of His inheritance in the saints."

Paul applied truth from Scripture and asked God specifically to work those truths into the lives of people he cared for. Every time you read your Bible, jot down the lessons and promises that you read. The next time you pray for someone, ask God to show him what you learned, enriching him with knowledge of God's Word. You'll discover a whole new dimension of communication with the Lord.

Dear Lord, I pray that others will experience what I am learning and be enriched with the knowledge of Your Word.

Meeting with God

SCRIPTURE READING: Ephesians 3:14–21   KEY VERSE: Psalm 55:17

Evening and morning and at noon
I will pray, and cry aloud,
And He shall hear my voice.

Some people are afraid to ask God for the little things. They think that some-how He is too big and too busy to care about the trivialities of their lives. Nothing could be farther from the truth. Catherine Marshall explains in her book *Adventures in Prayer:*

> Oddly, we who are afraid to ask that the pain of rheumatism be removed or a lost contact lens be found, often do not hesitate to pray for world peace or the salvation of souls or a revival to change the face of our time. It never occurs to us that if God's power is lacking for these everyday prayers, His power to handle big, all-inclusive petitions will be lacking too.
>
> In order to make sure that we are not retreating from the tension of faith, it is helpful to ask ourselves as we pray, "Do I really expect anything to hap-pen?" This will prevent us from going window-shopping in prayer. At times window-shopping can be enjoyable, but there it ends . . .
>
> So we decide to ask His help with some small immediate need. Our ask-ing is like stepping into a tiny anteroom. Taking a hesitant step forward, we discover that the anteroom leads into the King's spacious reception hall.
>
> To our astonishment, the King Himself comes forward to meet us, offer-ing a gift so momentous as to be worthy only of the King.

Lord, thank You for the invitation to come into Your presence to meet and fellowship with You.

Everyday Opportunities

SCRIPTURE READING: Psalm 61:1–8   KEY VERSE: Ephesians 2:10

We are His workmanship, created in Christ Jesus for good works, which God prepared beforehand that we should walk in them.

Changing your life to be more like Christ is called Sanctification.

The Holy Spirit is always at work in your life, conforming you to the image of Christ; that's called sanctification. And though you do not enhance this development through self-effort, God wants you to pay close attention to what He's doing, even asking Him specifically to show you the aspects of His activity.

His goals for you are not mysterious; God is not trying to hide His plans for you. When you ask Him to give you direction, whether it's for coping with daily activities or for grasping His larger vision, He will give you the guidance you request (James 1:5).

All of us have sin habits and negative behaviors that aren't readily apparent to us. God may use the words of friends to point out such problem areas to you, as painful as that may be. Or He may choose to quietly convict your heart without outside assistance. Either way, He'll let you know what He wants to change next.

Did you know that God has already planned spiritual activities for you (Eph. 2:10)? Ask Him to open your eyes to everyday opportunities to demonstrate His love to others. He'll even give you creative ideas for ministry. Remember, all of His riches are yours for the asking.

Dear Lord, as I wait in Your presence today, show me where I need to change. Open my eyes to everyday opportunities to demonstrate Your love to others.

Transforming Prayer

SCRIPTURE READING: Colossians 4:2–4   KEY VERSE: Isaiah 26:3

You will keep him in perfect peace,
Whose mind is stayed on You,
Because he trusts in You.

In the movie version of *Shadowlands,* which portrays the endearing relationship between Christian apologist C. S. Lewis and Joy Gresham, a friend comments to Lewis that God finally answered his prayers. As part of his response, Lewis says, "Prayer doesn't change God; it changes me."

How profound and true that is! Your communication with God is your intimate connection with Him, and He allows you to participate in the work that He is doing and even to see His actions in relationship to your prayers. God hears and answers every prayer, but His purposes in prayer go far beyond giving you a measurable response.

God wants to transform your life through the process of prayer. Your personal relationship with Christ is deepened and enlarged when you spend time talking to Him. As you come into His presence with reverence and a quiet heart, ready to listen, He begins to purify your heart and sift your priorities. You develop a passion for obedience to God, and you begin to see Him as the Provider for all your needs.

Most important, you experience the peace that comes from knowing God is in control (Phil. 4:6–7). Your anxiety melts away as you learn to trust Him. These are just some of the ways God uses prayer to change your heart. The more you pray, the more transformations you'll discover.

Change me, Lord, as I wait in Your presence. Let my anxiety melt away and let me learn to trust You.

Giving God Glory

SCRIPTURE READING: Psalm 24:1–10   KEY VERSE: Revelation 19:1

After these things I heard a loud voice of a great multitude in heaven, saying, "Alleluia! Salvation and glory and honor and power belong to the Lord our God!"

Jesus condemned the actions of the religious leaders who prayed loudly in the streets so that they would be seen and admired by others. The purpose of prayer is to communicate humbly with God, not to gain the praise of men. In her book *A Journey into Prayer*, Evelyn Christenson relates her personal concerns in this area:

Wanting something for our own glory, not God's, is one reason why a prayer, although scripturally accurate and acceptable to God, is ruined by our reason for praying it.

Some years ago, as I prayed my birthday prayer for the coming year, my words simply were these: "God, You be glorified, not me!" And when the year ended, my praying for only His glory did not end. Praying the "right prayer" about God getting all the glory has been a learning process for me for a long time.

Through the years, I have prayed before speaking that I will not be seen as I speak—only Jesus . . . The greatest compliment I ever receive is when someone steps up to me and quietly says, "I saw Jesus standing there instead of you today." For His glory!

My illustration or point may be very good in itself, but if my motive for bringing it is for my glory, God will not use it to move in the lives of those in my audience. It has to be for His glory.

Lord, reveal the motives behind my prayers. I don't want to pray for something for my own glory. I want my life to reflect Your glory.

The Righteous Judge

SCRIPTURE READING: Luke 18:1–8   KEY VERSE: Matthew 7:8

Everyone who asks receives, and he who seeks finds, and to him who knocks it will be opened.

The widow had made a complete nuisance of herself. She just wouldn't take no for an answer, and the judge was becoming irate. He didn't care whether she had a case, and he didn't want to be bothered with the facts. All he knew was that if he granted her the legal protection she asked for, she would finally leave him alone.

Why would Jesus tell this parable to help explain why you should be persistent in prayer? The judge in the story isn't at all like your heavenly Father and that is Jesus' point: "Hear what the unjust judge said. And shall not God avenge His own elect who cry out day and night to Him, though He bears long with them? I tell you that He will avenge them speedily" (Luke 18:6–8).

If an earthly judge without a conscience gives in because someone keeps after him, how much more will God the righteous and loving Judge listen to you, His own child? God is not deaf to your appeals. You may feel that He is not listening, but in reality He may be asking you to wait. Sometimes He withholds an answer for a time so that you will draw closer to Him and develop the habit of talking to Him through prayer.

Remember, God's priority is always your relationship with Him. Keep going to your heavenly Father, the just Judge. Your case is on His heart.

Father, how I thank You that You are a just judge. Help me persevere in prayer, knowing that You will answer in due time and Your answer will be just and right.

The High-Priestly Prayer

SCRIPTURE READING: John 17:1–26 KEY VERSE: John 17:20

I do not pray for these alone, but also for those who will believe in Me through their word.

This Scripture forms what scholars call the High-Priestly prayer. In it Jesus prayed for us and made His requests to the Father on our behalf. Warren Wiersbe discusses it:

> This is the greatest prayer ever prayed on earth and the greatest prayer recorded anywhere in Scripture. John 17 is certainly the "holy of holies" of the Gospel record, and we must approach this chapter in a spirit of humility and worship. To think that we are privileged to listen in as God the Son converses with His Father just as He is about to give His life as a ransom for sinners!
>
> No matter what events occurred later that evening, this prayer makes it clear that Jesus was and is the Overcomer. He was not a "victim"; He was and is the Victor! "Be of good cheer," He had encouraged His disciples; "I have overcome the world" (John 16:33) . . .
>
> Why did Jesus pray this prayer? Certainly He was preparing Himself for the sufferings that lay ahead. As He contemplated the glory that the Father promised Him, He would receive new strength for His sacrifice (Hebrews 12:1–3). But He also had His disciples in mind (John 17:13).
>
> What an encouragement this prayer should have been to them! He prayed about their security, their joy, their unity, and their future glory! He also prayed it for us today, so that we would know all that He has done for us.

Jesus, thank You for Your prayers for me! Thank You for Your concern about my security, joy, unity, and future glory.

The Presence of God

SCRIPTURE READING: Acts 17:22–31   KEY VERSE: Matthew 28:20

And lo, I am with you always, even to the end of the age.

One of the most debilitating emotions is loneliness. Maybe you've felt that way in a hospital or emergency room, in a new city or job, or even in the midst of friends and family. Feeling as if there is no one to care or share with is a terrifying sensation. It can even be deadly.

That is why one of the most comforting names given to our Savior is Immanuel, "God with us." Because of the indwelling Christ, believers are never separated from His permanent presence. We are in Christ and He is in us. What an encouragement! What a comfort! What an assurance! We always have a shoulder to lean on, the broad shoulders of Immanuel. We always have Someone to listen to our heartache, our constant Companion, Friend Jesus.

The gods of other religions are usually in some far-off, remote corner, stoically seated in a seat of perfection. Not so with our Creator and Redeemer. Once in us, He will never leave us, abandon us, or forget us.

Don't let our adversary and accuser rob you of the peace and joy that come from experiencing and enjoying the sweet presence of our God. No sin, no deed, no trial can ever diminish the full presence and acceptance of Christ once you have become His child through faith. God is for you. God loves you. Allow His presence to fill any void.

Lord, I am so thankful that I can lean upon You in prayer today. No trial can diminish the sweetness of Your presence in my life.

Intercessory Prayer

SCRIPTURE READING: Matthew 5:38–45   KEY VERSE: Job 42:10

The LORD restored Job's losses when he prayed for his friends. Indeed the LORD gave Job twice as much as he had before.

U sually, the last thing we do for individuals who rub us the wrong way is to pray for them. We would rather gossip, grumble, or backbite in such instances. Have you ever thought why that is true?

Of course, the power of sin within us is one culprit, but there is an even more ominous perpetrator at work. Our crafty and deadly adversary, the devil, busily plies his trade in such strained relationships, realizing that intercessory prayer on behalf of others is the one supernatural ingredient that can tear down his stronghold.

Without Christ, the unbeliever is in the terminal death grip of Satan and sin. With Christ, the believer is freed from the devil's mastery but is still susceptible to his evil influence.

Behind the behavior of those who offend you is the deceiver at work. As long as you refuse or resist to pray on their behalf, it is unlikely you will see real change in them or in you. Rather than verbally or mentally slur or badger those who irritate you, you must mount an assault on the evil one through regular, sincere intercession. Your petitions can spell the difference between freedom and bondage—for you and them.

Freedom or bondage—my prayers can make the difference! Thank You, dear Lord, for the privilege of interceding for others.

APRIL

Your Inheritance and Identity in Christ

MOUNTAIN: The mountain of the Lord's inheritance in the promised land

KEY VERSES:

Exodus 15:17–18

You will bring them in and plant them
In the mountain of Your inheritance,
In the place, O LORD, which You have made
For Your own dwelling,
The sanctuary, O LORD, which Your hands have
established.
The LORD shall reign forever and ever.

Ephesians 1:17–18

That the God of our Lord Jesus Christ, the Father of glory, may give to you the spirit of wisdom and revelation in the knowledge of Him, the eyes of your understanding being enlightened; that you may know what is the hope of His calling, what are the riches of the glory of His inheritance in the saints.

Discovering Your True Identity

SCRIPTURE READING: Ephesians 2:8–10   KEY VERSE: Psalm 139:14

I will praise You, for I am fearfully and wonderfully made;
Marvelous are Your works,
And that my soul knows very well.

The alarm clock rings. Another day awaits. The early morning news brings word of the newest economic summit, the nominees for this year's Nobel Peace Prize, and a report on the national gathering of governors.

Meanwhile, the only financial summit you have is a monthly talk with your spouse to reconcile the checkbook. The only peace you are interested in is stopping the constant bickering between your teenagers. And the only gathering of important people you attended was the recent family reunion.

You can feel small and insignificant in a world of six billion people, millions of worthwhile developments, and thousands of news clips of notable happenings that make your contribution seem almost meaningless.

Although God cares about financial stability, world peace, and social justice, He has one great thing on His mind today—you. You are His workmanship, His masterpiece. There is no one else like you, and God cares for you with infinite watchfulness. He knows exactly how many hairs came out in your brush this morning. Your checkbook matters as much as the federal budget, harmony in your home as much as harmony among nations.

I am Your workmanship! I am Your masterpiece. There is no one else like me, Lord, and You care for me with infinite watchfulness.

The Favor of God

SCRIPTURE READING: 1 Samuel 3:1–10   KEY VERSE: Psalm 90:12

Teach us to number our days,
That we may gain a heart of wisdom.

Does God care more for you than anybody else? No. Does He care less for you than anybody else? No.

God cares for you in precisely the same manner He does for each of His children—with complete justice, fairness, goodness, and equality.

His forgiveness is just for you. His love is custom designed to meet your most excruciating emotional and spiritual needs. His Word speaks to you personally.

He calls you by name as He did Samuel (1 Sam. 3). He is intimately acquainted with every single one of your peculiar ways (Ps. 139) and has numbered each of your days on planet earth (Ps. 90:12).

Yet you are not to stand still and bask in all this attention lavished on you. God takes care of you, His workmanship, so that you may engage in a lifetime of extending His goodness to others.

Assured of Christ's unstinting, unreserved grace and favor toward you in every circumstance, you may wake up each day with a positive outlook and the knowledge that He is at work through you to accomplish His objectives.

God has some good works for you to do today. No one can do them but you.

Thank You, dear Lord, that You know me by name. You are intimately acquainted with every one of my ways and have numbered each of my days.

God's Immeasurable Riches

SCRIPTURE READING: Colossians 2:1–10   KEY VERSE: Hebrews 1:2

[God] has in these last days spoken to us by His Son, whom He has appointed heir of all things, through whom also He made the worlds.

The word *heir* evokes thoughts of money or property handed down from generation to generation, with some special person receiving a legacy from a parent or relative. The heir is granted full benefits and ownership privileges and has the gratifying knowledge that he is unique, blessed, chosen for honor in some way.

Not many of us will inherit a vast estate or get a surprise phone call from a wealthy relation. But with Jesus as your Savior, you are already an heir with Him of all God's immeasurable riches. God the Father gave everything to Jesus, "whom He has appointed heir of all things, through whom also He made the worlds" (Heb. 1:2). He is your fullness and abundant supply for every part of your being.

Do you need strength? God has all power and gives energy for every task. Do you lack wisdom? He provides discernment and insight that cut through even the densest fog of confusion. Are you searching for contentment? Jesus gives you peace beyond human understanding.

A bank account can be depleted; a fortune can dwindle away; houses and property can be taken. But the inheritance you have in Christ is untouchable, unchanging, and inexhaustible.

Thank You, dear Lord, that my inheritance in You is untouchable, unchanging, and inexhaustible. You are all I need!

The Wellspring of Spiritual Blessings

SCRIPTURE READING: 1 Peter 5:5–6   KEY VERSE: James 4:10

Humble yourselves in the sight of the Lord, and He will lift you up.

The grace of God is the wellspring of all spiritual blessings. Grace gives and gives, superabounding in its measure and effectiveness. How then can you cease striving, get off the performance treadmill, and learn to walk in such rich and plentiful grace?

Here is the key: the more you humble yourself before God, the more you receive the fullness of God's grace.

God "gives grace to the humble" (1 Peter 5:5). Not to the strong, but to the weak. Not to the self-sufficient, but to the dependent. Not to the proud, but to the poor of spirit. You humble yourself by realizing the majesty of God, worshiping Him as the mighty God. The more you adore and praise the Savior, the more highly you think of Him. You can do much, but it is so little when compared to what You may accomplish when God directs and empowers you.

Humbling yourself does not belittle your self-esteem or worth to God. It positions you to receive your sustenance from the Source of all good things, Jesus Christ. As a humble believer, you fling yourself on the grace of God, leaning your full weight on Him. You draw all your strength, peace, joy, and security from the sufficiency of God's generous grace.

I fling myself upon Your mercy, O Lord. I lean on You and draw my strength, peace, joy, and security from Your sufficiency.

The Gift of Grace

SCRIPTURE READING: Titus 3:4–7   KEY VERSE: Proverbs 3:34

Surely He scorns the scornful,
But gives grace to the humble.

If God's offer of grace is so rich and free, why do so many people fail to receive the gift of salvation? The inability to receive the grace of God is almost always connected with an overdose of pride.

It is often difficult for some persons to receive a helping hand from another person in regard to material matters. They would rather earn the gift offered on their own initiative and can even be insulted by the generosity of the giver.

Perhaps you can identify with that feeling. You may have had a definite need. Someone graciously volunteered to meet that need, but you refused the offer because it wounded your pride, your sense of self-esteem.

Perhaps in some way you devised a means to satisfy your need. But in the spiritual realm, there is no substitute for grace. You cannot supplant good works or performance for grace. You can either receive it or reject it. It is yours to enjoy by faith or yours to turn away by pride.

Do not refuse the offer of God's grace in salvation. There is no other ground by which a man can be saved. Let go of pride and receive the grace of God.

Take my pride, Lord. I want to receive the fullness of Your grace.

The Wings of Grace

SCRIPTURE READING: 1 Corinthians 9:24–27   KEY VERSE: Hebrews 12:1

Therefore we also, since we are surrounded by so great a cloud of witnesses, let us lay aside every weight, and the sin which so easily ensnares us, and let us run with endurance the race that is set before us.

In the Scriptures, the Christian life is compared to a race. Paul called us to run the race so we may win (1 Cor. 9:24). The author of Hebrews told us to run our race with endurance (Heb. 12:1).

The only means by which believers can triumphantly run and finish the course God assigned for each of us is to run on the wings of grace. The legs of performance eventually grow weak. The muscles of legalism and religion weigh us down and become rigid hindrances. Our problem is that we can understand the need for grace in salvation and glorification, but we tend to rely on other means in the interim—our sanctification on earth.

Justification, the securing of a favorable verdict by Christ's death, is by grace. Glorification, the consummate conforming of our bodies and souls to Christ's glorious image, is by grace. Sanctification, the process of growing in Christlikeness, is also by grace.

In His grace, God supplies all the gear you need for running the spiritual race—His Spirit, His Word, prayer, and fellowship with other believers.

Be strong in grace. Throw off the leg irons of works and religion, and receive the power of God's grace.

Dear Lord, thank You for supplying all the spiritual gear I need for running the race—Your Spirit, Your Word, prayer, and fellowship with other believers.

The Riches of God's Grace

SCRIPTURE READING: Romans 6:1–3   KEY VERSE: John 1:16

Of His fullness we have all received, and grace for grace.

The gospel of God's grace, His full provision for man's sin—present life and eternal destiny—is frequently perverted and attacked. At the foundation of most false religions is a denial of the free gift of salvation and an embrace of good works.

Others caution that the good news of grace can lead to a lifestyle of sin without appropriate punishment. "I am saved by grace, so why does it matter how I live?" is the standard argument.

The Scriptures clearly refute both errors, citing man's inability to know God apart from the Savior's initiative and man's responsibility to live obediently. The rebellious believer reaps what he sows and is a most miserable creature.

However, we should never let such opposition dilute the overwhelming truth of amazing grace. Critics can never dampen the transforming, liberating power of God's free, unconditional, unmerited love and mercy.

The gospel of grace, though misunderstood, cannot be replaced. It is the cornerstone for all of life, illuminating the goodness of God and attracting us to Him. Delight yourself today in the God of all grace.

> *Dear Lord, today I will delight myself in Your grace that has made full provision for my present life and eternal destiny.*

An Infinite Treasury

SCRIPTURE READING: Romans 5:1–11   KEY VERSES: 2 Peter 1:2–3

Grace and peace be multiplied to you in the knowledge of God and of Jesus our Lord, as His divine power has given to us all things that pertain to life and godliness, through the knowledge of Him who called us by glory and virtue.

The elderly couple had lived modestly for years on their small farm. The land was not the best, but they always had raised enough to survive. They eventually sold the farm to a developer. Working on a hunch, the new owner drilled for and discovered oil—a well worth millions of dollars. For years, the couple had lived on top of untold wealth and never knew what they had been missing.

Many believers do not understand the vast riches they already possess in Jesus Christ, an infinite treasury of wisdom and knowledge and all good things. The moment you accept Him as your Savior you receive everything God is, everything God does, and everything God provides. You lack nothing; God's immeasurable, overflowing love and power are available to you by His grace for every trial, every decision, every challenge.

The apostle Peter explained how God gives you these astounding resources: "Grace and peace be multiplied to you in the knowledge of God and of Jesus our Lord, as His divine power has given to us all things that pertain to life and godliness" (2 Peter 1:2–3). Today, you can embrace the fullness of His grace and live the abundant life He has planned.

Lord, I embrace the fullness of Your grace today. I choose to live the abundant life You have planned for me.

The Sufficiency of Christ

SCRIPTURE READING: Romans 6:4–11   KEY VERSE: Romans 8:37

In all these things we are more than conquerors through Him who loved us.

The first five chapters of Romans overflow with the Bible doctrine of justification by faith, which is the foundation of our salvation. Through the Cross, we have been declared righteous, and we have been changed from our former relationship of enmity with God to friendship with God.

In Romans 6, Paul introduced a new truth that the believer must embrace by faith and apply if he is to experience a growing, victorious Christian life. It is the principle of identification, and affirming its meaning and relevance is the first step to becoming more than a conqueror through Jesus Christ (Rom. 8:37).

Identification means that you have been identified or placed by God into Christ's death, burial, and resurrection. In God's eye and mind your sin was on the cross with Jesus.

That's not all. You were raised with Christ (Eph. 2:6). Jesus' resurrection includes you because of your union with Him. This fact is just as certain as justification and reconciliation. To experience its reality, you must believe what the Bible says: you are crucified and risen with Christ (Rom. 6:4). Your role is to reckon or count it as done (Rom. 6:11).

Justification and reconciliation are mine through faith! Thank You, Father!

Divine Representation

SCRIPTURE READING: Romans 5:12–21   KEY VERSE: Romans 5:18

Therefore, as through one man's offense judgment came to all men, resulting in condemnation, even so through one Man's righteous act the free gift came to all men, resulting in justification of life.

Located in Washington, D.C., are one hundred U.S. senators and 435 members of the U.S. House of Representatives. Each represents the voting constituency of his or her home state. Some representatives from small districts represent only thousands of voters, while senators from large states—such as California and New York—represent many millions. Because they are our elected state officials, their votes legally represent their constituencies. For the record, their votes are our votes.

In a way this is how identification works. Jesus was not only our substitute on the cross, dying for us, but He was also our representative. John Stott, in his book *The Cross,* defines a representative as "one who acts on behalf of another in such a way as to involve the other in his action . . . As our representative, He [Christ] did what we, by being united to Him, have also done: We have died and risen with Him."

In His death, burial, and resurrection, Christ represented the entire human race. We are identified with Him, and we receive the merits of Christ's work when we place our faith in Him and His redemptive labor. We are freed from the guilt and penalty of sin (died with Him) and empowered to live (risen with Him) an overcoming life.

Jesus, thank You for representing me in Your death, burial, and resurrection. I praise You that I am a beneficiary of your redemptive labor, freed from the guilt and penalty of sin and empowered to live an overcoming life.

Your Source and Supply

SCRIPTURE READING: Matthew 6:25–34   KEY VERSE: Acts 17:28

In Him we live and move and have our being, as also some of your own poets have said, "For we are also His offspring."

What is your most pressing need today? Money for the mortgage, college tuition, or Christmas gifts? A new direction for your career? Peace with your children? Unity in your marriage? Whatever your need, God has an answer: seek first His kingdom and His righteousness (Matt. 6:33).

What does God have to do with schools, cars, relationships, money, or investments? Everything. As the Source and Supply of all your needs—material or otherwise—God is the Ultimate Giver. His wisdom, love, and sovereignty work on your behalf, regardless of the complexity, urgency, or practicality of your needs.

You seek God to meet your needs because He knows them even before you ask. He is fully aware of the problems you face and the demands they place on you. When you seek God first, He promises to supply every necessity, just as He does for the birds of the air (Matt. 6:26).

You seek Him first by depending upon His answer, refusing to manipulate your circumstances. When you want God's way—His path above all else—mortgage, school, and family fit into His plan and purpose. Therefore, He will provide in His time; He will meet every possible need. Anxiety over the future is replaced by confident trust in God's absolute goodness.

Lord, I have confident trust in Your goodness. I know You will provide all I need in Your time.

The Good Things in Life

SCRIPTURE READING: Psalm 34:1–10   KEY VERSE: Matthew 5:6

Blessed are those who hunger and thirst for righteousness,
For they shall be filled.

Everyone wants the good things in life. But God's idea of the good things is much different from most people's. Where some may pursue material gain or satisfaction in relationships, God knows real contentment comes elsewhere. In His eyes, sometimes even trial, heartache, and suffering are good things in our lives.

The best things in life are the things that fit within the purpose and plan God has for your life. They may include wealth or prestige. But they may also include tribulation that God uses to mold you into the servant He has long envisioned.

"Those who seek the LORD shall not lack any good thing" (Ps. 34:10). What does it mean to seek the Lord? Believers already have His Spirit living within us, right? Yes, but Jesus said in Matthew 5:6, "Blessed are those who hunger and thirst for righteousness, for they shall be filled." Seeking the Lord means longing and thirsting for Him, for a daily intimate relationship with Him.

This process is fascinating. In seeking worldly gain, many people find that the more they get, the more they want. The same is true with Jesus Christ. The more you understand your wonderful Savior and Lord, the more you long to know Him better still. The good things in life come when you seek Him and know you shall be filled.

My heart cries out for You, dear Lord. I hunger and thirst for your right-
eousness. I long for an intimate relationship with You.

The Inner Sanctum of Your Heart

SCRIPTURE READING: Psalm 16:1–11   KEY VERSE: Isaiah 26:3

You will keep him in perfect peace,
Whose mind is stayed on You,
Because he trusts in You.

God will meet any real need when you set your mind and focus on Him. But sometimes you can confuse a quest for worldly pleasures as need. False teachers have spawned entire movements out of errant philosophy that says all you must do is name your desire and God will fulfill your every wish.

In his book *Far from Home,* Joseph M. Stowell explains in a compelling illustration:

> We're like kids at Christmas, begging "Give me the gift! Give me the gift!" and forgetting that it's out of love that the gifts were given to us by our parents. Of course, our parents love to give to us and to bless us with gifts, but what they really want is a love relationship with us. Intimacy is about a relationship, not a gift exchange. When we live expectantly, serve Him purely, slow down and spend seasons on our knees with His Word in prayer and meditation, He fills our souls with Himself.
>
> God doesn't meet us at the mall. He seeks us in the inner sanctum of our hearts. If it's intimacy we want, we need to be more intrigued with the Giver than the gifts. It's not the stuff He does for us that we should be loving; it's Him. If we want to experience Him more than we do, we need to love Him more than we do, more than all those other things we are attracted to, more than all the provisions we expect from Him.

Help me to slow down and spend more time with You in prayer and in the Word. Come and meet with me in the inner sanctum of my heart, Father.

All Is Provided

SCRIPTURE READING: John 7:37–39   KEY VERSE: John 4:10

Jesus answered and said to her, "If you knew the gift of God, and who it is who says to you, 'Give Me a drink,' you would have asked Him, and He would have given you living water."

A scene from a children's musical depicts a group of angels discussing the believers on earth. One angel turns and asks the others, "Don't they know how much the Father loves them? Do they realize how much He cares?"

God promises to provide for our needs. But we must trust Him and seek His wisdom. Obedience is a condition of the heart. It proves that we know God cares about us and that we care about Him. Every need of Adam was attended to, but he disobeyed God by falling to a temptation he was warned to avoid.

Many times Satan tempts us into thinking that we have needs when in reality God has provided all. All that the Israelites could ever dream of obtaining was theirs, yet they abandoned their faith in God, thus setting the stage for disobedience to rule their hearts.

Throughout history, a discomforting glitch has remained in the heart of mankind. We have continued to seek the pleasures of other gods while pushing away what God offers so freely—His love and devotion.

The guarantee of love and provision He offers us is the same one He gave to Abraham, Isaac, David, Mary, and the disciples: "Come to Me . . . Drink."

Trace His provision through the Bible. Start with Genesis, and follow it through to Revelation. All you need He provides!

Father, all I need, You have already provided. Thank You for Your love for me and Your concern for my desires.

The Answer to Your Needs

SCRIPTURE READING: Luke 8:43–48   KEY VERSE: Psalm 111:4

He has made His wonderful works to be remembered;
The LORD is gracious and full of compassion.

Jesus is very holistic. A good example is found in Luke 8 when He heals a woman who has experienced hemorrhaging for twelve years. It's hard to imagine how this woman maintained her hope for healing, especially with the stigma that accompanied her illness. But she continued to look for a cure, and her determination brought her to the feet of the Savior.

A deep longing for love and acceptance is a normal need for any person, let alone someone who has been placed in forced isolation. The cruelty of Jewish tradition blocked this need from being met. Anyone who touched this woman was considered unclean.

The portrait Jesus provided is one of abundant mercy and grace. Not only did He heal her physical disease, but He also healed her spiritually and emotionally. Jesus was not repulsed by this woman's suffering. He saw her need and knew that only He could meet it. No matter how complex life may appear, God has an answer for your needs. This woman believed if she could just stretch out her hand far enough to touch the hem of Christ's outer garment, she would be healed. What a tremendous demonstration of faith!

In His compassion, Jesus turned to her and said, "Daughter, be of good cheer; your faith has made you well. Go in peace" (Luke 8:48). What is your need? Will you place it in the hands of the Savior and trust Him to meet it in His timing?

You are the answer to all my needs! Dear Lord, I place everything in Your hands and entrust it to Your loving care.

Loving Acceptance

SCRIPTURE READING: John 15:12–19   KEY VERSE: John 15:16

You did not choose Me, but I chose you and appointed you that you should go and bear fruit, and that your fruit should remain, that whatever you ask the Father in My name He may give you.

The youngster ran out the door to join his friends. Twenty minutes later he was back. "I thought you were meeting your friends down at the ball field," his mother commented. But before he could answer, she noticed the look of hurt on his face and asked, "Honey, what happened?"

"Mom, they didn't choose me to play on either one of their teams. Nobody likes me." This disappointment may seem trivial from an adult's perspective, but it's not. Rejection can leave a person feeling left out and disillusioned. Such an incident has the power to shape one's personality and self-image.

"I'm sorry you weren't chosen," replied the boy's mother. "Sometimes things happen that are hurtful, but always remember you mean a lot to me and your dad."

One of the greatest needs of our society is the need to belong. We want to know we matter to someone else. How we choose to meet this need is critical to our sense of self-worth and to our relationship with God.

Jesus Christ holds the greatest amount of acceptance you could ever hope to find. No matter what turns your life has taken or who has rejected you, God promises to love and accept you when you come to Him. And the fact remains that He will always choose you to be on His team!

Dear Lord, please heal the emotional scars left by rejection. Thank You for loving and accepting me just as I am.

Our Source of Identity

SCRIPTURE READING: Luke 9:23–26   KEY VERSE: Luke 9:24

For whoever desires to save his life will lose it, but whoever loses his life for My sake will save it.

Teenagers often search for identity through role models such as actors and sports figures. However, these may be the very people whose lives are coming apart at the seams. Adults do the same thing, only they are more likely to seek self-gratification through financial gain and social position.

Because we are Christians, our only true source of identity is Jesus Christ. He is our example for successful living. Searching for this in another person or social position leads only to disappointment. But many who profess to know Jesus as their Savior refuse to acknowledge Him as Lord over every area of their lives. Attitudes such as pride, selfishness, greed, and materialism arise from hearts that are not fully committed to Christ. Jesus made it clear that in order for us to save our lives, we must be willing to lose them unto Him (Luke 9:24).

Peter reminded us that we are really aliens, strangers to this world because of our love and devotion to Jesus Christ. Therefore, we are not to seek gratification in temporal pleasures. God chose us to know Him and to experience the wonder of His mercy and grace. Our identity is secure because of who lives inside us and not who we are.

Have you settled the identity issue? If not, ask God to reveal the areas in your life that lack true commitment to Him.

> *Father, be Lord over every area of my life. Reveal areas of my life where I lack true commitment, and help me to surrender them to You.*

The Great Provider

SCRIPTURE READING: Exodus 23:22–28   KEY VERSE: Matthew 14:31

Immediately Jesus stretched out His hand and caught him, and said to him, "O you of little faith, why did you doubt?"

He was determined to buy a new car and overlooked the fact that his financial stresses were growing. Friends encouraged him to buy a cheaper used car, but he pressed on with his plan. Six months later he was in financial trouble.

God is committed to meeting your needs. However, He is not committed to giving you all your wants. Several things can work against you in this area of needs:

Disobedience. When you disobey God, you must face the consequences of your wrong decisions. However, the moment you turn to the Lord and seek His forgiveness, He restores the joy of your fellowship with Him.

Doubt. Failing to trust God diffuses God's plan for your life. It also signals a lack of faith in His ability to provide for your needs

Manipulation. Trying to meet your needs your way is spiritual idolatry. Manipulation breeds deceit. Be willing to be honest with God, no matter how painful it seems.

Wrong motivation. Motives that are not God centered are self-centered. Set your focus on God and receive His blessing.

Ignoring responsibility. When you ignore your God-given responsibilities—family, friends, and job—your fellowship with God wanes, and you struggle spiritually. Let Christ be your Provider, and He will meet all your needs.

Cleanse me from disobedience, doubt, manipulation, and wrong motives, O Lord. I look to You as my Provider.

Your Greatest Need

SCRIPTURE READING: John 3:1–17   KEY VERSE: John 3:17

*For God did not send His Son into the world to condemn the world,
but that the world through Him might be saved.*

Throughout the Bible, we see God reaching out to His creation in an effort to save and restore. Of course, nowhere is this more evident than in the New Testament, especially in the Gospels through the life of His Son.

Jesus came to earth to seek and save those who were spiritually lost and bound by sin. By His own profession, He made that clear when He told His disciples that He did not come to judge mankind, but to save the lost from an eternal death (John 3:17).

We may be tempted to think that God is too caught up in the details of the universe to be concerned about our problems. But this is not true. Jesus was and still is totally interested in our lives.

Even after His crucifixion, His intimate concern was for those He loved. One example was His compassion for Mary as she searched for Him at the empty tomb. Jesus had not yet ascended to the Father. He witnessed Mary's deep sorrow and was moved with compassion. "Mary!" Jesus called out to her.

"Rabboni!" (which means "Teacher") was her reply (John 20:16). When she saw the Lord, she knew her prayers had been answered. Jesus was alive! That was her greatest need—to know that what He had promised was true.

What is your greatest need? Call out to the Savior, and He will meet that need.

*Lord, I bring to You my greatest need today. I know Your promises are true.
I wait expectantly for fulfillment.*

Blessings Abounding

SCRIPTURE READING: Judges 16:1–31   KEY VERSE: Judges 16:28

Then Samson called to the LORD, saying, "O Lord GOD, remember me, I pray! Strengthen me, I pray, just this once, O God, that I may with one blow take vengeance on the Philistines for my two eyes!"

Samson was a man of supernatural strength. Yet even this gift from God did not keep him from seeking to meet his needs his way. And as the result of his wayward living, Samson died a tragic death.

God understands that we have needs, but He wants us to bring those needs to Him. Even the desires we experience are opportunities for God to answer prayer and provide for us in mighty ways.

Unfortunately, sometimes we allow our passions to control us. We overlook the fact that we belong to God, and He has a pathway for us to follow. We strike out on our own only to meet a costly defeat.

Samson had a deep need. Delilah was not the answer. Perhaps his need was to feel that someone loved him. Or it could have been that he had a need to feel worthy. All sin has a root, and that root runs directly to a basic need. When we choose to meet our needs in illegitimate ways, we suffer the consequences of our wrong decisions.

The way Samson's life ended was not what God desired for him. Yet the Lord knew that Samson would turn back to Him. And at the very end, that was what God's prophet did.

Don't wait until the end of your life to enjoy God's goodness. Make a vital decision to allow Him to meet your needs. When He is in control, blessings abound.

Heavenly Father, when you are in control, blessings abound. So please, take control of every aspect of my life.

Seeking God First

SCRIPTURE READING: Matthew 14:14–21   KEY VERSE: John 6:26

Jesus answered them and said, "Most assuredly, I say to you, you seek Me, not because you saw the signs, but because you ate of the loaves and were filled."

How many times have you thought: *I wish God would bless me?* Maybe those words came to you when you were asking God to answer a specific prayer or when you sensed some type of adversity approaching. There are many different ways to receive God's blessings, but most often we think of it from a material sense. The people who followed Jesus did the same thing.

After feeding the five thousand, Jesus exposed this materialistic attitude: "Most assuredly, I say to you, you seek Me, not because you saw the signs, but because you ate of the loaves and were filled" (John 6:26). Many followed the Lord in order to receive something. Their eyes were set on seeing miracles and material provisions. But Jesus wanted them to see Him as the Bread of Life in whom all their needs would be met.

The greatest of all God's blessings has nothing to do with material wealth and social position, and everything to do with the closeness of His presence. That was why He instructed His disciples by saying, "Seek Me first, and all these things will be added to you."

Are your eyes set on the Savior because of what He provides or because you love Him? The test of true love is this: abiding with the One you love regardless of anything else. Learn to love Him and Him alone; then all your cares will be satisfied.

Dear Lord, I am not seeking things. I am not pursuing blessings. I am seeking You and You alone.

Experiencing God's Best

SCRIPTURE READING: Luke 12:22–32   KEY VERSE: James 1:17

Every good gift and every perfect gift is from above, and comes down from the Father of lights, with whom there is no variation or shadow of turning.

Everything we do in life requires a decision. Some have said that even when we refuse to make a decision, we have decided what we will or will not do. The same is true when it comes to experiencing God's best for our lives.

Jesus taught us that it was God's good pleasure to give us the kingdom of God. This means that all we could ever hope or want is ours to enjoy. Of course, there are guidelines for us to follow.

For example, God will never give us things that lead to self-indulgence and greed. On the other hand, there are many Christians living in spiritual poverty because they have never learned to enjoy the goodness of God's blessing.

This in no way solely focuses on financial wealth, though God may choose to bless many in this area. Nor does it mean that we should feel guilty when God blesses us in some area of material value. God's blessings are not limited to any one category. They are endless, and it is our responsibility to enjoy them when they come.

Therefore, instead of denying the gifts He sends your way, ask the Lord to help you correctly handle them so that He will be glorified in your life. Jesus taught us that God gives good things to His children. Therefore, never refuse His gifts when they come because each one is wrapped in eternal love for you.

Thank You for Your precious gifts to me, dear Lord. They are wrapped in Your eternal love for me. I praise You for each one!

Your Hopes and Dreams

SCRIPTURE READING: John 16:23–24   KEY VERSE: Jeremiah 29:11

I know the thoughts that I think toward you, says the LORD, thoughts of peace and not of evil, to give you a future and a hope.

Some of the requirements to experiencing God's best include the following: *An open and willing heart.* Before you can experience the blessings of God, you must be open to His love and will for your life. He takes joy in blessing those who love Him. "Ask and you shall receive" were the words Jesus spoke to His disciples. Being open to God's blessings does not mean just being open to receive something good from Him. It means being willing to receive whatever He sends your way. And in some cases, He may send something that you did not wish to receive. However, you can be sure that every gift is ultimately good and sent from a loving Father who has your best interests in mind.

Obedience. This is a key to receiving and enjoying the goodness of God. Many times the obedience that you exercise is not noticeable to others, but God knows. When you take a step forward in obedience, the Lord always sends His blessings your way.

The ability to dream. God wants you to look forward to His blessings. When you lose the ability to dream and think on the goodness of God, something inside dies. No matter how small your dream for the future appears, refuse to let go of it. Allow God to reshape it if necessary, but always believe in His loving ability to supply answers to your hopes and dreams.

Father, give me an open and willing heart. Make me obedient to Your Word. Give me the ability to dream.

Strength for All Times

SCRIPTURE READING: Isaiah 40:28–31   KEY VERSE: 2 Corinthians 12:9

He said to me, "My grace is sufficient for you, for My strength is made perfect in weakness." Therefore most gladly I will rather boast in my infirmities, that the power of Christ may rest upon me.

When the Bible talks of strength, it means inner fortitude of spirit, mind, will, and emotion. It is the actual energizing work of the Holy Spirit to undergird and sustain us. We receive God's strength when we are weak. Isaiah encouraged us that God "gives power to the weak, and to those who have no might He increases strength" (Isa. 40:29). Paul said that "strength is made perfect in weakness" (2 Cor. 12:9).

The emotionally drained believer doesn't have to be swept into the undertow of stressful times. God will give you the strength you don't have if you will lean fully on His resources.

You experience the strength God gives as you praise Him. Something about praise is invigorating and enlivening. Although it is the very thing you don't feel like doing, praise is God's way to spiritually nourish you. Nehemiah declared that the "joy of the LORD is your strength" (Neh. 8:10).

In your weakest moments, when you feel like giving in to temptation or just giving up, realize your weakness is your opportunity to draw upon God's supernatural strength. Praise Him, as feebly as that may be, and you will be renewed and restored. His Word is His sure bond.

Thank You for Your strength, dear Lord. In my weakest moments, remind me that Your strength is my inheritance, and help me to draw upon it.

Contentment in All Circumstances

SCRIPTURE READING: Philippians 4:11–19   KEY VERSE: Philippians 4:19

My God shall supply all your need according to His riches in glory by Christ Jesus.

Our materially oriented culture is programmed to generate discontentment. That is why each year brings new cars, new fashions, new improvements, all designed to make us dissatisfied with our present status or possessions.

Cultivating contentment in the Christian life begins with understanding that things never define your value. Your job, neighborhood, or net worth does not figure into God's equation for value and worth. Your value lies in your priceless relationship with God as your Father.

Still more, you can counter the anxious and stressful tug of discontentment with a solid understanding of several basic scriptural truths.

God cares for you. Because you are His child, He has assumed responsibility for providing for your emotional, spiritual, and physical needs. He will do so as you trust Him without reservation while you go about the routine tasks of each day.

God is in control. When a job is terminated, a mate quits, a friend deserts, God is quietly but sovereignly at work for your good. You are not a victim of the economy or another's decision.

You can be content in any circumstance when you are sure of God's unceasing care and absolute control of every detail. Rest in His ability, and contentment will follow.

Father, I am so thankful that You are in control of every circumstance of my life. You care for me and have assumed responsibility for me as Your child.

An Ambassador of Peace

SCRIPTURE READING: Ephesians 2:11–14   KEY VERSE: 2 Corinthians 5:20

We are ambassadors for Christ, as though God were pleading through us: we implore you on Christ's behalf, be reconciled to God.

Since the collapse of communism, many extraordinary events have occurred, most exemplary. However, there has been a darker side that exposes one of sin's most subtle, yet heinous, streaks.

In parts of Europe, there is now much hatred and rivalry between nationalities formerly separated by political barriers. Various ethnic groups that were kept in check by the oppression of Communist rule now rage against each other.

Paul wrote that Christ broke down all barriers between Jew and Gentile—every man, woman, or child of non-Jewish descent. The cross of Christ transcends cultural obstacles.

As a Christian, you must realize that once you receive Christ, you have been placed into the body of Christ. All believers of every ethnic origin who put their faith in Christ are members together of that body.

As a believer, you are to work for peaceful relationships with the unsaved as well. You are an ambassador for Christ who looks at the souls of individuals, not skin color or cultural heritage. Only the Christian is equipped to bring true peace—God's peace—to a world steeped in the evil of sin.

Thank You for making me a member of Your body, dear Lord. Make me an ambassador of Your peace who looks at the souls of individuals, not skin color or cultural heritage.

The Fullness of Your Position

SCRIPTURE READING: Ephesians 3:11–13   KEY VERSE: Hebrews 10:10

By that will we have been sanctified through the offering of the body of Jesus Christ once for all.

Up until they accepted the Son of God as their Savior, Gentiles existed in a world of paganism. Paul wrote that their god had been their appetites or stomachs (Phil. 3:19). He meant that their selfish, lustful desires ruled their lives.

However, when the mystery of salvation was revealed, God established a new basis for spiritual living. Man's emotions and desires were no longer to have charge over him. Once he became a believer, he was given a new nature with a built-in desire for the things of God. Paul called early Christians *saints,* a word strongly related to *sanctification.* Both words mean to be "set apart" for God. When we trust Christ as our Savior, we are spiritually taken out of the world and "set apart" for God in Christ.

Paul cautioned early believers to stand firm in their new faith because their citizenship was no longer of this world but of heaven. Therefore, they should live accordingly and not be drawn aside by the temptations of a pagan society.

God's redemptive plan is no longer a mystery! Ask Him to help you understand the fullness of your position in Christ. Only then can you enjoy living completely committed to all He calls you to do.

Dear heavenly Father, help me to stand firm in my faith. Help me to understand the fullness of my position in Christ.

God's Best for Your Life

SCRIPTURE READING: Ephesians 4:14–21 KEY VERSE: Ephesians 1:3

Blessed be the God and Father of our Lord Jesus Christ, who has blessed us with every spiritual blessing in the heavenly places in Christ.

The discovery of King Tut's tomb is considered one of the richest in history. However, archaeologists had no idea what waited for them beyond the first chamber; robbers had earlier plundered it. Yet a closer examination revealed an undisturbed sepulchral chamber and treasure room.

Excavators found priceless gold and silver items along with precious stones. There was also an abundance of rings and bracelets so ingenious and perfect in design that even a magnifying glass could not reveal the soldered joints.

With gold, silver, and priceless jewelry surrounding them, archaeologists could not help wondering why earlier intruders had stopped at the outer chamber. Did they not realize they had entered the burial chamber of a king?

As puzzling as this may seem, many of us do the same thing in our Christian walk. We plunder the outer chamber of God's blessings, never realizing there is an entire throne room waiting for us if only we would seek Him above all else.

Don't allow yourself to be robbed of God's best for your life. Ask Him to make you aware of the blessings He has for you. As you seek His will, submit all that you are to all that He is; and His wealth of eternal blessings will be yours.

I don't want to be robbed of Your best, God. Make me aware of the blessings You have for me. I submit all that I am to all that You are.

Treasure in Heaven

SCRIPTURE READING: Colossians 1:12–17   KEY VERSES: 1 Peter 1:3–4

Blessed be the God and Father of our Lord Jesus Christ, who according to His abundant mercy has begotten us again to a living hope through the resurrection of Jesus Christ from the dead, to an inheritance incorruptible and undefiled and that does not fade away, reserved in heaven for you.

In his book *The Weight of Glory,* C. S. Lewis noted how believers often underestimate the full riches that God has for His children:

> "If we consider . . . the staggering nature of the rewards promised in the Gospels, it would seem that our Lord finds our desires, not too strong, but too weak. We are half-hearted creatures . . . like an ignorant child who wants to go on making mud pies in a slum because he cannot imagine what is meant by the offer of a holiday at the sea. We are far too easily pleased."

When you understand the vast riches God has promised you as His child, you are motivated to take hold of all He has available. When you trusted Jesus as your Savior and Lord, you received a priceless inheritance, prepared especially for you, that will never fade or lose its value (1 Peter 1:3–4).

In His tremendous love, Jesus has equipped and fitted you to enjoy many of these treasures right now. Salvation, an abundance of grace, and the gift of righteousness are special blessings for you today.

God also gives you the privilege of laying up treasure in heaven. The more you are faithful with the talents, skills, and opportunities He affords you today, the more rewards He bestows in heaven to enjoy with Him forever.

Father, help me to use my talents, skills, and opportunities to the greatest extent possible. Show me how to lay up treasure in heaven.

Recipients of His Riches

SCRIPTURE READING: Ephesians 3:14–21   KEY VERSE: Romans 9:23

That He might make known the riches of His glory on the vessels of mercy, which He had prepared beforehand for glory.

The apostle Paul wrote the book of Ephesians as a practical guide to the Christian life. It provides rich insight into our position in Christ, the advantages of that relationship, and instructions for protecting ourselves from the enemy's snares.

However, Paul knew that some of the enemy's ploys would leak through to engage us in a spiritual battle. A much-used subtlety of Satan is to blind us to the truth of God concerning our heritage in Christ and the riches He has stored up for us.

Paul's purpose in writing to the Ephesians was to get them to grasp the truth of their position in Christ. He knew once they understood their relationship to God through Jesus Christ, they would begin to live in the power that was theirs through the Holy Spirit. God never meant for us to limp along as wounded Christians struggling to gain victory in life.

The world is in constant competition for wealth and riches in hopes of finding purpose and true meaning. God deposited the unfathomable riches of heaven to your account the moment you placed your trust in His Son. Ask Him to help you claim all He has for you today.

Father, thank You for the unfathomable riches of heaven that You have deposited into my account. I want to claim all You have for me today!

MAY

Praise, Worship, and Meditation

MOUNTAIN: Mount Moriah where Abraham went to worship

KEY VERSES: Genesis 22:1–14

Now it came to pass after these things that God tested Abraham, and said to him, "Abraham!" And he said, "Here I am." Then He said, "Take now your son, your only son Isaac, whom you love, and go to the land of Moriah, and offer him there as a burnt offering on one of the mountains of which I shall tell you." . . . So Abraham took the wood of the burnt offering and laid it on Isaac his son; and he took the fire in his hand, and a knife, and the two of them went together. But Isaac spoke to Abraham his father and said, "My father!" And he said, "Here I am, my son." Then he said, "Look, the fire and the wood, but where is the lamb for a burnt offering?" And Abraham said, "My son, God will provide for Himself the lamb for a burnt offering." So the two of them went together. Then they came to the place of which God had told him. And Abraham built an altar there and placed the wood in order; and he bound Isaac his son and laid him on the altar, upon the wood. And Abraham stretched out his hand and took the knife to slay his son. But the Angel of the Lord called to him from heaven and said, "Abraham, Abraham!" And he said, "Here I am." And He said, "Do not lay your hand on the lad, or do anything to him; for now I know that you fear God, since you have not withheld your son, your only son, from Me." Then Abraham lifted his eyes and looked, and there behind him was a ram caught in a thicket by its horns. So Abraham went and took the ram, and offered it up for a burnt offering instead of his son. And Abraham called the name of the place, The-LORD-Will-Provide; as it is said to this day, "In the Mount of The LORD it shall be provided."

His Deeds and Greatness

SCRIPTURE READING: Psalm 150:1–6   KEY VERSE: Psalm 95:6

Oh come, let us worship and bow down;
Let us kneel before the LORD our Maker.

Two basic truths can lead to sincere worship, changing the perspective on problems and giving hope for endurance:

"Praise Him for His mighty acts" (Ps. 150:2). God created the heavens and earth. He created you. He sent His Son to earth to bear your sin so you might receive eternal life. He has filled you with the Holy Spirit, who always extends the mercy and grace of God for your every need. The list goes on. Think of those special times when God answered your prayers, provided guidance in critical situations, protected you from harm, and specifically worked in your life. Thank Him that He is still working in your present circumstances to bring about positive future results, even though that may seem impossible right now.

"Praise Him according to His excellent greatness!" (Ps. 150:2). God never changes. He is always loving, always caring, always working for your good. His power stands firm in the midst of any storm. Spend time thanking Him for who He is.

Praise lights the candle of hope and encouragement in the midst of blackness that no ill wind can snuff out. Worship is the way to put your problems in God's capable hands.

I praise You for Your mighty deeds, Father. I thank You that You have answered prayer and that You are working in my present circumstances to bring positive future results.

Close to the Father's Heart

SCRIPTURE READING: John 17:1–8   KEY VERSE: Psalm 145:18

The LORD is near to all who call upon Him,
To all who call upon Him in truth.

The believer who lives close to the Father's heart is free to express his feelings to Him. You do not have to be uptight with God. He knew every detail of your life the moment He created you. When you were saved, the Lord Jesus Christ understood all of your past failures and hang-ups and your future struggles.

Because you are now His child for all eternity, you can be completely honest with Him. You can pour out your hurts, your anger, your disappointments, your secrets, and your dreams to the Lord. He will never reject you (Heb. 13:5). You can never turn away His steadfast love.

There will be times when you do not understand what God is up to in your life. God's presence may seem distant. Because you have God's assurance of His presence and because of His unceasing activity on your behalf, you can still cling to Him and worship Him in the knowledge of His love for you. Refuse the advances of competing lovers—money, fame, power—and deny doubt and unbelief.

Have you the kind of intimacy with God so that the Father is your most adored Friend? Does your unswerving allegiance belong to Him? If not, confess your need for such a relationship, let Him gather you into His waiting arms, and worship Him.

Father, let me learn to worship You even when Your presence seems distant.
Help me deny doubt and unbelief and refuse the advances of money, fame,
and power.

Loving God

SCRIPTURE READING: Matthew 22:34–40   KEY VERSE: Psalm 107:1

Oh, give thanks to the LORD, for He is good!
For His mercy endures forever.

Some people have problems with the Lord Jesus Christ's command to love Him with all of their hearts, all of their souls, and all of their minds: "I do not like someone—even if that Someone is God—commanding me to love him. I want my love to come freely."

Such a reservation melts when we consider why God sets the commandment of love above all others. As we allow the Holy Spirit to love Him through us, we love God with all of our strength because He is worthy of our worship and devotion.

The Lord created the heavens and the earth and all that is in them, including us (Gen. 1:1; 2:7, 22). Christ has saved us from eternal destruction. He supplies all of our needs (Phil. 4:19). Christ Jesus died and rose again for you and me.

Understanding God's majesty and glory is the wellspring of our love. He has done so much for us. How can we not love and worship such a One?

We also love God with all of our hearts because He knows that devotion given to any other person or thing besides Himself is harmful. God created us for Himself. When our highest and noblest love is directed to something or someone else, we have been seduced into treachery. Loving God frees us from competing idols, which only enslave us.

Free me from competing idols, Lord. Set me free to worship You with all my heart.

Practical Obedience

SCRIPTURE READING: John 14:15–21   KEY VERSE: John 14:15

If you love Me, keep My commandments.

Just before you leave the house for an overnight trip, your son hugs you and says, "I love you, Dad. Have a good trip."

"I love you, too, Son. Don't forget to clean out the garage like I told you, okay?"

"You bet, Dad."

The next evening you arrive at the door. Your son greets you.

"We missed you, Dad. We love you so much."

"I missed you, too, Son. It's good to see you. Did you get the garage clean as I told you?"

The boy lowers his head.

"No, sir."

Loving God, while definitely a matter of the heart, is gauged ultimately by our obedience to Him. Words of praise and adoration are pleasing to the Father, but the practical test of our love for our heavenly Father comes in whether we do what He asks.

Has God asked you to correct an area of disobedience in your life? Are you participating in an activity that He forbids in His Word? Are you living out the truths of the Scriptures by allowing the Lord Jesus Christ to express His life through you by loving unconditionally, giving generously, serving others, providing godly direction for your children?

Loving and worshiping God are emotional, but without practical obedience they are incomplete.

Dear God, I cannot worship You the way I should without obedience. Help me learn to obey—loving unconditionally, giving generously, and serving others.

A Divine Dimension

SCRIPTURE READING: Psalm 9:1–4   KEY VERSE: Philippians 4:6

Be anxious for nothing, but in everything by prayer and supplication, with thanksgiving, let your requests be made known to God.

Just as we can neglect our bodies or minds through lack of physical or mental exercise, we can easily neglect the vital spiritual exercise of praise and worship. *Why?* Why do we avoid the one dimension of our spiritual existence that Scripture prioritizes as essential to our Christian well-being?

One reason is that we fail to recognize its importance. Sure, we pray over our meals, in church, or in emergencies, but somehow we fail to realize that God has given us prayer, praise, and worship as a direct means of communication with Him.

What value do you place on prayer? How important are talking with Him, sharing with Him, praising Him, and worshiping God?

Another factor in our shunning of prayer and praise is the failure to perceive their relevance to all of life. Jesus taught us to pray for our daily bread. That includes the whole spectrum of our needs: financial, physical, emotional, relational, and vocational. He taught us by example and precept to praise and worship God.

When you are alone with God, you can bring every need, dream, hurt, and longing to Someone who hears, cares, and desires to work through every circumstance. You can praise and worship Him because you know He is at work in the circumstances of your life. When you do this, all of life takes on a divine dimension.

Dear God, thank You for the opportunity to fellowship with You daily in prayer, praise, and worship.

In Times of Distress

SCRIPTURE READING: Psalm 22:1–22   KEY VERSE: Psalm 28:7

The LORD is my strength and my shield;
My heart trusted in Him, and I am helped;
Therefore my heart greatly rejoices,
And with my song I will praise Him.

Worship is often associated with cheerful, happy occasions in our lives. Blessed by God, we gladly praise Him for His goodness. However, a review of the Scriptures reveals another aspect of worship that is as important and perhaps more meaningful. In times of distress, trial, and discouragement, that worship is essential to maintain spiritual stability.

- The Psalms burst with worship of God while the psalmists were in the throes of affliction. When David was up against the wall with no way out, he consistently sang praises after pouring out his heartaches.
- When Jehoshaphat saw that he was surrounded by militant hordes, God instructed him to arrange a praise service.
- At the stroke of midnight in a rank jail, Paul and Silas started a sing-along of praise hymns.

Are you depressed? Is your outlook gloomy? Are you in a tight place with no obvious escape route? Right now is the time to turn your heart toward worship. Deliberately overrule your feelings of despondency and heaviness, and worship God.

Nothing is too hard for God, and nothing like worship awakens you to that reality.

Nothing is too hard for You, O God. I worship You right now in spite of my circumstances.

Hope for Every Situation

SCRIPTURE READING: Numbers 13:25–33   KEY VERSE: Psalm 7:17

I will praise the LORD according to His righteousness,
And will sing praise to the name of the LORD Most High.

God instructed Israel to send twelve spies to survey the promised land, a land that was already theirs. He had given it to them as a result of His covenant with Abraham (Num. 13:2).

The spies confirmed what God had told them. The land flowed with milk and honey. A single cluster of grapes was so large, two men were required to carry it. However, the report of the spies filled the people's hearts with discouragement. They told how the land was populated by strong and mighty people. The cities, they said, were "fortified and very large" (Num. 13:28).

God's people became frightened and begged Moses to take them back into the desert. The victory that was theirs was lost, and they chose to believe Satan's lie and doubted God's ability to grant them victory.

God allows obstacles so you can learn to trust Him and praise Him in every circumstance. His goal is not to harm you but to bless you. Don't allow life's obstacles to keep you from enjoying God's plan for your life. God has allowed them for a purpose. Trust Him, and realize that when you feel out of control, He is never shaken. He is your sovereign Deliverer, and in Him there is eternal hope for every situation—so praise Him!

I praise You, Lord, that You are my sovereign Deliverer, and in You there is hope for every situation.

He Never Slumbers

SCRIPTURE READING: Acts 17:22–31   KEY VERSE: Psalm 121:3

He will not allow your foot to be moved;
He who keeps you will not slumber.

At no time are you outside the presence of God. The apostle Paul made that clear while speaking to the philosophers on Mars Hill. Near there they had erected an altar to the "unknown god."

The Athenians were zealous in their pagan worship and wanted to make sure no god was overlooked. Thus, they made a place of worship for those who remained unknown. Realizing they would not understand the basis of Christianity, Paul shifted his delivery of the gospel to include this peculiarity of their pagan beliefs. He explained that the true God, the one they deemed as "unknown," was really the Creator of all things.

The Lord is a personal God, not limited by time or space, One who inhabits the hearts of all who believe in Him. Therefore, no temple or building can contain His presence because He is eternally present throughout the universe.

Have you ever thought that God is with you in all you do and say throughout the day? He is not just present in the morning when you awake. He is with you in the grocery store, in the doctor's office, at work, even at play. No matter where you go, God goes with you. Praise Him for His care over your life, for His devotion that never slumbers.

Father, thank You for Your constant care over me. Your devotion never slumbers. You are with me every moment of each day.

An Act of the Will

SCRIPTURE READING: 1 Thessalonians 5:16–18   KEY VERSE: Psalm 22:22

I will declare Your name to My brethren;
In the midst of the assembly I will praise You.

The error comes in believing that to give thanks, one has to feel thankful or happy. But that was not what Paul was talking about in his first letter to the Thessalonian church.

When the car breaks down without warning or the children are sick or your husband loses his job or a good friend rejects you, your emotions are tender. You do not feel as if you are walking on cloud nine; and most important, the Lord does not expect you to. Jesus knows what it is like to experience grief and heart pain so deep that it tears at the fiber of your being.

If giving thanks is not always an expression of emotion, then what is it? Thanksgiving is an act of the will. It means looking at a negative circumstance and acknowledging that God allowed it into your life for a reason and an ultimately good purpose. You can thank Him in full faith because you know that the current pain is an opportunity for Him to demonstrate His grace on your behalf.

Have you ever met a fellow believer who felt as though he had to manipulate his emotions into a constant "high" in order to be obedient and joyful? Such a state is unnatural, and it is only a matter of time until he comes to the realization that God is not requiring artificial displays of passion. God desires your faith and trust that He will bring a blessing.

Father, I thank You that my current pain is an opportunity for You to demonstrate Your grace on my behalf.

The Fear of God

SCRIPTURE READING: Isaiah 66:1–2   KEY VERSES: Isaiah 11:2

The Spirit of the LORD shall rest upon Him,
The Spirit of wisdom and understanding,
The Spirit of counsel and might,
The Spirit of knowledge and of the fear of the LORD.

The fear of God is a subject that draws little attention today. Many misinterpret its implications while others believe it to be an Old Testament revelation that no longer applies under the new law of grace.

Understood properly, however, the fear of God revitalizes our worship, heightens our often low view of God, and sensitizes us to the true nature of evil. A right concept of the fear of God involves a sense of awe and wonder at the majesty of God.

Fearing God does not mean that we shake in horror but that we bow in adoration at His feet. Jesus is described in Isaiah as having "the Spirit of knowledge and of the fear of the LORD" (Isa. 11:2). Certainly, Jesus was not afraid of the Father, but He knew the awesome power and identity of the Eternal One.

Fearing God also leads us into a new hatred of evil. We tolerate sin in our lives because we are not fully aware of how vile it is in the eyes of a holy, just God.

How awesome is God in your eyes? How reverently do you treat His Word and His people? How humbly do you come into His presence? How menacing does sin appear? Ask God to give you a proper "fear of God" that steers you into the contrite spirit that God favors and blesses and inspires you to true praise and worship.

Lord, I come humbly into Your presence. Give me a contrite spirit that will release me to praise and worship You.

Praying with Confidence

SCRIPTURE READING: 1 John 5:13-15   KEY VERSE: Hebrews 10:35

Do not cast away your confidence, which has great reward.

Too often we approach prayer and worship like a child entering his first day of school—very tentatively. That certainly is not the concept of prayer and worship presented in the Scriptures. Like a proven champion, the believer should exude confidence in his rapport with God: "This is the confidence that we have in Him, that if we ask anything according to His will, He hears us" (1 John 5:14).

Perhaps one reason for your hesitancy is your uncertainty over what is God's will in a given situation. You want God's direction; you seek to obey Him. But how far should you go when you don't have the path clearly marked? You may not always know God's will in a particular circumstance, but you can still pray with confidence when you are willing to do the following:

- Let God have His way. You work and act in a specific manner, but You are ever ready to change course. God knows what is best for you, and you accept His plan, even if you disagree.
- Glorify Him more than obtain your answer. Your chief purpose is to honor God. Whatever route exalts Him—not just blesses you—is the path you seek to walk.
- Praise Him regardless of the outcome. You can confidently give thanks in all things, knowing that God is in control.

Dear Lord, search my heart and reveal my true motives. I want to glorify You more than just obtain answers to my problems.

Approaching God

SCRIPTURE READING: Hebrews 10:19–22   KEY VERSE: Hebrews 4:16

Let us therefore come boldly to the throne of grace, that we may obtain mercy and find grace to help in time of need.

Orel Hershiser was the confident catalyst who led the Los Angeles Dodgers to a World Series victory in 1988. He was so aggressive that his teammates nicknamed him "Bulldog." Hershiser displayed the boldness and tenacity that should characterize the Christian's relationship with God.

Your prayer life should not be weak and indecisive. You can approach God and present your needs, desires, and petitions with reverent assurance. You now have unhindered access into the Lord's presence to praise and worship Him. Previously shrouded in fear and trembling, His presence is entered freely by the person whose sin is forgiven through Christ's shed blood. You need not fear anymore.

You can be confident in approaching God to worship because Christ is now your sympathetic, understanding High Priest. You come to a throne of grace, which floods you with His tender mercy.

The Lord Jesus Christ is for you, not against you. He understands your frailties, your mood swings, your habits. He does not ever condemn you, for He was condemned in your stead (Rom. 8:1). Your confidence is also in the sure promises of God. He will do what He says in His Word. Praise Him for that today!

Lord, I praise You that I can come into Your presence to worship and commune with confidence, knowing You will do all You have promised.

Personal Intimacy

SCRIPTURE READING: Psalm 142:1–7   KEY VERSE: Psalm 142:5

I cried out to You, O LORD:
I said, "You are my refuge,
My portion in the land of the living."

The goal of a married couple is not just to stay married but to develop a personal intimacy that touches body, soul, and spirit. Likewise, the goal of a believer is not just to be a Christian but to cultivate an intimate, devoted relationship with the heavenly Father.

In both instances honest, sincere, and consistent communication is the key to such oneness and nearness. The Christian experiences that process through a deepening, growing, expanding experience of praise, worship, and prayer.

God's goal in intimacy is not just to answer your petitions or hear your complaints or solve your problems. Although He does address each of these needs, they are only a part of the Lord Jesus Christ's ultimate purpose—oneness and union with Him.

God wants you to know Him; to enjoy Him; to live continually in the light of His favor, wisdom, and truth. He desires a genuine relationship with you, His child. Daily worship and prayer are the spiritual closet where you and the Father are drawn into a personal intimacy in which God's love for you and your love for Him become the bedrock of your faith.

Make it your goal to know God intimately. Learn to worship and praise Him—then watch your prayer life move into a new dimension.

Heavenly Father, my goal is to know You intimately. Teach me how to worship. Teach me how to pray.

Communion with God

SCRIPTURE READING: John 1:1–14   KEY VERSE: Revelation 21:3

I heard a loud voice from heaven saying, "Behold, the tabernacle of God is with men, and He will dwell with them, and they shall be His people. God Himself will be with them and be their God."

God's compelling desire since the creation of the world is to live in communion with man. Think of the grandeur and majesty of a God who yearns to befriend man in such a way that man's entire life is lived out in the presence of the awesome, loving God.

So great is His desire to fellowship with man that He has made every provision possible for that intimacy. When sin severed man's union with God and brought spiritual and physical death, God provided a tabernacle. The tabernacle was a place where man could still relate to Him under a divinely imposed order.

When John wrote that "the Word [Christ] became flesh and dwelt among us" (John 1:14), he was referring to the incarnation of Christ. It represents the most passionate means by which God could restore fellowship with man through Jesus' life, death, and resurrection.

The zenith of God's desire to live and dwell among man is found in Revelation 21:3: "Behold, the tabernacle of God is with men, and He will dwell with them, and they shall be His people. God Himself will be with them."

Salvation does much more than bring you out of darkness and death; it ushers you into the presence of God to experience divine communion in prayer, praise, and worship.

Thank You, Lord, that You made every provision possible for me to experience intimacy with You. I praise You that You dwell in me, I am Yours, and You are my God.

New Levels of Praise

SCRIPTURE READING: Exodus 3:1–6   KEY VERSE: Hebrews 3:15

While it is said:
"Today, if you will hear His voice,
Do not harden your hearts as in the rebellion."

A river that runs through one U.S. city is extraordinarily clean and clear. Its pristine quality can be attributed to a large watershed area in which rainfall gradually seeps through a thick layer of forest and rock before trickling into the river's ecosystem.

This is illustrative of the biblical practice of meditation. It is the absorption and retention of truth that distills the essence of Scripture, making it clear, relevant, and applicable to personal needs.

Meditating—thinking through what God has said, why He said it, and what it means to us today—is the means by which we weave the power and life of God's Word into our spiritual and emotional fabric. God's Word is alive, so full of spiritual truth and wisdom that even a single passage can be digested for a lifetime.

God has something to say to you personally, but you must have ears to hear. You can behold wonderful things from God's Word if you are willing to quietly and thoroughly examine its content through biblical meditation.

Put God's Word to work in your innermost being—your mind, will, and emotions. Allow it to seep into your spirit, receiving its full richness, and you will be inspired to new levels of praise.

Father, as I meditate on Your Word today, quicken it to my innermost being
so that I can receive its richness. Lift me to new levels of praise and worship.

When the Word Comes Alive

SCRIPTURE READING: Psalm 19:1–14   KEY VERSE: Psalm 19:14

Let the words of my mouth and the meditation of my heart
Be acceptable in Your sight,
O LORD, my strength and my Redeemer.

On a scale of one to ten (with ten indicating the highest frequency), where do you rank your practice of meditation on Scripture? Despite the value God places upon musing on and pondering His truth (Josh. 1:8), the Christian seldom prioritizes meditation.

Dr. J. I. Packer describes one reason for our poor spiritual health in this area.

"If I were the devil, one of my first aims would be to stop folk from digging into the Bible . . . I should do all that I could to surround it with the spiritual equivalent of pits, thorn hedges, and man traps, to frighten people off."

R. Kent Hughes highlights the profit of meditation on the Bible in his book *Disciplines of a Godly Man.*

We may be challenged, convicted, and exhilarated with the call to meditation. The question is, how is this to be done? . . . Ideally, we are to make meditation a part of our regular devotion, giving hidden time to reverently muttering [speaking to ourselves] God's Word.

But even our busy schedules can be punctuated with Scriptural meditation—in the car, at lunch break, or waiting for a bus. Select a choice text, write it on a card, and slip it into your pocket. Pull it out in those spare moments. Murmur it. Memorize it. Pray it. Say it. Share it.

When the Word really comes alive in your heart, you will enter a new dimension of prayer, praise, and worship.

Dear Lord, as I meditate on Your truths today, let the Word come alive in my heart.

Divine Purposes

SCRIPTURE READING: Psalm 67:1–7   KEY VERSE: Psalm 66:1

Make a joyful shout to God, all the earth!

George Bernard accepted Jesus as his Savior at the age of sixteen. He served for a time in the Salvation Army and was later ordained as a minister, leading many revivals throughout Michigan and New York. Then, in 1913, he experienced a time of extreme crisis.

Bernard did what he had done for years—he turned to the Lord. He spent much time in prayer, worship, and Bible study, meditating deeply about the Cross. Wanting to share the truth he discovered, Bernard wrote his thoughts in verse form with music to accompany them. His work is a spiritual legacy to believers everywhere, the beloved hymn "The Old Rugged Cross."

The Lord used His dealings with one man to bless countless others. When God deals with us individually, He has divine purposes in mind. God blesses His children and works in our lives because He loves us dearly, and He wants His goodness to go even farther. His plan for you fits perfectly with His plan for the world.

Recognizing God's overall plan is a key to a growing relationship with Him. You see yourself as He sees you, a much-loved child with talents and gifts to use for His service. When you understand His higher purposes for your life, you are a useful tool in His hands as you exercise your talents to glorify Him.

God, I know You have divine purposes in mind in every aspect of my life.
Help me to use each experience to leave a spiritual legacy to others.

An Opportunity to Worship

SCRIPTURE READING: 1 Samuel 26:21–31   KEY VERSES: 1 John 3:7–8

Little children, let no one deceive you. He who practices righteous-ness is righteous, just as He is righteous. He who sins is of the devil, for the devil has sinned from the beginning. For this purpose the Son of God was manifested, that He might destroy the works of the devil.

The erosion of Saul's life began subtly. The enemy never announces his plans to lure us away from our devotion to Christ. Instead, he uses small and seemingly harmless tactics to draw us into deception and compromise.

One careless event changed the course of Saul's life and eventually led to his denunciation by God and his death. Although God's grace keeps the believer, sin has its consequences, and many times the relationship with God suffers. Make sure your life is free of spiritual erosion by asking God to give you a deep love for Him and His Word.

Amy Carmichael once wrote,

> The story of Mary breaking her pot of ointment made me think of some among us who love their Savior and yet have not broken theirs (vessel of oil). Something is held back, and so there is no outpouring of that love, no fragrance in the house. It is shut up, not given.
>
> The days are passing so quickly. Soon it will be too late to pour all we have on His feet. How sorry Mary would have been if she had missed her opportunity that evening—an opportunity that would never come again: "But you do not always have Me." Soon He was among His foes. She could not have reached Him then.

Lord, I want to take every opportunity to worship You. I want to express my love to You right now. I pour out the fragrance of my life in a sacrifice of praise.

The Greatest Test

SCRIPTURE READING: Psalm 103:1–22   KEY VERSES: Psalm 103:1–2

Bless the LORD, O my soul;
And all that is within me, bless His holy name!
Bless the LORD, O my soul,
And forget not all His benefits.

C. S. Lewis declared, "Praise is inner health made audible." Psalm 103 begins with this same thought.

At times, it seems difficult to praise God. Trouble abounds and sorrow clouds our eyes. Before we know it, we cannot see the goodness of the Lord. Then our spiritual blindness places us in a position of direct attack from our adversary, the devil.

Satan's mission is one of discouragement. He knows he cannot have a believer's soul, but he does not give up. Therefore, he seeks to do the one thing that will render your life ineffective for the Lord, and that is to discourage you and rob you of your joy.

Discouragement is the enemy's highest goal, but praises spoken in adoration of the Lord change feelings of defeat into glorious triumph.

Is something burdening you? Take it to the Lord in prayer. Refreshment and encouragement await you. The secret of praise is not found in waiting until everything in your life is peaceful and calm. It is learning to praise God in the most difficult moments. This is the greatest test of faith and love. Can you sing your praises to the Lord regardless of the situation? If so, you will abide in the joy of the Lord.

I praise You, Lord, despite my circumstances. I worship You, despite my difficulties. In Your presence I seek refreshment and encouragement.

Requirements for Praise

SCRIPTURE READING: Psalm 24:1–10   KEY VERSE: Psalm 31:19

Oh, how great is Your goodness,
Which You have laid up for those who fear You,
Which You have prepared for those who trust in You
In the presence of the sons of men!

Before you can truly praise God for who He is and what He is doing in your life, you must have the right attitudes. Here are the requirements for praise:

- Submission to God. When you submit your life to the Lord, you will not argue about the circumstances that He brings your way. If there is hardship, you will ask Him to take the difficulty and teach you what you need to learn from it.
- Repentance of known sin. You cannot truly praise God for the life He has given you and live in sin at the same time. Sin builds a barrier between the Lord and you that only His forgiveness can remove.
- A deep abiding love for the Lord.
- No evidence of a critical spirit. Criticism of others implies that you are right and they are wrong. God is strong enough to deal with the situations that trouble you. Keep your focus on Him.
- A willingness to take captive any thought of fear. Fear isolates and paralyzes. As God's beloved, you have no reason to fear anyone or anything. The Lord is your strength, and He stands guard over your life.
- A desire to keep your life Christ centered by focusing on the Lord each day. No matter what kind of storm is building, God is in control.
- Christ-centered relationships with others. Praise is multiplied when shared with another person.

Lord, I submit my life to You today. I repent of my sin. Deliver me from a critical spirit and a spirit of fear. Help me keep my life centered on You. Set me free to worship You.

Marching into Battle

SCRIPTURE READING: 2 Chronicles 20:1–19   KEY VERSE: 2 Chronicles 20:17

You will not need to fight in this battle. Position yourselves, stand still and see the salvation of the LORD, who is with you, O Judah and Jerusalem! Do not fear or be dismayed; tomorrow go out against them, for the LORD is with you.

The massive enemy army was coming. We can only imagine how news traveled in Jehoshaphat's day—by messenger on foot or by rider on horseback. One day life was normal, filled with regular activity. The next day the nation of Judah awoke to news of enemy invasion.

Reports of the threat spread quickly, igniting feelings of panic. Even King Jehoshaphat became fearful, but he also recognized that no enemy was stronger than the Lord God.

He immediately proclaimed a fast, and then he called the people together to pray. The Lord's Spirit filled the temple area where the people were praying and spoke through the prophet Jahaziel: "Listen, all you of Judah . . . Thus says the Lord to you, 'Do not be afraid nor dismayed because of this great multitude, for the battle is not yours, but God's . . . Position yourselves . . . and see the salvation of the LORD, who is with you'" (2 Chron. 20:15–17).

God instructed Jehoshaphat to place the choir in front of the people as they marched into battle. What an act of faith by Jehoshaphat!

Can you do what Judah did—march into battle singing? They heard the word of the Lord and understood that the victory was theirs. All they were called to do was to watch, pray, and praise. When we praise Him, God works in miraculous ways!

Lord, as I march into the battles of this day, I praise You! The victory is mine!

A Taste of Heaven

SCRIPTURE READING: Revelation 21:1–8   KEY VERSE: Revelation 7:11

All the angels stood around the throne and the elders and the four living creatures, and fell on their faces before the throne and worshiped God.

Some dear saints long for a glimpse of heaven. The apostle John had this very experience. Momentarily, God allowed John to taste the goodness of His heavenly presence while remaining on earth. What an honor for a faithful servant of the Lord Jesus Christ.

Heaven is a place of worship and praise. The overwhelming scene that opened before John's eyes was one of true glory. John wrote: "When I saw [Jesus], I fell at His feet as dead. But He laid His right hand on me, saying to me, 'Do not be afraid; I am the First and the Last. I am He who lives, and was dead, and behold, I am alive forevermore. Amen. And I have the keys of Hades and of Death'" (Rev. 1:17–18).

The emotion that swept through John as he saw the risen Savior and Lord was one of awesome fear and worship. It was not fear as we experience it in everyday life. Instead, it was a reverent fear that recognized the power and strength of almighty God.

When you are called to stand in God's presence, life on earth and all its troubles will seem small and insignificant. There will be only one issue at hand—the need to bow down and worship the Savior.

You can enjoy a taste of heavenly worship here and now. Enter God's presence with a grateful heart as you meditate on the goodness of His affections toward you.

Thank You for Your goodness to me, Lord. As I enter into Your presence to worship today, give me a taste of what awaits me in heaven.

The Focus of Your Life

SCRIPTURE READING: Psalm 27:1–14   KEY VERSE: Psalm 27:14

Wait on the LORD;
Be of good courage,
And He shall strengthen your heart;
Wait, I say, on the LORD!

In Psalm 27, David was in the process of rousing his faith back to the point where he could say without a doubt that "the LORD is my light and my salvation; whom shall I fear?"

However, in Psalm 26, things did not appear so bright, and David pleaded his case before the Lord. When you face doubts and fears, what do you think of? Are God's hope and intervention realities you believe? They should be.

God answers the heartfelt cries of His people. He wants you to know and believe that He will deliver you from all trouble. And even if the trouble remains for a season, He will provide and care for you.

Your responsibility is simply this: be willing to love and worship God. Sound too simplistic? Try it for a week. Let go of arguing your point of view. Put aside resentment, self-righteousness, and any pride that have placed enmity between you and others. Then set the focus of your life and heart on Jesus Christ. Doing this may be one of the toughest things you have ever done.

But over time you will notice small irritations have vanished. The need for recognition disappears, and there is an inner peace like nothing you have felt before. Instead of nervously worrying about tomorrow, you realize that God is the Captain of your soul. You can wait for God's blessing just as David did because you have tasted His goodness.

Thank You for the inner peace that comes in Your presence, Lord. Help me
to keep my focus on You instead of worrying about the future.

Deliverance Is Near

SCRIPTURE READING: Hebrews 12:1-4   KEY VERSE: Hebrews 11:39

All these, having obtained a good testimony through faith, did not receive the promise.

It's hard to read Hebrews 11:39 without feeling pain of sorrow. In chapter 11, the writer of Hebrews recounted the faithfulness of the Old Testament saints. He told of the faith exhibited by Sarah and Abraham, of Jacob and Joseph, of King David, and many in between. There's a passage about Enoch and Abel—two names we rarely mention in our day-to-day conversations.

Each had one thought in mind, and that was to receive God's promise. Their eyes were turned to the future with the expectation that their generation might witness Messiah's arrival. However, the writer of Hebrews told us that each died without seeing or physically touching His hand. But in Hebrews 12:1, our dismay is turned into great joy: "Therefore we also, since we are surrounded by so great a cloud of witnesses, let us lay aside every weight, and . . . let us run with endurance the race that is set before us."

Were these Old Testament saints disappointed because they missed Jesus' arrival? Not in the least. Their prayers were answered the moment they entered the presence of God. The burden you bear, the tears you shed, the sorrow you carry—God knows it all, and He has assembled a great and mighty host of experienced witnesses to cheer you on to victory.

Therefore, you can praise Him today and wait for Him in peace and joy, for His deliverance is near.

I praise You, Lord, because my deliverance is near. You know my burdens, tears, and sorrows. I humbly bow before You and worship.

A Passion for God

SCRIPTURE READING: Revelation 3:14–22 KEY VERSES: Revelation 3:15–16

I know your works, that you are neither cold nor hot. I could wish you were cold or hot. So then, because you are lukewarm, and neither cold nor hot, I will vomit you out of My mouth.

Christianity is not for fence-sitters. Once rescued from sin's penalty by faith in Christ, the believer enters an engaging, transforming relationship with God that should be marked with unparalleled intensity and zeal.

The apostle John recorded Jesus' rebuke of the church at Laodicea for its mediocrity: "I know your works, that you are neither cold nor hot . . . Because you are lukewarm . . . I will vomit you out of My mouth" (Rev. 3:15–16).

The Greek word used for "hot" means literally "boiling hot." Nonchalance or apathy is repulsive to God.

God gave His all to save us. In return, without coercion, He asks us to love Him with all of our hearts, souls, and minds; to serve Him cheerfully and wholeheartedly; to worship Him with grateful fervor.

Why? Because God wants the best for us. He desires that we experience His fullness of life each day. That is impossible if we seek Him feebly, love and worship Him casually, or pray sporadically.

If your relationship with the Savior is tepid, your Christian experience will be lackluster, impotent, and uncompelling to a world awash with mediocrity. But the fire is lit. You can find new passion for God and fulfillment in His service, if you desire.

Lord, I love You with all of my heart, soul, and mind. I want to serve You cheerfully and wholeheartedly and worship You with grateful fervor. Restore my passion.

The Wellspring of Worship

SCRIPTURE READING: 1 Samuel 15:1–23   KEY VERSE: John 21:15

When they had eaten breakfast, Jesus said to Simon Peter, "Simon, son of Jonah, do you love Me more than these?" He said to Him, "Yes, Lord; You know that I love You." He said to him, "Feed My lambs."

Joni Eareckson Tada, the gifted author and artist who was paralyzed in an accident as a teenager, was once asked to share her favorite Scripture. Her response was precise:

"My favorite verse in the Bible is Jesus' terse question to Peter: 'Lovest thou Me?'" (John 21:15).

Herein is the heart of an obedient life—love and devotion for God. Obedience to Christ was not designed as a chore. While we may initially submit due to fear or a sense of obligation, God desires compliance from sheer delight in Him.

David exclaimed, "I delight to do Your will, O my God, and Your law is within my heart" (Ps. 40:8).

Can you join in that joyful refrain? Is obedience to God a drudgery, motivated by fear of retribution? Do you comply only so you will not feel guilty? The wellspring of genuine Christianity and true worship is a passion to please the Savior who redeemed you and now indwells you through His Spirit.

Fear or duty will carry you only so far, but love for God will carry you through everything. Obedience still may be hard at times, but it will never again be toilsome. Lovest thou God? If your answer is yes, obedience will be spontaneous.

I delight to do Your will, O God. Your law is within my heart. Give me a passion to please You.

Devotion to God

SCRIPTURE READING: 2 Corinthians 11:22–28   KEY VERSE: Psalm 26:3

Your lovingkindness is before my eyes,
And I have walked in Your truth.

Love for God is the foundation for true obedience. Likewise, your obedience to Christ demonstrates the reality of your love for Him. Both parts of the equation are true, but devotion to God not dread or duty, properly primes and fuels the disciple of Jesus Christ. When you heed God's Word and keep His ways because you love Him, you declare your reverence and honor for who He is.

God is the almighty One, the Alpha and Omega, the Creator and Redeemer, the Lord and King of both heaven and earth. Who cannot love such a God whose lovingkindness and faithfulness are always perfectly expressed toward His people? He is worthy of your sincere adoration and explicit love.

When you obey God out of a heart of devotion, you affirm your allegiance to Him. He is the Master of all, but is He your Master? Your loving obedience demonstrates your joyful, voluntary servanthood to the Lord Jesus Christ.

Each act of obedience confirms your willing servitude to the gracious Lord. God sets you free to follow Him. The more you love and obey Him, the more exciting and rewarding your journey of discipleship and your worship experience will become.

You are worthy of my praise, O Lord. Thank You for Your lovingkindness and faithfulness to me. Give me a heart that obeys You out of love rather than dread or duty.

Rejoicing in Salvation

SCRIPTURE READING: 1 Timothy 1:12–15   KEY VERSE: Psalm 55:9

Destroy, O Lord, and divide their tongues,
For I have seen violence and strife in the city.

The person who used the word *joy* more than any other writer of Scripture was the apostle Paul. That appears incredible. Wasn't Paul beaten, stoned, ridiculed, and mocked wherever he preached? Wasn't Paul the fellow who knew the inside of a prison cell better than the average criminal?

How could he even think of rejoicing, much less use it so liberally in his epistles? Paul's delight came from an overwhelming gratitude for God's work of salvation: "The grace of our Lord was exceedingly abundant . . . This is a faithful saying and worthy of all acceptance, that Christ Jesus came into the world to save sinners, of whom I am chief" (1 Tim. 1:14–15).

If you have placed your faith in Christ as Savior, think of the supernatural transformation that transpired. You were brought from the domain of Satan into the kingdom of God; you were delivered from unending punishment and gifted with everlasting life.

You became God's friend, His child. He became your heavenly Father because through the agency of His Spirit, you were born again. Consider the greatness of your salvation, then rejoice in it today.

God, You are my Friend and my heavenly Father. I rejoice in You and my salvation.

The Throne Room of God

SCRIPTURE READING: Psalm 55:1–3   KEY VERSE: Psalm 57:7

My heart is steadfast, O God, my heart is steadfast;
I will sing and give praise.

Our first course of action when facing a problem should be to take our burden to God in prayer and praise Him for the answer. Believers in Jesus Christ can avail ourselves of the wisdom, power, and counsel of God Himself through the supernatural gift of prayer. Unbelievers have no such resource. They must deal with crises in their limited strength and wisdom.

As a follower of Christ, you have the immeasurable, fathomless power of prayer at your disposal. When you were saved by faith in Christ through the riches of His grace, you were given access to God: "Therefore, brethren, having boldness to enter the Holiest by the blood of Jesus . . . draw near with a true heart in full assurance of faith" (Heb. 10:19, 22). You are reconciled to Christ forever.

You are His friend. You are forgiven of all your sins—past, present, and future. The moment you placed your faith in Christ, the doors of heaven were opened for you to approach the heavenly Father with complete assurance.

You can bring anything to Him. He will not reject you. As you turn to Him with your problems in prayer, the Lord Jesus Christ providentially works to supply your needs and help you.

Bring it all to Him in prayer. Praise Him for the answer. The red carpet of Christ's blood has paved Your way into the throne room of God.

Dear Lord, thank You for access into Your throne room. Christ's blood has paved the way for me.

Glorifying God

SCRIPTURE READING: Psalm 63:1–8   KEY VERSE: Romans 8:28

We know that all things work together for good to those who love God, to those who are the called according to His purpose.

Glorifying God seems to be such a titanic goal that it can frighten us into inaction: "My life is a mess. I am so erratic. How can I ever glorify God?"

Lao-tzu once said, "A journey of a thousand miles must begin with a single step." Glorifying God is an eternal process that begins on earth and continues in heaven. Our heavenly existence will be forever focused on exalting God. Realizing that, we can take the initiative to begin glorifying Him one day, one act, one thought at a time.

Each day is God's gift. You have multitudes of opportunities to honor God through your conduct and conversation. Thus, glorifying God means seeking to maximize each occasion with a deliberate step of obedience. When you falter, which will be often, you confess your disobedience, thank Him for His complete forgiveness, and move on with the task.

What could be more pleasing to your heavenly Father than to daily glorify Him? Establish that lofty aim as your supreme objective, and then live each day in humble dependence on the power of the Holy Spirit and obedience to His revealed truth.

Dear Lord, help me to glorify You today one act and one thought at a time. If I falter, forgive me, and help me to move on with the task.

Obedience Is the Only Way

SCRIPTURE READING: Psalm 61:1–24   KEY VERSE: Philippians 3:10

That I may know Him and the power of His resurrection, and the fellowship of His sufferings, being conformed to His death.

Sometimes obedience is tremendously difficult. You know what God requires of you, but from where you stand, obeying Him appears much too painful. You try to find a way out or around the situation, but nothing works. You must decide if you will obey God or give in to disobedience. For the believer, there's only one decision, and that is obedience. Anything less is disobedience.

In the devotional book *Daily with the King*, Glyn Evans writes,

> Some things I do in the Christian life are effortless . . . preach a sermon, lead a soul to Christ, write an article. Other things—vastly more important—are so difficult they command my whole strength and time . . . learn about God, know God, imitate and obey God. Those are the abiding things, like faith, hope, and love . . .
>
> God, You never told me how hard the way was. You let me find that out for myself. If I had known, I never would have followed. But having begun, I cannot turn back.
>
> That backward road leads to nowhere and to nothingness. To go forward is hard but it promises its reward. "That I might know Him" was Paul's cry (Philippians 3:10). So it is mine. Life's greatest reward is to know Him! The joy of the captured heart!

True worship springs from an obedient heart. Remember that God always places a blessing within the things He requires of you. Never forget that His strength is available to all who trust and obey Him.

Dear Lord, help me to obey Your Word so the bond of our relationship is strengthened each day.

JUNE

Temptation

MOUNTAIN: Mount of Temptation where
Jesus was tempted

KEY VERSES: Matthew 4:1–11

Then Jesus was led up by the Spirit into the wilderness to be tempted by the devil. And when He had fasted forty days and forty nights, afterward He was hungry. Now when the tempter came to Him, he said, "If You are the Son of God, command that these stones become bread." But He answered and said, "It is written, 'Man shall not live by bread alone, but by every word that proceeds from the mouth of God.'"

Then the devil took Him up into the holy city, set Him on the pinnacle of the temple, and said to Him, "If You are the Son of God, throw Yourself down. For it is written: 'He shall give His angels charge over you,' and, 'In their hands they shall bear you up, lest you dash your foot against a stone.'"

Jesus said to him, "It is written again, 'You shall not tempt the Lord your God.'" Again, the devil took Him up on an exceedingly high mountain, and showed Him all the kingdoms of the world and their glory. And he said to Him, "All these things I will give You if You will fall down and worship me." Then Jesus said to him, "Away with you, Satan! For it is written, 'You shall worship the Lord your God, and Him only you shall serve.'"

Then the devil left Him, and behold, angels came and ministered to Him.

In Times of Temptation

SCRIPTURE READING: Luke 4:1–14   KEY VERSE: Luke 4:14

Jesus returned in the power of the Spirit to Galilee, and news of Him went out through all the surrounding region.

Everyone faces temptation. Even the Son of God was tempted by Satan to turn away from God. But Jesus saw through the enemy's schemes and remained firm in His love and devotion to the Father (Luke 4:1–13).

One of the reasons Jesus came to live among us was to personally identify with our needs and struggles. He understands how we feel under the weight of temptation. He has faced the tempter and overcome the darkness and adversity associated with Satan's fiery trials.

When you face temptation, know that you do not face it alone. Jesus is with you, and He provides the strength you need to say no to every dark thought or evil imagination.

In times of temptation, when the enemy whispers lies to defeat and discourage you, take your stand against him by clothing yourself in the mighty armor of God (Eph. 6). Also know that you can never disappoint God. He knows exactly what you are doing even before you do it, and He loves you still.

Being tempted is not a sin. Sin is the result of acting on the temptation. God provides the strength you need to steer clear of temptation. You can say no to all evil because Jesus lives in you, and He has given you the Holy Spirit to lead you into all truth and knowledge. Therefore, take your stand as a child of God, and claim His strength and victory!

> *Thank You, Lord, that I have the power to say no to all evil because You live in me. You have given me the Holy Spirit to lead me into all truth and knowledge, so I take my stand as Your child and claim Your strength and victory.*

A Supernatural Change Agent

SCRIPTURE READING: Ephesians 4:17–29   KEY VERSE: Proverbs 23:7

For as he thinks in his heart, so is he.

Long before the pounding of hammers and buzzing of saws come to a residential or commercial building site, the contractor has an architectural blueprint in hand. Pipes, nails, shingles, studs, joists, ceilings, rooms, windows—in essence, the entire finished product—merely follow the detailed rendering.

Our growth as Christians has this one striking similarity: our measurable, visible behavior inevitably follows our mental blueprint. What we do and what others see are expressions of our mind-sets.

That is why Jesus said obviously identifiable acts such as murder, theft, and adultery stem from an inner evil. The thought precedes the act. Thus, real change proceeds from the inside out, from our thinking to our living.

You must abandon the world's bent toward greed and self-protection. You can no longer trust old habits that have cut deep thought patterns into your psychological and emotional grid systems.

Christ's death for your sins makes possible not just a new destiny but a radically new outlook on all of life. Your mind must be made wholly new each day. Such transformation begins, continues, and ends through the daily intake of God's supernatural change agent—divine truth.

Change me from the inside out, dear Lord. Use Your supernatural change agent of divine truth to make me a new creature in You.

Building Truth into Your Life

SCRIPTURE READING: 2 Timothy 2:15–19   KEY VERSE: Ephesians 1:13

In Him you also trusted, after you heard the word of truth, the gospel of your salvation; in whom also, having believed, you were sealed with the Holy Spirit of promise.

How do you build truth into your life?

First, you must rely on the conviction and instruction of the Holy Spirit. "The Spirit of truth" alone can reveal your personal inconsistencies and impart transforming truth (John 14:17). He guides you into the otherwise inscrutable ways of God.

Second, you must develop an unceasing concentration on God's Word. The body of Scriptures—from Genesis to Revelation—is "the word of truth" (2 Tim. 2:15). The Word of God is your complete specification list for abundant living.

Third, you must be committed to a life of prayer. Through communion and interaction with the heavenly Father, you allow the Spirit and the Word to do their transforming work. Prayer allows you to sift your needs, desires, and troubles through the mind and will of God, gaining His discernment and guidance.

Fourth, you must have the courage to act. Truth can never be left on the table. It must be applied if you are to receive its consequences. It is not just knowing but doing that makes truth relevant.

In cultivating these disciplines, your entire thought processes are altered to conform to God's pattern for living, and your life becomes a solid reflection of His image.

Dear heavenly Father, help me rely on the conviction and instruction of the Holy Spirit, develop an unceasing concentration on Your Word, and be committed to prayer. Then give me the courage to act.

A Winnable War

SCRIPTURE READING: Colossians 3:8–11   KEY VERSE: Romans 7:17

It is no longer I who do it, but sin that dwells in me.

In the 1860s our nation was embroiled in a bitter civil war—one part of our country pitted against the other. In the twentieth century, America fought in wars with and against other nations.

As a believer, you participate in a spiritual battle with consequences that are just as deadly. Understanding the nature of the conflict, however, can greatly alter the outcome.

Here's why: when you received Christ as Savior, you received a new spirit, and you became a distinctly new person. Your old identity apart from Christ was done away with.

How does that affect your walk with Christ? Tremendously. As a new creature in Christ, you are no longer at war with yourself. It is not a civil war—the old John Doe versus the new John Doe. If that were the case, you would always be at odds with yourself, and that would be frustrating at best. Such tension often leads to a mediocre Christian experience—winning some and losing a lot.

The truth that sets you free is this: the battle you face is partisan—the new you against the principle and power of sin that still indwell you. This is a winnable war.

Thank You, Lord, for the truth that sets me free. I praise You that I am a new creature in Christ.

The New You

SCRIPTURE READING: 1 Cor. 15:21–22, 45   KEY VERSES: Romans 7:24–25

O wretched man that I am! Who will deliver me from this body of death? I thank God—through Jesus Christ our Lord! So then, with the mind I myself serve the law of God, but with the flesh the law of sin.

Trying to live a victorious Christian life while fighting yourself is a losing proposition. But experiencing Christ's triumph on a consistent basis against the power of sin makes the abundant life feasible.

The Bible speaks of it this way. Before you were saved, you were "in Adam." That means you were totally apart from Christ, separated from His life, dead to His presence. You were an enemy of the Cross.

Once saved by a supernatural act of God, you were placed "in Christ." That means you are now entirely pleasing to the heavenly Father. You are totally accepted in the Beloved because your old sin nature (what you were before Christ) has been crucified with Christ.

Even more, the triumph of Christ over sin is now available to each of His children. Since you are in Him, all of His divine resources—His Word, His Spirit, His power—are yours to conquer the power of sin that indwells you but is no longer your master or your identity.

For the Christian, it is Christ and you against the power of sin, not Christ and you against you and sin. Your victory over dominating habits, treacherous passions, and emotional strongholds is entirely possible, for Christ is in you and for you.

Christ is in me and for me! I have authority over all the power of sin. Thank You for this freedom, dear Lord.

Who You Are in Christ

SCRIPTURE READING: 1 Corinthians 1:1–9   KEY VERSE: Romans 8:6

To be carnally minded is death, but to be spiritually minded is life and peace.

You are locked into a bad habit that you cannot seem to overcome. The more you try to do what God says is right, the tighter the vise. You struggle—for months, for years. There is some measure of release at times, but you still feel captive to the problem.

If that sounds like a familiar scenario to you, don't give up. God has provided a way of escape, no matter how deep the bondage. He is the Rescuer. There is help in the battle. Knowing the truth, not struggling against the lie, sets you free. Receiving the victory, not trying to attain it, is Christ's liberating message.

When the apostle Paul penned his first epistle to the Corinthians, the church was in a mess. The people lived in immorality, were involved in idol worship, and quarreled about their leadership.

You would think Paul would immediately berate the Corinthians. Instead, he began his letter with a remarkable description of their identity in Christ. He called them "saints" or "holy ones." He said they had been "sanctified." He continued to remind them of the grace richly available to them.

Paul spoke the truth that sets men free. Knowing who you are in Christ will change your behavior.

Dear heavenly Father, help me to realize who I am in You, so I will be able to change. Reveal the truth that will set me free.

Don't Believe A Lie

SCRIPTURE READING: Colossians 3:1–5   KEY VERSE: Matthew 16:23

But He turned and said to Peter, "Get behind Me, Satan! You are an offense to Me, for you are not mindful of the things of God, but the things of men."

Paul reminded the Corinthians of their position in Christ—holy, righteous, and blameless—because he knew their thinking must to change before their behavior could be altered.

Here is where many fail to overcome unwanted habits. We try to change our actions without conforming our thinking to God's truth.

We inevitably act the way we perceive ourselves. If we feel like unworthy sinners, then we will usually act like them—guilt-ridden, erratic, and unhappy. Satan points his dirty finger at our actions and accuses us as vile sinners until we finally believe him.

Don't believe a lie! Don't yield to the father of lies and the accuser of the brethren who has no truth in him.

This is the truth: You are a saint who occasionally sins. However, nothing you did yesterday, today, or tomorrow can change your position in Christ. When you do sin, even habitually, you are not acting according to your true desires or identity as God's holy one. You are acting inconsistently with your new nature in Christ.

God says you are a saint now that you have received Christ. That is why you can experience victory over all sin. Christ is in you. He will make you more than a conqueror as you know the truth that sets you free.

Dear Lord, help me to walk in the victory that is mine. Make me more than a conqueror over sin.

The Roots of Rebellion

SCRIPTURE READING: 1 Samuel 15:1–23   KEY VERSE: 1 Samuel 15:23

> *For rebellion is as the sin of witchcraft,*
> *And stubbornness is as iniquity and idolatry.*
> *Because you have rejected the word of the LORD,*
> *He also has rejected you from being king.*

Partial obedience is not obedience. It is rebellion that turns aside to selfish desires while ignoring the wishes of those in authority over us. At first glance rebellion may appear insignificant, but don't be fooled. The roots of rebellion grow quickly and run deep.

God directed Saul to destroy the Amalekites. When the dust on the battlefield settled, however, Saul and his army spared the Amalekite king and the best of his flocks. With disobedience standing between him and God, Saul tried in vain to explain his actions. He claimed he saved the best of the spoil as a sacrifice to God, but the true intent of Saul's heart was selfish gain. This one act of rebellion cost him the throne. Years later, it cost Israel the lives of some of its strongest fighting men.

Ultimately, all rebellion circumvents God's control even though its aim is usually directed at human authority. It quenches our fellowship with God and derails His blessings. You may think your rebellion is justifiable, but God never blesses anything that contradicts His will. Rebellion is always at enmity with God.

Ask Him to surface any hidden rebellion within your heart. When you come to Him in repentance, He always responds in love and grace.

Father, please surface any hidden rebellion in my heart, then help me repent of it. Let me respond with obedience to You and those in authority over me.

The Way of the Cross

SCRIPTURE READING: 1 Peter 5:1–11   KEY VERSE: 1 Peter 5:6

Therefore humble yourselves under the mighty hand of God, that He may exalt you in due time.

The apostle Peter had a streak of rebellion that lay hidden until Jesus announced His impending death. Then it surfaced in prideful array (Matt. 16:23). Peter did not understand God's plan nor did he respond to Christ's words in faith.

He thought only of the ensuing political unrest facing the Jews. His entire life was apprehended by the thought of the Messiah sitting on the throne of David instead of personal fellowship he shared with Jesus.

Had the Lord not rebuked Peter's actions, the other disciples might have begun nursing a rebellious attitude as well. But in obedience, Peter yielded himself to Christ and thus begun a deeper journey into a loving relationship with his Lord.

God's way is not the way of rebellion, but the way of obedience. It is not the way of pride, but the way of humility. Years later and long after the death of Christ, Peter wrote, "Humble yourselves under the mighty hand of God, that He may exalt you in due time" (1 Peter 5:6).

The secret to submission is not fighting back in rebellion but drawing close to Jesus. The way of the Cross is not the way of rebellion, but the way of humble submission. Will you submit all that you are to Him today?

I humbly submit to You, Lord. Draw me close to Jesus. Bring me by the way of the Cross.

Yes, Lord

SCRIPTURE READING: Read: Jonah 1:1–5   KEY VERSE: Psalm 139:7

Where can I go from Your Spirit?
Or where can I flee from Your presence?

God instructed Jonah to go east to Nineveh. Instead, he headed west to Tarshish and into the pathway of rebellion. He knew if he preached God's message, the Ninevites would turn from their wickedness and follow God. They were Israel's dire enemies, and Jonah could not bear the thought of their repentance. So he refused to obey, and in his rebellion he found he was the one separated from God.

Disobedience does not cancel God's commands. Our lack of obedience does not alter His plan. There is no such thing as "getting off the hook" with God. We can't escape the presence of God. Even in the belly of a whale, God was there to convict Jonah of his sin. Resistance to God's will brings suffering to others. Rebellion has a ripple effect and erodes relationships with God and others. It steals our joy, divides our minds, and causes guilt.

Many times we are given a second chance. Jonah was, but that is not always the case. God wants us to respond to His will by faith and obedience. God always accomplishes His will. Nothing we do or say alters His plan. There is only one way to answer the call of God and that is to say, "Yes, Lord." Anything else results in disobedience.

I say yes today, Lord—to Your will and Your way. Help me walk in obedience to Your Word and Your plan for my life.

God Is in Everything

SCRIPTURE READING: Psalm 89:1–17   KEY VERSE: Psalm 89:11

The heavens are Yours, the earth also is Yours;
The world and all its fullness, You have founded them.

God is involved in every area of your life. And while this may be easy to understand in joyful times, it is just as true in times of sorrow and heartache. God will never abandon you to the harsh forces of this world without some form of help and support.

In 1 Corinthians 10:13, the apostle Paul told us: "No temptation has overtaken you except such as is common to man; but God is faithful, who will not allow you to be tempted beyond what you are able, but with the temptation will also make the way of escape, that you may be able to bear it."

Let the Holy Spirit show you a deeper meaning of this word. Temptation can come in the form of a testing of your faith. It may involve something that suddenly appears and leaves you feeling helplessly overwhelmed.

Often you cannot see the outcome of the testing of your faith. God stretches you in your relationships, job, and other areas to see if you will remain steadfast and true to Him and the others involved. Ultimately, the outcome of your testing is tremendous blessing.

Is God in everything? The answer is a hardy yes! He is not the One who causes the pain you feel or the disappointment you experience, but He promises to use each one for your good and His glory. Therefore, you can trust Him in times of rain, wind, and sunshine.

I trust You, Lord, in good times and in bad. You have promised to use everything for my good and Your glory.

Accusations of the Enemy

SCRIPTURE READING: Ephesians 3:14–19   KEY VERSE: Jeremiah 29:11

I know the thoughts that I think toward you, says the LORD, thoughts of peace and not of evil, to give you a future and a hope.

Satan has a long record when it comes to discouraging the saints of God. He enjoys telling us that we are weak and of little use to the kingdom of God. He whispers lying thoughts to our minds, trying to deceive us into believing that God cannot possibly love us because of past failures and sins. These accusations are completely false, and the enemy of our souls knows it.

God's love for you is so great that He sent His only Son to earth to die for your sins (John 3:16). Through Jesus Christ, you now have the opportunity to live free from Satan's shame and condemnation.

The love of God holds you safe and keeps you motivated in your relationship with Jesus Christ. Feelings of inferiority may tell you that you are worthless and there is no hope for your future. But God says the opposite: "I know the thoughts that I think toward you . . . thoughts of peace and not of evil, to give you a future and a hope" (Jer. 29:11).

Neil Anderson writes: "You are not the helpless victim caught between two nearly equal but opposite heavenly super-powers. Satan is a deceiver. Only God is omnipotent (all-powerful), omnipresent (always present), and omniscient (all-knowing) . . . A true knowledge of God and our identity in Christ are the greatest determinants of our mental health."

In the name of Jesus, I rebuke the accusations of the enemy today. I am set free from Satan's shame and condemnation.

Learning to Forgive

SCRIPTURE READING: Mark 11:23–26   KEY VERSE: Hebrews 13:5

Let your conduct be without covetousness; be content with such things as you have. For He Himself has said, "I will never leave you nor forsake you."

Satan delights in seeing you hurt not only once, but also in attempting to have you relive your hurt for days, weeks, months, even years afterward. Sometimes you may feel you're on the road to recovery when the enemy attacks you on the same issue again.

One of his methods of churning your life and emotions is to convince you that someone "owes you." Perhaps you were legitimately wronged. You're hurting and don't know what to do about it. And perhaps you're certain the only way you'll ever have true peace is for the person who hurt you to pay for what happened.

Many horrible sins leave people, even children, as helpless victims. Perhaps you are one of these victims, and perhaps your life seemingly has spiraled out of control ever since you were wronged. Perhaps you're also consumed with blaming others.

Please remember that God has promised He will never leave or forsake you (Heb. 13:5), and His edicts from His judgment seat are absolutely perfect. You cannot control what happened in the past, but you can control your current responses and attitude.

Harboring blame or resentment promotes disharmony and bitterness. Worse, it harms your testimony and fellowship with God. So far as it depends on you, forgive and allow God to handle the rest.

Lord, I am tempted to harbor unforgiveness and bitterness. Teach me to forgive and allow You to handle all the rest.

A Path to Forgiveness

SCRIPTURE READING: 1 John 2:1–9   KEY VERSE: 1 John 1:9

*If we confess our sins, He is faithful and just to forgive us our sins
and to cleanse us from all unrighteousness.*

Just as God has made the way to salvation through faith in the Lord Jesus
Christ clear, He also has provided a straight path for forgiveness when you do
sin. Forgiveness is not obtained through emotional regret or renewed fervor. It
is experienced personally by sincere confession of your sin to the Father.

First, you realize you have sinned against God. While your sin affects you
and others, its chief offense is the violation of the Lord's commands behind
which is God Himself. You have grieved Him personally.

Second, you confess your transgressions. As long as you refuse to admit
your sin, you are in bondage to it. You must bring it to the Father, agreeing with
His view of sin.

Third, you rely on the full provision of your forgiveness from sin in Jesus
Christ. He is your Advocate, always pointing to His sufficient work on Calvary
as the sole grounds for your redemption. Then you are cleansed, refreshed, and
restored by God's unconditional love. You rejoice in His grace that makes such
forgiveness possible, worshiping Him for His indescribable mercy.

Are you refusing to confess a sin to the Lord? Your rebellion and misery
can end today if you will admit your sin and receive His forgiveness.

*I realize I have sinned against You, God. I confess my transgressions to You.
I rely on the full provision of Jesus Christ for forgiveness.*

Sinning After Salvation

SCRIPTURE READING: Galatians 6:7–9   KEY VERSE: Romans 6:2

Certainly not! How shall we who died to sin live any longer in it?

When we understand the grounds for salvation (the cross of Christ) and the eternal security it brings, the inevitable question is: Can we then sin freely? Paul's reply to such wrong thinking is clear: "Certainly not! How shall we who died to sin live any longer in it?" (Rom. 6:2).

Sin is a curse to all believers. Our new relationship as children of God should radically alter our view of sin and our participation in it. Why? Although the penalty of sin, which is death, has been removed for the Christian, sin still has severe consequences for those who engage in it.

- The adulterer will be shamed by his family.
- The abusive parent will experience the pain of emotionally alienated children.
- We will reap what we sow (Gal. 6:7).

That law is in effect for Christian and unbeliever alike. The consequences of sin are as severe as ever. Though the Christian will not experience eternal death, he can experience a living death on earth if he sins habitually.

When you sin, you position yourself under the Lord's discipline, which can be painful, though He administers it with a loving, not angry, hand. Sin is always destructive; you can never get away with it.

Forgive me of my sins, dear Lord. Cleanse me. Set me free. Help me not to become weighed down again with the yoke of bondage.

Rebuke and Restoration

SCRIPTURE READING: Psalm 51:1–19   KEY VERSE: Job 4:8

Even as I have seen,
Those who plow iniquity
And sow trouble reap the same.

Can you get away with sin?

Sin is disobedience. Disobedience is a violation of God's Word and ways. Violating His commands places you in confrontation with God's character, which is the foundation for all His decrees.

Thus, when you sin, small or large, you sin against God Himself—holy, perfect, and just. In His righteousness, He is compelled to deal with your iniquity. Ignoring your sin would be tantamount to changing God's immutable character and attributes, which He has declared cannot happen.

You can always depend on God to remain the same. When you obey Him, you can expect His blessings. Similarly, when you disobey Him you can anticipate His correction. God's unvarying character is your cornerstone and compass. His chastisement for sin is certain and sure, but always given with loving discipline.

Your parents might have condoned certain actions when you were a child. In reality, they were not doing you a favor. God does not overlook any sin. His holiness is your foundation for Christian growth. His rebuke and restoration keep you on His course, protecting you from even greater disaster.

Dear Lord, thank You for rebuking my sin to keep me from greater disaster.
I praise You for restoration through the blood of Jesus Christ.

A Lifestyle of Sin

SCRIPTURE READING: Psalm 119:65–72   KEY VERSE: Proverbs 28:13

He who covers his sins will not prosper,
But whoever confesses and forsakes them will have mercy.

We may travel seventy miles per hour in a sixty-five-mile-per-hour speed zone and not be caught by the police.

We may not report cash income on our income tax statement and fail to be summoned by the Internal Revenue Service.

But we can never fudge on God's Word and avoid the consequences. God means what He says and says what He means.

Although the consequences of sin will vary according to its nature, God hates all sin.

Unfortunately, because the consequences of gossip at the office, the lustful look at the shopping mall, or the outburst of temper in the home seem minor, we can develop a lifestyle of disobedience.

There may appear to be no repercussions, but all sin disrupts and interferes in our fellowship with Jesus Christ. Our intimacy wanes. Our devotion flickers. Our sense of God's peace, joy, and love fades. Conversation with Him diminishes. Above all, our hearts are not right with Him. The severest effect of sin is a dulling of our relationship with Christ.

If you have sinned against God, humbly acknowledge your sin, receive His forgiveness, and rekindle the heart of your salvation—intimacy with Christ.

Lord, forgive me for a lifestyle of disobedience. I humbly acknowledge my
sin. I receive Your forgiveness. Rekindle my intimacy with You.

Your Strength and Shield

SCRIPTURE READING: 2 Cor. 12:7–10   KEY VERSE: 1 Cor. 1:27

God has chosen the foolish things of the world to put to shame the wise, and God has chosen the weak things of the world to put to shame the things which are mighty.

Every Christian has a weakness, a soft spiritual underbelly. Satan, though not omniscient, is keen on probing for our spiritual chinks and mounting unrelenting assaults. Frequently, we are caught in the vicious and futile circle of failure, repentance, renewed commitment, and repeated relapse. As long as we are kept in this dizzying and frustrating mode, the devil can keep us off balance, taking the loving edge off our relationship with Christ and our effectiveness in His work.

God's ways, however, are not ours. His solution for our weakness is radically different. Instead of our buckling up our spiritual chin strap one more notch, Christ asks us to admit our weakness and concentrate on His strength. This may sound simple, but it is not simplistic.

Grace saved us from sin, and grace will deliver us. We need Christ's power, not our own resolve, to defeat our foe and overcome our weakness.

Take your weakness, whatever its nature, to Christ. Do not give up to your problem but give in to Christ, yielding to His Spirit who can fortify your frailty with supernatural grace. You are weak, but He is strong. Jesus is your Strength and your Shield. Lean on His grace.

Jesus, You are my Strength and my Shield. You are the One who can fortify my human frailty with supernatural grace. I lean on You today.

The Great Divorce

SCRIPTURE READING: Genesis 3:22–24   KEY VERSE: Romans 5:12

Just as through one man sin entered the world, and death through sin, and thus death spread to all men, because all sinned.

Divorce has become too common in our fractured age. Its disabling effects—financially, emotionally, and socially—are well documented in various studies.

In a real sense, sin has effected a divorce between man and God. When the original couple, Adam and Eve, sinned in the Garden, God evicted man from His presence: "He drove out the man" (Gen. 3:24). The Hebrew word for "drove" is also used in the Old Testament on five occasions for divorce.

God and man—united at Creation in intimacy, fellowship, and purpose—were separated by sin. The holiness of God and the sin of man are incompatible. The Creator and the creation, man, can no longer live together in harmony apart from faith in Christ. Sin drives unbelieving man out of God's presence and into chaos and evil.

The great divorce, as author C. S. Lewis put it, has fixed a gulf, a chasm, between God and man. Born into sin, man suffers from the emotional and spiritual wreckage of life apart from God, driven by wayward desires and instincts, walking in the darkness of his own counsel.

The truth about sin is ugly. But you must know the truth, the good and the bad, before you can be set free.

Set me free from sin, dear Lord. Restore my fellowship with You. Lead me from darkness into Your glorious light.

The Reality of Sin

SCRIPTURE READING: 2 Corinthians 4:1–7   KEY VERSE: 2 Corinthians 4:7

We have this treasure in earthen vessels, that the excellence of the power may be of God and not of us.

Malcolm Muggeridge, the late British author who converted to Christianity, once said that the evening news was proof enough for the reality of sin.

Entering the human race through Adam's rebellion in the Garden, sin pervades our planet, expressing itself most vividly in the twisted, tainted actions of men.

We sin because we are sinners. Every man and woman conceived on planet earth is born with a sin nature—a bent away from God that seeks to live independently of Him, either passively or actively rejecting Him.

If you trace your human heritage, you would ultimately arrive at Adam and Eve, the fountainhead of the human race. When they sinned, we all were dragged down with them, for our humanity was bound up in them.

The evidence that we are sinners is, as Muggeridge attested, quite obvious. Crime, drugs, war, greed, and corruption of every sort are the staple of our media diet. But the greater problem is that we as individuals experience the ravages of sin. After all, a society's problems are but the culmination of individual ills. Its cure can be found only in Christ.

Dear Lord, I recognize that my basic nature is sinful. Only through Your provision for redemption am I set free from sin. Help me walk in this freedom instead of being a slave to sin.

The Disaster of Wrong Desire

SCRIPTURE READING: Psalm 106:1–15   KEY VERSE: Numbers 11:1

When the people complained, it displeased the LORD; for the LORD heard it, and His anger was aroused. So the fire of the LORD burned among them, and consumed some in the outskirts of the camp.

A wise Christian once remarked: "You may get what you want, but you may not want what you get."

That certainly was the case when the Israelites demanded meat to spice up their diet of manna. Even as they were savoring the first bite, God struck them with a deadly plague.

Wrong desires are still a clear and present danger for us today. We can manipulate circumstances or people to attain our wants. Though we may be momentarily satisfied, we will eventually reap the distasteful consequences.

How can you avoid the pitfalls of asking the heavenly Father for things that will be to our detriment?

First, delight yourself in the Lord on a regular basis (Ps. 37:4). When you make loving God your chief desire, you will find your requests aligned with His will the majority of the time.

Second, find your contentment in Christ. You may be prone to think if you had this object or knew this person or could accomplish this goal, life would be far better. God may grant your desire, but He wants you to find your contentment in your relationship with Christ.

Third, rest in the goodness and faithfulness of God. God will give you only what is for your welfare, and He will do so with perfect faithfulness.

Father, I will delight myself in You today. I will find contentment in Christ and rest in Your goodness and faithfulness.

Dealing with Immorality

SCRIPTURE READING: 1 Corinthians 4:1–7   KEY VERSE: Romans 6:11

You also, reckon yourselves to be dead indeed to sin, but alive to God in Christ Jesus our Lord.

A pilot flying a plane through a massive thunderstorm where the horizon is obscured may experience a sensation known as vertigo. Though he is upside down, he feels as if he is flying upright. Correction depends upon his reliance on his instruments, which indicate otherwise.

Similarly, while we may not feel dead to sin (specifically immorality), the Word of God says we are, and His Word is always accurate, even in the midst of storms of passion. This is what the Scriptures refer to as "reckoning," counting a fact true apart from any emotion or affection. That is why we are called to reckon ourselves dead to sin and alive to God (Rom. 6:11).

Successfully handling immorality begins with reckoning yourself dead to its power, but you must continue by reckoning yourself alive to Christ. You put on this new man, this new identity, by faith in God's Word.

For sexual immorality, the Scripture says, "God did not call us to uncleanness, but in holiness" (1 Thess. 4:7). For unethical conduct, the Scripture says we should desire "to live honorably" (Heb. 13:18). You deal with immorality by understanding your new holy nature in Christ and appropriating its transforming truth.

Dear Lord, help me die to sin and come alive to You and Your Word. Let me understand and appropriate the truth of my new nature.

New Gods, New Arrivals

SCRIPTURE READING: Deuteronomy 32:15–17   KEY VERSE: Exodus 20:5

You shall not bow down to them nor serve them. For I, the LORD your God, am a jealous God, visiting the iniquity of the fathers on the children to the third and fourth generations of those who hate Me.

Our modern culture relegates the concept of idols to pagan or Eastern religions. Certainly, we, in our enlightened society, do not worship ornate statues or sacred artifacts, we may think. Yet our idols are just as real. The Bible describes an idol as anything to which we give our time, energy, and attention to the exclusion of Jehovah God.

In rebuking the Israelites for their idolatry, Moses described such impostors as "new gods, new arrivals" (Deut. 32:17). The "new gods" can be career, prestige, money, and/or pleasure. Given preeminence, they become demanding gods that increasingly command our adoration and service.

The root evil in idolatry is that our worship is ultimately laid at Satan's feet. He always competes for our allegiance. He deceives us into thinking that we are following our own ambitions or pleasures.

God demands our worship and devotion. Sacrifices given to fulfill our agendas are given to a false god.

If you have carved an idol, return to your first love, Jesus Christ. Place Him first in all you do; and He will order your life with dignity, integrity, and joy.

Take every idol from my life, dear Lord. Order my life with dignity, integrity, and joy.

Staying Alert

SCRIPTURE READING: 2 Samuel 11:1–27   KEY VERSE: Proverbs 4:23

Keep your heart with all diligence,
For out of it spring the issues of life.

King David was on top of the world; his years of hiding from Saul were over. Both the Northern and the Southern Kingdoms were united. Israel was victorious in battle and, for the first time in years, secure from her enemies. Then David's moment of weakness struck. Here are lessons for all. David had become complacent in his success. Instead of leading his army in battle as was his custom, he stayed behind, sending his captains.

We must always be alert for Satan's snares. We never grow so spiritually mature that we are excluded from his assaults. The moment we depend too heavily on our strength, position, or integrity, we are ripe targets for failure.

David failed to do spiritual battle when temptation surfaced. He looked at Bathsheba and kept looking. All of us have moments of weakness when temptation strikes with hurricane force. It is in the initial stages, however, that the battle is won or lost (2 Tim. 2:22; Matt. 26:41). Our only defense is by a sheer act of the will—trusting in the Lord Jesus Christ (James 4:7)—to resist the devil's deceitful overtures.

Be on the alert against Satan. He is "a roaring lion" (1 Peter 5:8), but he can be resisted when you depend on God (Ephesians 6:13).

Heavenly Father, help me resist the attacks of the enemy today. Keep me alert against Satan and his diabolical strategies.

Consider the Consequences

SCRIPTURE READING: 2 Samuel 12:10–18   KEY VERSE: Numbers 32:23

But if you do not do so, then take note, you have sinned against the
LORD; and be sure your sin will find you out.

The fundamental law of physics is this: for every action, there is an opposite and equal reaction. Just as universally applicable is this unchanging spiritual principle: for every sin, there are corresponding, continuing consequences. In other words, we reap what we sow.

Sin's most blinding deception is that we can avoid any ramifications. We think we can get away with immorality, indiscretion, or indecency without paying the consequences. Because our loving God understands the inevitable results of sin, He persistently seeks our holiness. Sin has a price. If you are thinking of violating the law of God, think of these sobering truths:

Grace does not cancel sin's consequences. God will forgive us when we sin. He will still love us and use us, but the damage will not always be erased. A one-night stand can yield a lifetime of regret; a moment of anger can wreak havoc for years. Sin's consequences affect others as well. Even the next generation can be adversely impacted by our unwise choices.

If you are tempted to disobey, consider the consequences. If you have sinned and you are suffering the aftereffects, turn to God with a repentant heart. He will restore you.

Dear Lord, keep me from sin and its consequences. Help me understand the
ramifications of disobedience.

Freedom from Bondage

SCRIPTURE READING: Psalm 101:1–8   KEY VERSES: Ephesians 4:31–32

Let all bitterness, wrath, anger, clamor, and evil speaking be put away from you, with all malice. And be kind to one another, tender-hearted, forgiving one another, just as God in Christ forgave you.

The young man told of the anger and bitterness consuming his life. Finally, in frustration he said, "I feel trapped just like a bird tied to a short tether. I want to be free, but it doesn't seem possible."

Many believers feel just as trapped as this man. For years they have been bound by old habits, feelings, or physical addictions that God never meant for them to bear.

One of the first steps to freedom from bondage is acceptance. You must accept God's personal love for you. No matter what your circumstances may be, Jesus loves you.

The second step is to ask God to forgive and cleanse you from any sin in your life. Forgiveness of others is also a key factor. Until you forgive those who have hurt you, you will never experience true freedom.

A third step is to be honest with God about your feelings and weaknesses. If you have suffered disappointment, tell Him about it. He cares and wants you to know that you can bring anything to Him in prayer.

A final step toward freedom is to ask God to help you gain His perspective on your situation. God is your dearest Friend. He promises to take care of you and provide for your deepest needs. Ask Him to reveal His personal love for you and the grace that is yours in Christ.

Father, help me be honest with You about my feelings and weaknesses. Cleanse me from any sin in my life and help me forgive others.

The Victory That Is Yours

SCRIPTURE READING: John 8:32–37   KEY VERSE: John 8:12

Jesus spoke to them again, saying, "I am the light of the world. He who follows Me shall not walk in darkness, but have the light of life."

Jesus told His disciples: "If you abide in My word . . . you shall know the truth, and the truth shall make you free" (John 8:31–32). Christ knew His followers would face many temptations after He was gone. That was why He wanted them to focus on the truth of His Word, not the instability and spiritual darkness of the world around them.

As long as Christ was with them, the disciples followed with ease. Then came the night of His arrest, and Jesus was gone. However, instead of walking in the light of His truth, they allowed fear to capture their hearts. Many people struggle with emotional or physical bondage because they walk in the dim light of their own desires and resources, not the light of God's Word.

Christ said, "I am the light of the world. He who follows Me shall not walk in darkness, but have the light of life" (John 8:12). Our hope as believers is the fact that Christ is our Source of light.

You may be struggling with something that has held you captive for years. Now is the time to ask God to help you face it and deal with it by submitting it to His control. Then claim the victory that is yours through the power of His Spirit. No matter what you are facing, there is hope in the light of God's truth.

God, I submit the bondage in my life to Your control. I claim the victory that is mine today through the power of Your Spirit.

A Divine Sin-Blocker

SCRIPTURE READING: Romans 5:17–21   KEY VERSE: 2 Corinthians 8:7

As you abound in everything—in faith, in speech, in knowledge, in all diligence, and in your love for us—see that you abound in this grace also.

For years she was entangled in an immoral lifestyle. Finally, through a friend, she came to know Jesus as her Savior. Several years passed before there was any hint of trouble; then friends discovered she was concealing a deep emotional hurt.

Instead of being transparent with God or talking her feelings out with a pastor or counselor, she allowed anger to fester and infect her emotional well-being. Sin resurfaced; only this time it was far more consuming.

Jesus loves us unconditionally. His grace is sufficient. We can lay all our hurts safely at His feet, knowing He will support and carry us through the difficulties of life.

The problem in this woman's life stemmed from a lack of communication. Out of fear of rejection, she failed to communicate her need to God. Did He know of it? Yes, but He wants us to bring every tear, every heartache, to Him in prayer. It is a matter of yielding and loving Him above all else.

The chain reaction from an inner hurt can move quickly from self-pity to feelings of rebellion and then a return to sinful behavior. But God's grace applied to your life is a divine sin-blocker. All you need to do is to walk in the light of His forgiveness.

Apply Your grace to my life, Lord. Let me walk in the light of Your forgiveness.

Evidences of the Flesh

SCRIPTURE READING: Galatians 5:16–21 KEY VERSE: Galatians 5:1

Stand fast therefore in the liberty by which Christ has made us free, and do not be entangled again with a yoke of bondage.

In Galatians 5, Paul used the term flesh to describe the part of our lives that stands in opposition to God. The fruit of the Spirit, or the evidence of Christ's life in us, includes love, joy, peace, patience, kindness, goodness, faithfulness, gentleness, and self-control. The evidence of the flesh includes immorality, impurity, sensuality, idolatry, sorcery, hatred, strife, jealousy, outbursts of anger, disputes, dissension in our relationships, factions, envying, drunkenness, carousing, and other things like these.

The flesh is not so much tangible in nature as it is revealed in our attitudes, desires, and lifestyles. Never think that just because you serve the Lord, you won't be caught up in the trappings of the flesh. A person can serve God, make a wonderful public impression, and still be living in the flesh.

The central focus of the Spirit-filled life must always be Jesus Christ, while the primary focus of the flesh is self-will, self-assertion, self-love, self-indulgence, self-pity, self-reliance, self-consciousness, self-righteousness, and self-glorification.

However, we do not have to serve the desires of the flesh. As children of God, we have been given the power to say no to our old way of living and thinking. Ask the Lord to reveal any evidences of the flesh in your life. Be willing to allow Him to strip away all that does not glorify Him.

Father, please reveal any evidences of the flesh in my life. Strip away all that does not glorify You.

Power of the Flesh

SCRIPTURE READING: Romans 8:12–18   KEY VERSE: Romans 8:8

So then, those who are in the flesh cannot please God.

The part of man that is called the flesh can surface at any time in many ways. However, we can know one thing for sure: the goal of the flesh is to elevate self. We call it the flesh because it has to do with our fallen nature, which is in direct opposition to the things of God.

The fleshly attitudes within us can become quite obvious. They always prompt us to seek to be heard first and noticed above those around us. In dealing with the flesh, we quickly discover that not only does the flesh want its way, but it becomes indignant if others do not agree with it.

The flesh cannot be improved, disciplined, changed, or redeemed. It is the part of man that represents the fallen state of Adam. Only God can deal successfully with the flesh, and He has done this by eliminating its power.

Jesus has overcome the power of every fleshly action that we struggle against. When we pray and confess our need for Christ, He comes to us and abides with us through the power of the Holy Spirit. We are no longer under the rule of the flesh.

No longer are we reduced to pushing, planning, and plotting to be noticed or to attain worldly treasures. The very best is ours because we belong to almighty God. And His love for us is everlasting.

Lord, I realize that I cannot improve, discipline, change, or redeem my flesh. I submit my flesh to You. I am no longer under its rule.

JULY

THEME
___

Faith

MOUNTAIN: Mountains removed by faith

KEY VERSE: Matthew 17:20

Jesus said to them . . . "I say to you, if you have faith as a mustard seed, you will say to this mountain, 'Move from here to there,' and it will move; and nothing will be impossible for you."

Mustard Seed Faith

SCRIPTURE READING: Mark 11:23–26   KEY VERSE: Matthew 17:20

Jesus said to them, "Because of your unbelief; for assuredly, I say to you, if you have faith as a mustard seed, you will say to this mountain, 'Move from here to there,' and it will move; and nothing will be impossible for you."

Mary Damron refuses to stare at her mountain, not even the impoverished one she calls home. Mary is from the poor coal mining hollows of West Virginia, but she is rich beyond measure.

In his book *Living Beyond the Limits*, Franklin Graham devotes a chapter to Mary, who is a walking testimony of the life-changing power of faith in Christ. In 1994, Mary learned Graham needed gift-filled shoe boxes to distribute to the war-scarred children of Bosnia. Instead of focusing on her struggling Appalachian family, Mary traversed her community, asking for donations from churches and groups.

The day after Thanksgiving, she delivered to Graham twelve hundred shoe boxes in a twenty-ton truck. A year later, Mary delivered more than six thousand shoe boxes in time for Christmas. Her devotion and uncanny faith resulted not only in Graham's sending her to Bosnia to help deliver gifts, but also in President Bill Clinton's honoring her at the White House. Mary boldly asked the president for permission to pray for him, and she did.

The story of Mary Damron can be duplicated by anybody. She started small, with a mustard seed of faith and a mountain-sized heart for Jesus. And just as He will do for you whenever you are within His will, He made sure nothing stopped Mary's twenty-ton truck full of shoe boxes.

Lord, give me mustard seed faith to move mountains. Use me for Your glory!

Childlike Faith

SCRIPTURE READING: John 3:1–17   KEY VERSES: Ephesians 2:8–9

By grace you have been saved through faith, and that not of your-
selves; it is the gift of God, not of works, lest anyone should boast.

Every once in a while you hear someone say, "God helps those who help themselves." However, the truth is, God helps those who are quick to admit their need and absolute dependency on Him. As long as we think we can somehow work our way into heaven or perform some great deed on our own, we receive very little from the hand of God.

Jesus instructed the disciples to become like children in their approach to God. The issue He was addressing was one of pride. A child looks to his mother or father for support and help. He may try to do things on his own, but when frustration comes, he knows he can turn to his parents for a solution.

A young father told how he secretly watched his three-year-old daughter struggling to put on her shoes. The more she tried lacing and tying the shoes on her own, the more frustrated she became. Finally in desperation, she dropped back on her bed and loudly proclaimed: "Help me, God. I just can't do it."

Nicodemus had a hard time understanding Jesus' concept of a new birth. As a member of the Sanhedrin, he was highly educated. Still the only way he could expect to spend eternity with God was to place his childlike faith in Jesus Christ. It was not a matter of intellect; it was a matter of humble faith and grace. Take time to tell the Savior you need Him more than anything else.

Give me childlike faith in You, dear Lord. I need You more than anything else.

Peace with God

SCRIPTURE READING: Romans 5:1–11   KEY VERSE: Romans 5:10

For if when we were enemies we were reconciled to God through the death of His Son, much more, having been reconciled, we shall be saved by His life.

Thirty years after the crime, he was finally apprehended, tried, and found guilty by a jury. The arrest and conviction shocked both family and community. His life had been pleasant enough, raising a family, working as a salesman, even participating in many civic activities.

Men and women who are separated from God are in a similar predicament. While they may enjoy reasonably happy and successful lives, they live at enmity with their Creator and Judge.

Paul noted, "For if when we were enemies we were reconciled to God through the death of His Son" (Rom. 5:10). Other passages refer to man's alienation from God and his position as an enemy of "the cross of Christ" (Phil. 3:18).

Yet the love of God stretches across the chasm of sin and offers a solution to the hostility. The only path to true peace is faith in Christ's death, burial, and resurrection. That decision alone gives a person peace with God, establishing an eternal relationship with Christ.

True peace—the kind that lasts forever, the kind that reconciles God and man—is yours through faith in Christ. Don't deceive yourself or others with false appearances. Trust Him today.

Dear Lord, I thank You that true peace is mine through faith in Jesus Christ. I trust Him today!

Unshakable Peace

SCRIPTURE READING: Philippians 4:5–7   KEY VERSE: John 14:27

Peace I leave with you, My peace I give to you; not as the world gives do I give to you. Let not your heart be troubled, neither let it be afraid.

Charles Spurgeon. Martin Luther. John Wesley. Prominent names of Christendom, yet not without great personal struggles.

Spurgeon, known for his compelling sermons at the Metropolitan Tabernacle, battled recurring seasons of depression throughout his splendid ministry.

Luther, whose emphasis on justification by faith alone shattered centuries of false ideology, struggled with numerous physical afflictions.

Wesley, whose preaching filled the towns and villages of colonial America, endured a difficult marriage that created an unstable family life at best.

Their legacies, however, are noble and their achievements memorable. Despite their problems, the peace of God was rooted deeply in their spirits, serving as both rudder and stabilizer for their ministry and lives.

It is perfectly normal to have your cage rattled by strained relationships, financial tremors, or emotional surges. Jesus told us to expect such predicaments. But because you have Christ, you have unshakable peace in your innermost being. You can wade through dilemmas without yielding to irrational fears or anxiety. Keep Him at the center of your life, and you will reflect the peace of Christ.

Thank You, Lord, that Your unshakable peace will sustain me throughout the challenges of this day.

The Peace of God

SCRIPTURE READING: Ephesians 2:14–16   KEY VERSE: 1 Peter 5:7

Casting all your care upon Him, for He cares for you.

The peace of God is usually lost when we lose our perspective of God's over-riding, unceasing care of us.

Writing to a church under intense strain capable of dismantling any semblance of contentment, Peter closed his first letter by telling them to give their troubles to God because "He cares for you."

What a relief of pressure! What troubles me and upsets my spiritual well-being, even the slightest irritant, matters to God. He is so concerned that He invites me to give Him every care.

Cast your burdens on Him in prayer. Tell God what bothers you, what robs your joy and peace, and then really believe that He has heard you and will answer. If you truly trust Him to handle the problem, then experiencing His peace is a supernatural result. The situation is in God's hands. He is in control despite appearances. He is able to bring about a solution, whenever and however He chooses.

When you reach that point, the peace of God is yours. The storms may brew, but God is very concerned about you and has taken your cares upon Himself. When the pressure mounts, you cast every burden on Him. All is in His care, and that settles your soul as no other thought.

> *Father, when the pressures mount today, help me remember that You have taken all my cares upon Yourself. I cast my burdens on You, knowing that everything is in Your care.*

Our Heavenly Father

SCRIPTURE READING: Luke 20:1–8   KEY VERSES: Matthew 7:28–29

And so it was, when Jesus had ended these sayings, that the people were astonished at His teaching, for He taught them as one having authority, and not as the scribes.

The authority of Jesus' teaching staggered the Jews of His day. His miracles of healing and control over nature's forces awed hearers and disciples. But there was nothing more stunning to His audience than His constant reference to God as Father.

God was revealed in the Old Testament through very reverent and awe-inspiring names such as El Shaddai (God almighty), Elohim (Strong One), and Adonai (Lord of all). The most frequent title given to Him was Yahweh. So sacred was the Jewish concept of this name that the devout Jew would not pronounce it; the scribe who wrote it immediately washed his hands.

Imagine how startled Jesus' hearers were when the Messiah referred to God as "My Father," attesting to the deity of Christ and His oneness with God. When conversing with the disciples, Jesus often called God "your Father," referring to their membership in God's family and their intimacy with Him.

God is your Father. God is not distant, aloof, or impersonal, but longs for the depth of a Father-child relationship with you—no condemnation, no rejection, just unconditional love and acceptance.

You will not trust God greatly unless you love Him. You will not love Him freely until you come to know His fatherly embrace as a son or daughter.

No condemnation. No rejection. Unconditional love and acceptance. Thank You, Father!

The Fatherhood of God

SCRIPTURE READING: Hebrews 12:7–11   KEY VERSE: 1 John 3:1

Behold what manner of love the Father has bestowed on us, that we should be called children of God! Therefore the world does not know us, because it did not know Him.

J. I. Packer writes of the significance of the fatherhood of God in his book *Knowing God:*

> "If you want to judge how well a person understands Christianity, find out how much he makes of the thought of being God's child and having God as his father. If this is not the thought that prompts and controls his worship and prayers and his whole outlook on life, it means that he does not understand Christianity well at all."

Christianity is about family relationship. Once estranged from the fatherly love and presence of God, the believer is adopted into God's household and interacts with holy God as his heavenly Father. No other religion in the world offers this endearing personal affection.

When you come to God in prayer, you approach a Father who hears the heartbeat of His children and delights in giving them good and wholesome gifts (Matt. 6:6; 7:11).

Your basic needs for a productive, meaningful life on earth are provided by a gracious, caring Father who promises to provide for you, freeing you from distracting worry and draining fears (Matt. 6:24–34). Correction and discipline for the times you sin and err are administered not by a stern celestial sergeant, but a firm, loving, and wise Father who seeks your best interests (Heb. 12:7–11). The great love of the Father is amazingly yours.

Heavenly Father, help me respond properly to Your correction and discipline. Thank You for Your love that seeks my best interests.

Your Ultimate Welfare

SCRIPTURE READING: Psalm 139:1–24 KEY VERSE: Psalm 100:5

The LORD is good;
His mercy is everlasting,
And His truth endures to all generations.

Have you ever asked God for something that He did not give you? At first, you might have felt slighted or upset, but perhaps much later you saw the reason why God said no.

God promises to give only what is good for you and no less. Why? The Lord loves you with an affection beyond imagination, and He fashioned every intricate fiber of your being (Ps. 139). It makes sense, then, that He knows exactly what you need and what blessings would benefit you.

Imagine a father taking his four-year-old son through a toy store. The little boy is overwhelmed by all the sights and sounds and points everywhere, shouting and dragging his dad down the aisles. In the sports section, the boy spots a sleek air gun and goes wild with delight. "Please, Dad, please!" he begs.

Of course, the wise father knows his son is far too young to handle such equipment safely and says no. After the son has finished pouting about the answer, the father takes him down another aisle and helps him select a gift that suits his age and abilities.

What would you think of a father who gave in without considering the consequences? Not much. Your heavenly Father is careful. You can relax in the assurance that God answers your requests in absolute wisdom and tenderness and always with regard to your ultimate welfare.

Father, give me the faith to understand that You answer my prayers with
regard to my ultimate welfare.

When the Odds Are Against You

SCRIPTURE READING: Nehemiah 4:1–14   KEY VERSE: Nehemiah 8:10

Then he said to them, "Go your way, eat the fat, drink the sweet, and send portions to those for whom nothing is prepared; for this day is holy to our Lord. Do not sorrow, for the joy of the LORD is your strength."

After a horrifying accident while mountain climbing, Tim Hansel came to a profound conclusion: the joy of the Lord was his only strength (Neh. 8:10). With pain filtering through his body, Hansel sought help from God. In *You Gotta Keep Dancin'* he writes,

> My rage [desire] to live was real, but I had, without knowing or intending it, put a lid on it by saying to myself, "When I am strong, then I'll be joyful. When the pain eases, then I'll be joyful." I had enough excuses to last a lifetime.
>
> The problem was reality. The pain didn't subside. And I had placed myself in the position of waiting until things got better, waiting until I knew more of God, waiting until I had enough strength to be joyful.
>
> But through this profound and simple passage from Nehemiah God reminded me again and again that I cannot choose to be strong, but I can choose to be joyful. And when I am willing to do that, strength will follow . . . It wasn't the pain that was thwarting me as much as it was my attitude toward the pain. I realized that though the difficulties were undeniably real and would remain so for the rest of my life, I had the opportunity to choose a new freedom and joy if I wanted to.

Lasting joy and true faith are based only in Jesus Christ and not your circumstances. If the odds are against you, He will be your strength.

Lord, help me understand that lasting joy is based on You—not my circumstances. Strengthen my faith when the odds are against me.

Fear and Faith

SCRIPTURE READING: Judges 7:1–23   KEY VERSE: Judges 7:21

And every man stood in his place all around the camp; and the whole army ran and cried out and fled.

Judges 7 provides insight for those of us facing overwhelming circumstances. Gideon's army was surrounded and completely outnumbered by the enemy. The odds were definitely stacked against him. In the heat of the moment, it would have been understandable for him to panic and become frightened, but he didn't.

Fear is the opposite of faith. It is also one of the surest routes to defeat and discouragement. God told Gideon to send those struggling with fear away from the others because fear paralyzes people. A lion in the jungle doesn't just stalk his prey; he comes up on it and looks it in the eye. He literally paralyzes it with fear so that it becomes an easy lunch.

Fear and faith are not compatible. If left unchecked, fear quickly turns into anxiety and worry. Once the fear issue was dealt with, God began to work in a mighty way. He guided Gideon as to whom to take into battle with him.

Because of Israel's willingness to trust in the Lord, God delivered the people from their attackers by throwing the enemy into total confusion. The victory was won by faith. If the odds are stacked against you, there is really only one thing you can do to experience complete victory, and that is to place your trust in the One who will never let you down—the Lord Jesus Christ.

I know fear and faith are not compatible, Lord. So please, replace my fear with confident faith in You.

An Anxious Spirit

SCRIPTURE READING: Romans 6:1–8   KEY VERSE: Galatians 2:20

I have been crucified with Christ; it is no longer I who live, but Christ lives in me; and the life which I now live in the flesh I live by faith in the Son of God, who loved me and gave Himself for me.

Fear is really the natural by-product of an anxious spirit. An anxious spirit is the by-product of living under the false assumption that you can manage life by yourself, and that with effort you can maneuver circumstances into a satisfying outcome. This lifestyle, one of performance-based acceptance, is a sure prescription for feelings of failure.

In her book *The Confident Woman*, Anabel Gillham explains how she discovered the spiritual mind-set necessary for healthy confidence for every believer:

> I made a choice—with my mind, with my will—and it is your choice as well. I prayed, "Lord, I've done it my way for so long; I don't understand Galatians 2:20 and all that it means for me, but I want to claim its truth for my life.
>
> "You say that You now indwell me in the presence of the Holy Spirit; You say that I have been crucified, buried, and raised with You, and that the only One who ever lived the Christian life, You, promised to live that same life through me. By faith I receive what You have said in Your Word and I believe it . . . I thank You that You will do it all for me, through me."
>
> When I made that choice, my life didn't change overnight. I simply began to be consciously aware of my actions and thoughts; I began choosing His Way, trusting Him to be my strength, my power, my wisdom—my very life.

Lord, by faith I receive all You have said in Your Word, and I believe that You will do it all for me and through me.

Give It to God

SCRIPTURE READING: Philippians 4:6–9   KEY VERSE: Psalm 55:22

Cast your burden on the LORD,
And He shall sustain you;
He shall never permit the righteous to be moved.

That gnawing feeling of anxiety can grow from what we call the butterflies to full-blown panic if left unchecked. The Lord knows how critical it is that you get rid of anxiety. It destroys your peace, clouds your perception, robs your joy, and consumes your thinking.

Have you ever worried about something and then, after a time of mental agony, finally handed the concern over to God? The relief you felt was indescribable. What's amazing is that the next time a worry threatens to dominate, you are equally reluctant to let go.

Why? As human beings, we relish the sensation of being in control. We somehow feel that by pondering a problem continuously, thinking through all the options and possibilities, we will come up with good answers. That may be true sometimes, but the process saps all our energy. And when we rely on our limited resources and understanding, we discount completely the wisdom and sovereignty of God.

God wants you to give Him your perplexities, fears, worries, and impossible situations. He is the only One who can handle them, and He knows what is best for you. God has the big picture—you don't—and trying to manipulate things results in further confusion and anxiety.

If you're ready to trust Him, He is ready to listen. Pour out your heart to the Lord, and He will lift the burden. Give it to God.

Lord, I'm ready to trust You. Take my burdens, fears, and impossible situations. Give me confidence that You know best.

God at Work

SCRIPTURE READING: Isaiah 48:1–8   KEY VERSE: Isaiah 48:17

> *Thus says the LORD, your Redeemer,*
> *The Holy One of Israel:*
> *"I am the LORD your God,*
> *Who teaches you to profit,*
> *Who leads you by the way you should go."*

The children of Israel were stubborn. No matter how many times Isaiah warned them, they persisted in their disobedience and idolatry. Eventually, in approximately 586 B.C., the wicked nation of Babylon conquered Jerusalem and took the nation of Israel captive, just as Isaiah had prophesied.

Isaiah described part of God's purpose in giving them the prophecies:

> Because I knew that you were obstinate . . .
> Even from the beginning I have declared it to you;
> Before it came to pass I proclaimed it to you,
> Lest you should say, "My idol has done them,
> And my carved image and my molded image
> Have commanded them." (Isa. 48:4–5)

The Israelites refused to recognize God at work in their lives. They attributed the circumstances that befell them to the workings of their false gods. Why? The reasons are many, but a primary cause was an unwillingness to submit to the God of wisdom and authority, Someone they could not control, deceive, or manipulate.

The Israelites were certainly not an isolated case in this respect. Have you ever noticed a refusal to submit to God's direction in your life? The basic problem is a lack of understanding of the key principle in Isaiah 48:17. As you fully grasp the truth that God is all-wise and really does have the best in mind for you, obedience follows more naturally.

God, You are all-wise and have the best in mind for me. Help me walk by faith, even when I don't understand.

Trusting God

SCRIPTURE READING: Romans 4:16–21   KEY VERSE: Hebrews 11:3

By faith we understand that the worlds were framed by the word of God, so that the things which are seen were not made of things which are visible.

The four-year-old looked up at her aunt and asked, "What's wrong?" But her aunt was too busy trying to turn the doorknob to answer. Who would have thought that a quick look at a backyard play set would turn into "lock-out" day? But that was exactly what happened. With no one watching, the door had closed, and no one was inside to let them back in.

Peering through the back door, they could only imagine what it would be like to be back inside a secure house. Finally, her aunt prayed for God's help. While prayer may not always be the first thing we think of in times of emergency, it is our strongest source of hope. Simply put, God hears when we call to Him.

This story is simple and childlike. Did God answer? Yes, and while He did not send a miracle key to mysteriously open the door, He provided a lesson of faith and a way to trust in His provision. This time a rock through a small window was the catalyst to an open door.

"Well," you say, "that wasn't much of a provision." But it was! God provided something much more comforting than the material evidence of His power. He provided peace and the assurance that He was in control. We need a God like this, Someone who brings hope and calm to our storm-driven lives. Trust Him and you will be amazed at the peace He brings to your heart and life.

Help me to trust You, Lord. Give me faith in the face of difficult circumstances.

Friends and Your Faith

SCRIPTURE READING: Ephesians 4:1–6   KEY VERSE: Proverbs 16:18

Pride goes before destruction,
And a haughty spirit before a fall.

She hadn't felt emotional pain like that in years. She was numb inside from the shock of such hurtful words. Forgiveness wasn't the issue for her; she had already forgiven the offender. It wasn't anger that kept the words replaying inside her mind; it was their horrible truth.

Today at school, another teacher asked her what was wrong. She said, "Oh, I'm just a little under the weather today." After all, the teacher was just a casual acquaintance. Why should she dump it all on her?

At home that evening she realized something critical about herself. Her best friend called and immediately recognized the pain she was in. Still, she couldn't bring herself to open up. Finally, she realized the reason behind her reluctance to seek support—she was too proud to admit she had a need.

Is that a portrait of your inner struggle when something is wrong? You may think that it's easier to bear the pain than it is to show weakness or vulnerability. Sadly, that attitude prevents you from enjoying what God intended for you to experience, the comfort of your brothers and sisters in Christ.

If you are hurting today and your faith seems weak, go to a friend. Hiding the need doesn't make it go away, and you'll give someone else the opportunity to share with you.

Lord, when my faith is weak, help me to open up to others so they can strengthen me.

Trust for Tomorrow

SCRIPTURE READING: Luke 7:29–28   KEY VERSE: Luke 7:22

Jesus answered and said to them, "Go and tell John the things you have seen and heard: that the blind see, the lame walk, the lepers are cleansed, the deaf hear, the dead are raised, the poor have the gospel preached to them."

When you think of John the Baptist, you probably think first of his ministry by the Jordan River, calling people to repentance and faith in the coming Messiah.

Have you ever considered what happened to John after that time? He almost disappeared from the scene, except for the passage in Mark's gospel that described his death. King Herod had become angry over some of John's remarks about Herod's unlawful wife, Herodias, so Herod had John arrested. He languished in prison for a time, until the fateful night of Herod's birthday banquet. Herodias's daughter performed a special dance for the king, and in return Herod swore an oath to give her whatever she wanted.

When she finished dancing, she asked Herod (at her mother's suggestion) for John the Baptist's head on a platter. Afraid to back down in front of his guests, Herod had John beheaded.

John never got to see the fullness of Jesus' ministry. His part in it came at the very beginning, when Jesus presented Himself as the Messiah for baptism. How do you think John felt in prison, knowing he would probably die? No wonder he asked for Jesus' assurance as he awaited his sentence (Luke 7:19–28).

God's promises are true forever, and He wants you to trust Him for tomorrow—no matter what.

> *O Lord, Your promises are true forever. Help me to trust You for tomorrow—no matter what.*

Turning Pity into Praise

SCRIPTURE READING: Psalm 27:1–6   KEY VERSE: Psalm 29:2

Give unto the LORD the glory due to His name;
Worship the LORD in the beauty of holiness.

She spent most of the day moping in her favorite chair in her room. It was a rainy day, and the dark clouds and drumming of the drops on the roof only accentuated her gloomy mood.

"Why do these things have to happen to me?" she sighed to herself. She had gotten nothing but bad news the previous week. Her job was no longer secure, her car's engine needed to be replaced, and she was still bothered by a persistent and painful sinus infection.

The more she thought about her situation, the more she felt sorry for herself. She didn't want to hear the words of her best friend, who encouraged her to take her troubles to the Lord in prayer. Somehow, it seemed more comfortable to feel down and dwell on the negative.

Though she didn't know it, this woman was trapped in the pit of self-pity. This pit is especially deceptive because it often doesn't feel like a pit. It's much easier to focus on the pain than it is to examine God's solutions and seek His comfort. Sometimes it takes the tough words of a friend to pull you out of the pit onto the high ground of God's tender love.

Are you having a pity party today? Self-pity is actually a comfort blocker. Wallowing in depression keeps you from experiencing God's victory. Invite Him to join you, and He will turn your pity into His praise.

By faith, Lord, I choose to turn my self-pity into praise today. Thank You for Your faithfulness to me. Thank You for every blessing You have bestowed upon me.

Living by Faith

SCRIPTURE READING: Galatians 1:6–10   KEY VERSE: Galatians 3:1

O foolish Galatians! Who has bewitched you that you should not obey the truth, before whose eyes Jesus Christ was clearly portrayed among you as crucified?

In the apostle Paul's day, the Judaizers (Christian Jews who tried to impose the Jewish way of life on gentile believers) became indignant at the idea of salvation taking place by faith and God's grace. They viewed this concept as an affront to the Law of Moses and an open license to sin even more. But God's grace should never become a point of contention.

Warren Wiersbe asserts:

> First century Judaizers are not the only ones afraid to depend on God's grace. Legalists in our churches today warn that we dare not teach people about the liberty we have in Christ lest it result in religious anarchy. These people misunderstand Paul's teaching about grace, and it is to correct such misunderstanding that Paul wrote the final section of his Ephesian letter.
>
> Paul turns now from argument to application, from the doctrinal to the practical. The Christian who lives by faith is not going to become a rebel. Quite the contrary, he is going to experience the inner discipline of God that is far better than the outer discipline of man-made rules.
>
> No man could become a rebel who depends on God's grace, yields to God's Spirit, lives for others, and seeks to glorify God. The legalist is the one who eventually rebels, because he is living in bondage, depending on the flesh, living for self, and seeking the praise of men and not the glory of God.

Lord, I receive by faith Your gift of salvation. Thank You for delivering me from bondage, the flesh, self, and the praise of men.

Going Against the Flow

SCRIPTURE READING: Matthew 7:24–29   KEY VERSE: Luke 21:33

Heaven and earth will pass away, but My words will by no means pass away.

If you have witnessed the launching of a space shuttle from Cape Canaveral, Florida, you know that it is truly a spectacular sight. When not very high into the air, the shuttle begins a slight roll that positions it for later orbit.

Until the craft is out of the earth's atmosphere, the shuttle is under the control of computers. The astronauts are powerless to aid or assist its climb. Once in orbit, they man the controls, check the performance of onboard computers, and assist in vital experiments. When the mission is completed, the craft reenters the earth's gravitational pull and heads home. However, during reentry, NASA's computers stand silent. They trace the ship; but for a brief moment in time, the shuttle is an unpowered craft that relies on its gliding ability to make a safe landing.

Often we place our trust in things that are finite, fallible, and destructible. Yet we find it difficult to place our trust in God. The Bible tells us there is one thing that will never pass away, and that is the Word of God. Men and their ideas come and go, but Jesus Christ remains the same forever.

The same God who parted the Red Sea, spoke to the prophets, and came to us in the form of a baby invites you to come into His presence. Why not go against the flow of the world by placing your trust in something that never changes and will last for an eternity?

Father, I place my trust in what is infinite, infallible, and indestructible. I place my confidence in You, Your Word, and Your Son, Jesus Christ.

Faith for Today

SCRIPTURE READING: John 14:12–14   KEY VERSE: Hebrews 11:1

Faith is the substance of things hoped for, the evidence of things not seen.

In an emotionally taxing time, has someone ever told you to just "have faith"? It sounds like good advice, but the meaning is hazy. In her book *Glorious Intruder,* Joni Eareckson Tada talks about her struggle to come to grips with the real meaning of faith:

> "Have faith, Joni . . . one day it will all be better." I can't tell you how many times I heard words like those from sad-faced friends who clung to the guardrail of my hospital bed when I was first injured.
>
> . . . If being a woman of faith meant sitting around in my wheelchair longing for pie in the sky, I wanted no part of it. What a colossal misunderstanding!
>
> Faith, as the Bible defines it, is present-tense action. It's taking God's promises and acting on them today. This "right now" way of looking at God's assurances is the stuff of which great people of faith are made . . . To them, faith is pulled out of the abstract, out of the nebulous nowhere, out of the syrupy twilight, and lived with concrete certainty in the here and now.
>
> Somewhere along the line I realized that. On some dark night in a sterile room the words of Hebrews 11:1 began to seep through my stubborn defenses. I began to realize that faith means being sure of what we hope for now. It means knowing that something is real, this moment, all around you, even when you don't see it.

Lord, give me a faith that is sure of what I hope for. Give me faith that is real, even when I don't understand.

Perfect Faith

SCRIPTURE READING: Matthew 14:22–27   KEY VERSE: Matthew 14:27

Immediately Jesus spoke to them, saying, "Be of good cheer! It is I; do not be afraid."

Just as Peter did, we spend a good portion of our lives learning to live by faith. Peter was certain that he had unwavering faith in Christ. However, it was about to be tested. In the middle of a severe storm on the open Sea of Galilee, the disciples tried not to become overwhelmed with fear. They struggled furiously with the sails and longed for Jesus' help. But He was not with them on the trip, or at least that was what they perceived.

Suddenly, something caught their attention. An image that appeared to be a ghost was walking toward them on the water's raging surface. It was Jesus, but their frantic minds did not recognize Him.

They cried out in despair. Jesus, sensing their anguish called back, "Be of good cheer! It is I; do not be afraid" (Matt. 14:27). Peter exhibited real faith as he stepped out of the boat and walked toward Jesus.

It wasn't until he was a distance away from the boat that his faith began to crumble. The stormy swells and the winds created a curtain of doubt in Peter's mind. His attention shifted from the Lord to the storm, and he began to sink. Perfect faith is set on Christ. It does not waver. And the person who exhibits it will never sink, not because of his ability or strength, but because of God's faithfulness.

Perfect my faith, Lord. Give me a faith that does not waver. Give me a faith that is securely grounded in Your faithfulness.

A Heavenly Perspective

SCRIPTURE READING: Matthew 14:28–31   KEY VERSE: Matthew 21:21

Jesus answered and said to them, "Assuredly, I say to you, if you have faith and do not doubt, you will not only do what was done to the fig tree, but also if you say to this mountain, 'Be removed and be cast into the sea,' it will be done."

No one would deny the fact that faith is a battle. And at times we may feel as though we step forward to trust the Lord, only to stumble back several steps. As thoughts of doubt flood our minds, we wonder: *What if _____ happens? What if God doesn't do what He promised? Can I trust God even when I don't feel that He is close to me?"*

That was exactly where Peter found himself as he began to walk to Jesus across the stormy surface of the Sea of Galilee. As long as Peter's gaze was on the Lord, the waves and the wind meant nothing to him.

However, the moment he thought of the magnitude of the storm, he began to doubt and sink. We encourage fear and disbelief when we interpret a situation in light of our own knowledge and without regard to God's ability. What could have been a great moment of faith turned life-threatening as Peter caved in to thoughts of fear.

Another action that leads to increased anxiety is seeking the approval of others. A friend's counsel is fine, but first make sure you know God's will for your life. Many times another's point of view will not line up with God's. A heavenly perspective always leads to victory! All doubt is earmarked with discouraging lies of Satan. Keep your eyes on Jesus. Seek His will for your life through the light of His Word (Ps. 119:105).

Help me keep my eyes on You, Jesus, when faith is a battle. Give me the heavenly perspective that leads to victory.

Holding Out

SCRIPTURE READING: James 1:2–8   KEY VERSE: Hebrews 13:5

Let your conduct be without covetousness; be content with such things as you have. For He Himself has said, "I will never leave you nor forsake you."

James opened his book with encouraging news for a discouraged group of believers. His audience was the early church that, at the time this letter-turned-book was written, was under severe persecution.

However, James knew that emphasizing the church's trials would lead only to discouragement. Thus, he opened his letter with instruction about how we should handle the storms of life. It may surprise some that James highlighted joy and faith rather than anger and frustration.

James understood that God had a greater purpose in mind when He allowed the church to face various trials. He told us, "The testing of your faith produces patience. But let patience have its perfect work that you may be perfect and complete, lacking nothing" (James 1:3–4).

Often this lesson is not learned within a short period of time. But God is the Source of our hope, and He has said, "I will never leave you nor forsake you" (Heb. 13:5).

These early believers wavered in their faith, just as we will at times. But James indicated, as did the writer of Hebrews (Heb. 10:36), that if we hold out, believing that God will guide us through the darkest trial, we will certainly receive a lasting reward.

Dear Lord, strengthen my faith. Help me hold out in hard times, believing You will guide me through the darkest trial.

An Open Door

SCRIPTURE READING: 1 Corinthians 16:1–9   KEY VERSE: Revelation 3:8

I know your works. See, I have set before you an open door, and no one can shut it; for you have a little strength, have kept My word, and have not denied My name.

Here are some requirements of faith:

Listening to God. Whenever you face change or need to make a crucial decision, take time to pray, and if possible, be still before God. You may miss God's instructive voice because you have filled your life with noise and activity. Study His Word, and He will speak to you through the Scriptures.

Obeying God. It must have been difficult for Abraham to leave his home and loved ones in order to do what God wanted him to do. However, there was no other way. God instructed Abraham to leave Ur and travel to a place that God would reveal. Obedience is a direct doorway to blessings. It is something God takes very seriously and something He rewards generously.

Depending on God. God always is near. No matter what you face, He watches to see if you seek Him or chase after the affections of others. Allow Him to be your first choice in every situation, and He will bring blessings and hope to your life.

Waiting on God. God does not always answer your prayers immediately. He may make you wait. This testing is for a purpose: Will you cling to Him in faith or crumble in fear? Always hang on to your faith.

You never know when your Deliverer may open a door of immense hope.

Lord, I choose to listen to You, obey You, depend on You, and wait on You. I want to cling in faith rather than crumble in fear.

Waiting for the Answer

SCRIPTURE READING: Colossians 2:6–10 KEY VERSE: 1 Thessalonians 5:24

He who calls you is faithful, who also will do it.

Do you ever wonder whether you can trust God? Many deny their worry, but their actions speak differently. Have you ever prayed for something and felt as though your prayers were unanswered?

After a while, it is easy to think that maybe it would be okay to help God out—give Him a little shove to start things off. But you may want to consider the following: God is sovereign. He is both personal and loving. He has not forgotten you. Even though you may have to wait for the answer to your prayer, when it comes, it will be a wondrous blessing because you were willing to wait and trust the Lord for the answer.

God is infinitely wise. All knowledge about all things belongs to Him. A deep love and commitment toward those who have accepted His Son as their Savior are hallmarks of His personal care. Therefore, He has provided a way for sin to be eradicated from your life. In wisdom and mercy, He desires for you to live free from the bondage of sin and failure.

God loves perfectly and completely. He can meet all your needs. You may wonder how this can be, especially since you can't see or touch Him. Deep within the resources of His love, contentment and a sense of peace are waiting just for you. And nothing the world offers can duplicate these things.

Heavenly Father, I thank You that through faith, I can wait for my answer.

When God Says Go

SCRIPTURE READING: Genesis 12:1–9   KEY VERSES: Genesis 12:2–3

I will make you a great nation;
I will bless you
And make your name great;
And you shall be a blessing.
I will bless those who bless you,
And I will curse him who curses you;
And in you all the families of the earth shall be blessed.

Hannah Whitall Smith once wrote, "Sight is not faith, and hearing is not faith, neither is feeling faith; but believing when we neither see, hear, nor feel is faith . . . Therefore, we must believe before we feel, and often against our feelings if we would honor God by our faith."

As you read the account of Abram's life, you realize he was a man of extreme faith. God asked him to do something many would find difficult, and that was to leave his family and friends and go to an unfamiliar land.

Yet God's reassuring words in Genesis 12:2–3 lessened Abram's fear.

Abram—or Abraham as he was later called by God—gave little thought to the fact that his name would be made great. The most important thing to him was the exercise of his faith through obedience.

When God calls you to move in a certain direction by faith, He will provide you reassurance. Your responsibility is to obey and follow Him. Abram left everything because he heard God say, "Go." Are you willing to do the same? Pray that your response to the Lord is always one of faith, love, and obedience. That way you will never miss a single blessing.

God, give me the faith to obey and follow You when You say, "Go." I don't want to miss a single blessing You have for me!

He Is Faithful

SCRIPTURE READING: Hebrews 13:5–6   KEY VERSE: 2 Corinthians 5:7

We walk by faith, not by sight.

There will be times in your spiritual walk when you feel as though all of heaven is shut up before you. You may wonder whether God has forgotten you or you have done something to disappoint Him. But nothing you do surprises God. He is omniscient and perfectly aware of your every action.

Even in times of personal failure, God's love continues. He loves you unconditionally. His affections are based not on your performance but on His grace. You could never earn God's love. He cares for you just as much when you stumble as He does when you walk closely beside Him. This is not an excuse for sin but an opportunity to learn to love Him better.

Along the pathway of faith, you can expect to face times of trials and difficulty when you feel as though you are completely removed from God. However, you are not to walk by sight but in the reality of the promise that He will never leave or forsake you (Heb. 13:5–6).

Faith always looks beyond the immediate to the eternal. The times you feel God is doing nothing in your life are usually the times He is doing His greatest work. Take heart. He may have you protected under the cover of His hand while He works out the necessary details for your advancement. Trust Him, and you will find Him faithful.

> *Precious Lord, help me look beyond the immediate to the eternal. Help me realize that the times when I feel You are doing nothing in my life are when You are doing Your greatest work.*

Trusting with All Your Heart

SCRIPTURE READING: Proverbs 3:5–12   KEY VERSE: Proverbs 2:6

For the LORD gives wisdom;
From His mouth come knowledge and understanding.

Oswald Chambers wrote that our possessions and abilities are to be a matter of indifference to us:

> Having the proper outlook is evidence of the deeply rooted belief in the overshadowing of God's personal deliverance.
>
> The Sermon on the Mount indicates that when we are on a mission for Jesus Christ, there is not time to stand up for ourselves. Jesus says, in effect, "Don't worry about whether you are being treated justly." Looking for justice is actually a sign that we have been diverted from our devotion to Him. Never look for justice in this world, but never cease to give it. If we look for justice, we will only begin to complain and to indulge ourselves in the discontent of self-pity, as if to say, "Why should I be treated like this?"
>
> If we are devoted to Jesus Christ, we have nothing to do with what we encounter, whether it is just or unjust. In essence, Jesus says, "Continue steadily on with what I have told you to do, and I will guard your life. If you try to guide it yourself, you remove yourself from My deliverance." Even the most devout among us become atheistic in this regard—we do not believe Him. We put our common sense on the throne and then attach God's name to it. We lean to our own understanding, instead of trusting God with all our hearts.

Father, help me to trust You in faith with all my heart instead of leaning on my own understanding.

Faith to Wait

SCRIPTURE READING: Isaiah 40:28–31   KEY VERSE: Isaiah 5:21

Woe to those who are wise in their own eyes,
And prudent in their own sight!

Do you have a pride line? Have you inadvertently separated for yourself the facets of life that you feel you can most control?

On one side of the line, you may have bundled areas in which you have insecurity and surrendered them to the Lord. But do you have another side that you are consciously or subconsciously manipulating on your own? You say, "This is my specialty. This is what I am trained to do. I can handle this."

Can you really handle it? If your specialty is finances, can you really handle it if you lose your job or the stock market collapses? If you're good at your job, can you really handle it if your company reorganizes? If you're a good parent to your child, can you really handle it if he ultimately falls into the wrong crowd?

Obviously, nothing is really under your control. God laid the foundations of the heavens and the earth. He knitted you in your mother's womb. How could you ever presume to know more than He does?

The areas in which you feel most comfortable or most learned are the very areas in which we ultimately will prove most vulnerable. Woe to those who are wise in their own eyes.

Part of trusting in the Lord and having faith is waiting (Isa. 40:31). You must pause long enough not only to acknowledge Him and ask His guidance but also to hear His answer.

Lord, don't let me depend upon my own resources. Give me faith to wait
and trust in You.

God Has a Plan

Scripture reading: Matthew 6:25–34   Key verse: Philippians 4:19

My God shall supply all your need according to His riches in glory by Christ Jesus.

Matthew 6:25–34 is a portion of the Sermon on the Mount. As we read Christ's words to those who had gathered along the hillside, we discover a strong calmness emerging from the Son of God.

Essentially, Jesus told those gathered that it was a waste of time to worry. Why? Because God knew their needs, and He promised to provide for each one. The apostle Paul delivered the same message to the Philippian believers (Phil. 4:19).

The thought of God taking care of us is a victorious thought! We know that He has never failed to keep any of His promises. This fact alone should be the end of all doubt and worry, but it rarely is.

Often we become consumed with doubts and fears. When this happens, we have not transferred the ownership of our anxieties to Christ. Instead, we cling to doubt and fear with the hope of doing something to "help" God solve our problems.

If you want to "help God," try trusting Him. Let Him be God, and you become His faithful servant and friend.

Is there a pressing need in your life? Leave it at the altar of God. God is faithful. He takes into account all that you are facing and all that you will face in the future. He is omniscient, and He loves you perfectly. Whatever you need, God has a plan to solve it.

Lord, I rejoice that You have a plan to solve my every need. You know all I am facing today and in the future. I praise You!

In Difficult Times

SCRIPTURE READING: Psalm 4:1–8   KEY VERSE: Psalm 4:5

Offer the sacrifices of righteousness,
And put your trust in the LORD.

In her book *Abiding in Christ,* Cynthia Heald writes about her journey of faith during difficult times:

> The wise counsel of Proverbs 3:5–6 has been in my heart for over twenty-five years. Although it has become an old friend, its encouragement continues to be fresh and new in my life.
>
> During a recent struggle, it seemed that the Lord was saying to me, "Do you trust Me?" My response was, "Yes, Lord, I trust You. But can't You rephrase the question: Do you trust Me to work everything out so that you are happy? I think I could really trust You then."
>
> But the Lord was steadfast: the issue was my unconditional trust. No strings attached, no negotiating, no promises.
>
> In a deeper way, I began to understand what it means to trust God with all my heart. There is no room for bargaining for what I think is best, only implicit confidence and patience in His plan.
>
> The Scriptures do not guarantee that all will be well according to our human perspective. They do, however, promise that God will work all things for our good. As we learn to trust Him no matter what, He develops within us a deeply rooted confidence in Him. This confidence enables us to lean on His understanding and His ways of working in our lives.

Is God asking you to trust Him unconditionally?

Dear heavenly Father, let me trust You unconditionally—even in difficult times.

AUGUST

Spiritual Warfare

MOUNTAIN: Mount Carmel

KEY VERSES: 1 Kings 18

Ahab sent for all the children of Israel, and gathered the prophets together on Mount Carmel. And Elijah came to all the people, and said, "How long will you falter between two opinions? If the Lord is God, follow Him; but if Baal, follow him. . . . Therefore let them give us two bulls; and let them choose one bull for themselves, cut it in pieces, and lay it on the wood, but put no fire under it; and I will prepare the other bull, and lay it on the wood, but put no fire under it. Then you call on the name of your gods, and I will call on the name of the Lord; and the God who answers by fire, He is God."

. . . So they took the bull which was given them, and they prepared it, and called on the name of Baal from morning even till noon, saying, "O Baal, hear us!" But there was no voice; no one answered. And they leaped about the altar which they had made . . . But there was no voice; no one answered, no one paid attention.

. . . And it came to pass, at the time of the offering of the evening sacrifice, that Elijah the prophet came near and said, "LORD God of Abraham, Isaac, and Israel, let it be known this day that You are God in Israel and I am Your servant, and that I have done all these things at Your word. Hear me, O LORD, hear me, that this people may know that You are the LORD God, and that You have turned their hearts back to You again." Then the fire of the LORD fell and consumed the burnt sacrifice, and the wood and the stones and the dust, and it licked up the water that was in the trench. Now when all the people saw it, they fell on their faces; and they said, "The LORD, He is God! The LORD, He is God!"

Back on Course

SCRIPTURE READING: 1 Kings 19:9–15   KEY VERSE: 1 Kings 19:13

So it was, when Elijah heard it, that he wrapped his face in his mantle and went out and stood in the entrance of the cave. Suddenly a voice came to him, and said, "What are you doing here, Elijah?"

Elijah had just come away from a tremendous spiritual victory. In fact, the victory won on Mount Carmel was the highlight of his career as a prophet of God. However, immediately following the victory came a time of serious testing.

Elijah had stood firm in his faith, and God had destroyed all of the prophets of Baal, reaffirming the fact that He was Jehovah God. In a horrific fit of anger, Queen Jezebel sent a message to Elijah stating, "So let the gods do to me, and more also, if I do not make your life as the life of one of them [a prophet of Baal]" (1 Kings 19:2). In other words, Jezebel planned to kill Elijah. Filled with fear, Elijah fled.

Finally, at Mount Horeb he collapsed. That was where God spoke to him: "What are you doing here, Elijah?" It was a reasonable question to ask. Elijah was accustomed to living in the shadow of God's greatness and power. Why was he hiding out like a common criminal?

Maybe God is asking you the same question: "What are you doing here? Why are you running? Why are you fearful?" God did not let go of His prophet. Instead, He instructed Elijah to get back into the thick of things. And this is His word to you. If you have gotten off course, don't give up. Tell the Lord what you are struggling with, and He will send His encouragement and hope to you.

Lord, I am struggling, running, and fearful. Help me get back on course with You. Strengthen me with Your Word.

The Real War

SCRIPTURE READING: Psalm 140:1–8   KEY VERSE: Colossians 2:15

Having disarmed principalities and powers, He made a public spectacle of them, triumphing over them in it.

War is gruesome, agonizing, isolating, and often terrifying. Ask any veteran about his experiences in combat, and he will probably tell you stories that make you shudder. As horrible as open conflict with weapons can be, imagine how much worse a war would be if the enemy were invisible.

The truth is, each day you're in the middle of an ongoing spiritual war, and you can't even see the enemy with your physical eyes. There aren't many verses in the Bible that give details about the ways that Satan and his followers manifest themselves, but we do know that they are spirits, fallen angels. As eternal enemies of God, they are committed to disobedience and rebellion, and they delight in assisting us in making wrong choices.

First Peter 5:8 gives this warning: "Be sober, be vigilant; because your adversary the devil walks about like a roaring lion, seeking whom he may." But Christ has defeated him already at the cross, and you can claim His victory anytime you are assailed by spiritual enemies.

Are you aware of spiritual warfare? You need to be. Of course, the Lord does not want you focused on this realm improperly; your primary attention is to be given to your relationship with Christ. But the believer who is informed about spiritual battles is prepared when they come.

Help me be sober in spirit, dear Lord. Keep me alert to the tactics of the enemy who would seek to devour me spiritually.

Preparation for the Battle

SCRIPTURE READING: Ephesians 6:10–20   KEY VERSE: Ephesians 6:11

Put on the whole armor of God, that you may be able to stand against the wiles of the devil.

Imagine how foolish it would be for a soldier to go out to battle without his combat gear—no provisions, no weapon, no navigational tools.

In the spiritual realm, being equipped for the battle is equally essential. God does not intend for you to deal with the attacks of the opposition completely unarmed.

He has already given you His spiritual armor; your job is to be aware of the equipment He has provided and ask Him to dress you in it every day.

The helmet of salvation. You are secure in the knowledge that the Lord has sealed you as His forever. Even in the worst skirmish, your identity in Christ can never be taken by the enemy.

The breastplate of righteousness. The holiness of God transforms your inner being, renews your mind, and changes your desires. This solidity of Christlike character is a sure defense.

The girdle of truth. No lie can stand up to the sheer power of God's truth. Whether it's a subtle idea or a bold, outright declaration of falsehood, God's Word demolishes every stronghold.

The shield of faith. You have a shield that cannot be penetrated by even the most ingenious device. The strongest temptation can be repelled by the iron-clad fortress of belief in His power.

> *Lord, I put on the spiritual weapons You have provided for my battles today: the helmet of salvation, the breastplate of righteousness, the girdle of truth, and the shield of faith.*

The Breastplate of Righteousness

SCRIPTURE READING: 2 Corinthians 6:1–7   KEY VERSE: Romans 8:1

There is therefore now no condemnation to those who are in Christ Jesus, who do not walk according to the flesh, but according to the Spirit.

One of the most essential pieces of spiritual armor is the breastplate of righteousness. In her book *Lord, Is It Warfare?* Kay Arthur explains why it is so foundational to your defense:

> The Roman soldier's breastplate covered all his vital organs, protecting his body, front and back. Usually the breastplate was made of metal, unless the soldier could afford a scale or chain mail to cover his chest and hips . . . The breastplate of righteousness is a gift given to every child of God . . .
>
> When you were nothing but a sinner—helpless, ungodly, and without hope—God justified you . . . You were forgiven by God for all your sins: past, present, and future . . . Because your sins were absolutely forgiven, Satan no longer has the power of death over you . . .
>
> One of Satan's most effective strategies is to keep our sin before us. He'll remind us of sins we've already confessed or try to convince us that because of them God doesn't want us or cannot use us. Sometimes he tries to convince us that God will never forgive us, our sin is too terrible. To believe any of this is to go into battle without your breastplate.
>
> So, when condemnation or difficulties come and you think it's because God doesn't love you or is punishing you, you must recognize who's the instigator of those accusations.

Lord, thank You for Your forgiveness of my sins—past, present, and future. I praise You that Satan no longer has power over me.

The Gospel of Peace

SCRIPTURE READING: 1 Peter 3:13–22   KEY VERSES: 1 Peter 3:15–16

Sanctify the Lord God in your hearts, and always be ready to give a defense to everyone who asks you a reason for the hope that is in you, with meekness and fear; having a good conscience, that when they defame you as evildoers, those who revile your good conduct in Christ may be ashamed.

Do you think of the spiritual armor in largely symbolic terms? It's an excellent word picture to describe how God equips us for spiritual battle, but the concepts don't have to remain in the abstract.

For example, have you ever considered what it means to be armed with "the preparation of the gospel of peace" (Eph. 6:15)? How can something peaceful be a protection in a spiritual confrontation? The good news of Jesus is a message of love, and love quells many fiery darts, thus becoming a weapon. In many cases, a nonbeliever may be drawn to antagonizing you because he senses a peace in your life that is missing in his.

First Peter 3:15–16 gives us an idea of how God intends the "preparation of the gospel of peace" to be put into operation: "Sanctify the Lord God in your hearts, and always be ready to give a defense to everyone who asks you a reason for the hope that is in you, with meekness and fear; having a good conscience, that when they defame you as evildoers, those who revile your good conduct in Christ may be ashamed."

Don't be put off immediately when others seem to question your lifestyle or ask combative questions. They are probably trying to find out who you really are and what you believe. Always be armed with the gospel.

Father, arm me with the power of Your gospel. Prepare me to make a defense to people who question me about my spiritual experience. Let my godly behavior put them to shame.

The Sword of the Spirit

SCRIPTURE READING: Psalm 119:145–152   KEY VERSE: Hebrews 4:12

The word of God is living and powerful, and sharper than any two-edged sword, piercing even to the division of soul and spirit, and of joints and marrow, and is a discerner of the thoughts and intents of the heart.

To some, Scripture memorization is fun. To others, it is a chore comparable to facing an algebra test. If you find it difficult to retain Bible verses, perhaps a little motivation will help: when the devil is after you, it is essential that you know God's Word.

The fourth chapter of Matthew describes how Satan tempted a weakened, tired, hungry Jesus in the wilderness. Here, God Himself demonstrated the importance of knowing Scripture.

On each point of temptation that Satan foisted toward Him, Jesus answered first with three powerful words: "It is written." Jesus then recited Scripture. Each time, the enemy's hollow attempts crumbled under the weight of God's Word. Notice that Satan had no answer for any of Jesus' responses. He is the father of lies and can't handle the truth. When we invoke God's name and His Word, Christ becomes indomitable within us.

One of the Bible's most famous passages, Ephesians 6:13–17, informs believers how to dress for daily battle. Have you ever noticed that in the full armor of God the first implements are to be used for protection only? They are pieces of armor you are to don. The final element is "the sword of the Spirit." What is the sword of the Spirit? The Word of God. It is a weapon!

Father, I thank You for the sword of the Spirit, Your mighty Word. When Satan rises up against me today, help me to invoke Your name and Your Word.

A Winning Device

SCRIPTURE READING: Romans 8:35–39   KEY VERSE: Proverbs 6:27

Can a man take fire to his bosom,
And his clothes not be burned?

We constantly face situations that have the potential to cause us to compromise our walk with the Lord. Therefore, a good way to handle temptation is to view it as a warning device.

An alarm should go off blaring, "Warning! Warning!" In temptation, there is always a moment of decision when we must decide to yield and sin or to say no to the tempter of our souls. Proverbs 6:27 poses an interesting question: "Can a man take fire to his bosom, and his clothes not be burned?" Can you play with temptation, nurse it in your heart, bolster it with your thoughts, and not end up being burned? The obvious answer is no. And often the strength to endure temptation is far too great for you on your own.

But it is not too great for Jesus. He understands how Satan works in the life of a believer. Once you have accepted Jesus as your Savior, the enemy knows your life is sealed in Christ. There is nothing he can do to steal you away from God's powerful grip. However, Satan uses temptation to make you feel defeated and worthless before the throne of God.

God has given you a strong defense against the enemy. Ephesians 6 outlines God's plan. Memorize this chapter, and live each day victoriously in the armor of God.

Lord, thank You for the strong defensive weapons You have provided.
Thank You that I can live each day victoriously in Your armor.

Focused on the Battle

SCRIPTURE READING: James 1:12–16   KEY VERSE: Proverbs 1:10

My son, if sinners entice you,
Do not consent.

Is your consuming desire each day to please your Commanding Officer? Or do you become too involved in "civilian affairs"? In his book *Brave, Strong, and Tender,* Phil Downer explains the importance of spiritual focus, especially in spiritual warfare on the home front:

> God wants us focused on the battle. We are His soldiers, and a soldier thinking about something else is completely worthless in a fight.
>
> Not only are we God's soldiers, we are His servants, serving at His command. God is in the battle of the ages, fighting Satan and his forces all over this world . . .
>
> I've seen too many men in the ministry forget about their families, then have their ministries crumble because of the weakness in their family life . . . It's happening with Christian men today. Their sons are involved with the culture rather than Christ. Their daughters are more concerned with fashion and popularity than holiness and morality.
>
> We can't afford to lose a generation of believers. Satan wants to destroy our children as much as he wants to destroy us, so we've got to be focused on the battle.
>
> That means setting an example in front of our kids, letting them see Christ at work in us. It means making them part of our team . . . and letting them experience our ministry.

I am Your soldier, Lord. Keep me focused on the battle. Strengthen me, and give me the ability to strengthen my family and those who depend upon me.

Sin and Suffering

SCRIPTURE READING: Jonah 1:1–17   KEY VERSE: Jonah 2:2

And he said:
"I cried out to the LORD because of my affliction,
And He answered me.
Out of the belly of Sheol I cried,
And You heard my voice."

One of Satan's most deceptive lies is that sin impacts only the person committing the sin. It is a large part of today's philosophy of moral relativism, which says that whatever a person believes is right for him is indeed right. People believe in fewer and fewer absolutes.

"I'm not hurting anyone but myself" has been uttered under more than one rebellious breath. People should take time to examine that self-absorbed statement and consider why they would ever choose to hurt themselves anyway.

Sin's roots are those of wild weeds. They grow uncontrollably until they engulf not only the offender but also many others surrounding him. Sin can choke the life out of anyone, including a believer.

Jonah was the only prophet called of God who is on record as having rebelled against Him. The result was that his circumstances grew so bad that he twice preferred death over life. In addition, those innocent and unwitting people around him suffered. The sailors on the storm-tossed ship that carried Jonah had no idea about the baggage he was bringing onboard or he never would have made it through customs!

Although the temptation to sin sometimes seems irresistible, there are few occurrences in life as sobering as seeing an innocent person, especially a loved one, suffer for your rebellion.

Dear heavenly Father, I don't want to suffer for my rebellion or cause a loved one to suffer. When temptation seems irresistible, keep me from yielding to it.

The Danger of Deception

SCRIPTURE READING: 2 Peter 3:14–18   KEY VERSE: 2 Peter 1:8

If these things are yours and abound, you will be neither barren nor unfruitful in the knowledge of our Lord Jesus Christ.

Even mature believers can be sidetracked if they're not careful. That's why Peter gave this warning:

> Our beloved brother Paul, according to the wisdom given to him, has written to you, as also in all his epistles, speaking in them of these things, in which are some things hard to understand, which untaught and unstable people twist to their own destruction, as they do also the rest of the Scriptures. You therefore, beloved, wince you know this beforehand, beware lest you also fall from your own steadfastness, being led away with the error of the wicked. (2 Peter 3:15–17)

One of the greatest threats to spiritual growth is sidetracking through deception. When a believer fails to discern truth from error, he spends much time chasing falsehoods and structuring his life on untrue premises. Because what one member is involved in affects the whole body of Christ, others may be deceived or at least caught up in trying to free the one from the error.

How can you be sure that what you're hearing is okay? Always test it according to God's Word and the counsel of a strong, godly teacher whom you trust. As Paul said so powerfully in his letter to the Galatians: "But even if we, or an angel from heaven, preach any other gospel to you than what we have preached to you, let him be accursed!" (Gal. 1:8).

Don't let me be taken in by error, Lord. Protect me with Your truth.

Enslavement to Sin

SCRIPTURE READING: Psalm 119:129–136   KEY VERSE: Psalm 119:176

I have gone astray like a lost sheep;
Seek Your servant,
For I do not forget Your commandments.

Almost anyone who has ever been physically addicted to something will tell you that it all began with a small, innocent step—just one taste or one little moment of exposure. Then the experience gradually took over his mind and desires and body, until the addiction absorbed his attention day and night without relenting.

Maybe this was your experience or perhaps still is. And physical addiction isn't the only kind of consuming entrapment; any kind of sin or wrong desire can lead to emotional and spiritual enslavement. What is so devastating about bondage to sin is that it progresses slowly at first, allowing you the luxury to rationalize and justify what you perceive as your growing need. By the time you understand what is occurring, your problem has progressed to a serious condition.

King David experienced this process in his life in his sin with Bathsheba, a transgression that began when he first saw her bathing on her rooftop (2 Sam. 11). When he realized how far he had gone, he immediately repented, confessed his sin to God, and experienced God's grace anew. David had an advanced understanding of how sin operates.

He prayed:

> Direct my steps by Your word,
> And let no iniquity have dominion over me.
> Redeem me from the oppression of man,
> That I may keep Your precepts. (Ps. 119:133–34)

Direct my footsteps by Your Word, and do not let iniquity have dominion over me. Redeem me from the oppression of man so that I may keep Your precepts.

Spiritual Suicide

SCRIPTURE READING: Ephesians 5:6–14   KEY VERSES: John 12:31–32

Now is the judgment of this world; now the ruler of this world will be cast out. And I, if I am lifted up from the earth, will draw all peoples to Myself.

In *The Adversary*, Mark Bubeck discusses Satan:

> Satan and the kingdom of darkness over which he rules pose a constant challenge and threat to the effectiveness and stability of believers . . . Two extremes must be carefully avoided. The first extreme is the tendency to ignore this enemy and to treat the whole subject of demonology lightly.

> One of Satan's clever strategies against us is to keep us in ignorance of his power and working. A pastor friend once stated to me his conviction that if he would just occupy himself with the gospel, the winning of souls, and the Person of the Lord Jesus Christ, he would not have to be too concerned about Satan.

> Such a view sounds very pious and spiritual, but it is very unbiblical and dangerous. Any believer who determines to occupy himself with the gospel, the winning of the lost, and knowing the Lord Jesus Christ is going to be a special target of Satan. To ignore the weapons of our warfare provided by the Lord against Satan and his kingdom is spiritual suicide. We will soon meet spiritual disaster if we ignore this enemy.

> The other extreme to be avoided is a fearful preoccupation with Satan and his kingdom . . . Though recognizing the awesome power and cunning of Satan, the entire tenor of Scripture affirms that Satan is a defeated foe.

Keep me from extremes, dear Lord. Help me avoid fearful preoccupation with the enemy while at the same time being aware of his strategies.

A Defeated Foe

SCRIPTURE READING: Isaiah 14:12–15   KEY VERSE: Revelation 20:10

The devil, who deceived them, was cast into the lake of fire and brimstone where the beast and the false prophet are. And they will be tormented day and night forever and ever.

What is your mental picture of Satan? Is it the traditional cartoon image of a red horned figure in tights holding a pitchfork? However that cultural visualization developed, the Bible makes it clear that Satan is not simply a mischievous little creature with a bad temper. Satan was once a powerful angel, and most Bible scholars believe he was an archangel along with Michael. His pre-Fall splendor must have been beyond our imaginations. By the time we meet him in the pages of Genesis, tempting Eve in the Garden, he has already rebelled against God.

> How you have fallen from heaven,
> O Lucifer, son of the morning!
> How you are cut down to the ground,
> You who weakened the nations!
> For you have said in your heart:
> "I will ascend into heaven;
> I will exalt my throne above the stars of God" . . .
> Yet you shall be brought down to Sheol. (Isa. 14:12–15)

Today, Satan has power to influence events on earth as God allows, yet his end is sure—the fiery pit of hell. In the epic poem *Paradise Lost,* John Milton portrayed Satan vividly as a fallen angel, one who still possesses a dark splendor and evil abilities not to be underestimated. As you consider who Satan really is, remember not to be afraid. God has already defeated him.

Lord, I am not afraid! Satan is a defeated foe. All I must do is enforce the victory over him in my life today.

Satan's Limitations

SCRIPTURE READING: 1 Peter 5:8–11   KEY VERSE: 1 Peter 5:11

To Him [God] be the glory and the dominion forever and ever. Amen.

While God never wants you to become too focused on thinking about Satan and his role in the world, God does want you to be generally aware of how he operates. The worst position to take is "what I don't know can't hurt me." When it comes to spiritual issues, the very opposite is true.

The Lord has not revealed many details about Satan's specific abilities, but the Bible helps us understand his goals and his limitations. Satan is not omnipotent, omniscient, or omnipresent. These are characteristics of almighty God alone. Satan has a limited knowledge of the future, partly because he already dwells in the realm of the eternal. But ultimately, he can know only what God allows him to know.

Satan's mission is to divide and attempt to destroy the kingdom of God. Of course, he will not be successful; God has already laid forth his judgment and final doom (Rev. 20:10). In the meantime, however, he and his spiritual assistants are trying to do all the damage they can.

Satan can harass and lay snares for believers. That is why Scripture cautions us to be aware and discerning. Satan can never make you do anything wrong, but permitting his influence places you in the pathway of sin and its ill effects.

I reject every influence of Satan over my life today, Lord. I turn from the pathway of sin to the way of righteousness.

Strongholds for Satan

SCRIPTURE READING: 2 Corinthians 10:3–5   KEY VERSE: 1 Timothy 6:12

Fight the good fight of faith, lay hold on eternal life, to which you were also called and have confessed the good confession in the presence of many witnesses.

Another word for *fortresses* is *strongholds,* which, in the context of warfare, means "fortified places." In the spiritual realm, aspects of your behavior and thinking can become strongholds for Satan—hard-to-penetrate positions that furnish excellent ground for him to assault your inner being.

A stronghold may be found in any area of your life, from your speech to interpersonal relationships to eating habits. It may involve a weakness or a predisposition to a certain sin. In any case, a stronghold is something that you have never completely surrendered to the lordship or control of Jesus Christ.

Can you identify any strongholds in your life? It's not a mysterious subject. When you ask God to reveal His truth to you, He will reveal strongholds through the power of the Holy Spirit.

The Lord wants you to understand spiritual warfare so that you can end Satan's influence and move forward in your relationship with Him.

Dear heavenly Father, please reveal any spiritual strongholds in my life, and give me strength to deal with them.

Shattering Strongholds

SCRIPTURE READING: Matthew 4:1–11   KEY VERSE: Psalm 56:2

My enemies would hound me all day,
For there are many who fight against me, O Most High.

To tear down the enemy's strongholds so you can enjoy the freedom in Christ that belongs to you, you must first restrict his work and influence.

You remember from 2 Corinthians 10:3–5 that you cannot fight him by ordinary means. Bringing every thought captive to Christ is a job for Jesus Christ. Jesus does it for you when you use scriptural principles for warfare.

First, get rid of any objects and materials that belong to Satan. The Bible is clear that astrology and occult practices are Satan's domain (Deut. 18:10–14; Gal. 5:20). If you have any occult paraphernalia, destroy it at once. It would be a good idea to have a pastor or Christian friend with you as a witness.

Second, pray in Jesus' name for the stronghold to be shattered. Before you pray, find some Bible verses that pertain to your situation, and use them in your prayer. There is real power in the name and blood of Christ, and Satan cannot stand in the presence of the Son of God.

Always bear in mind that you are not the one doing the binding or crushing of Satan's influence. Pride or a desire for personal power has no place in battling the evil one. Your liberation lies only in humble faith in the power of Christ. Jesus came to set you free; claim that freedom today.

In the name of Jesus, every stronghold in my life is shattered by the power
of the blood! Jesus came to set me free, and I claim that freedom today!

A Casual View of Sin

SCRIPTURE READING: Romans 6:1–7   KEY VERSE: Romans 6:12

Therefore do not let sin reign in your mortal body, that you should obey it in its lusts.

How do you describe sin? Separation from God? Yielding to temptation? The bottom line to sin is rebellion against God where we make a conscious decision to step away from what we know is God's best for us.

Is anyone immune to temptation? No. Even Jesus was tempted to trust His own strength above the provision of God. However, the Son of God was not swayed by Satan's lies. He refused to listen to the enemy's words as viable options. Instead, He used Scripture as proof that God was and is sufficient for every need we have.

Sin begins when we fail to see God as our Provider. The enemy whispers lies, stating that we need something more than what we have. He appeals to our five senses (touching, hearing, smelling, tasting, and seeing) and sets emotional traps for us along the way, knowing that we will see his mile markers and be weakened in our desires to have and hold more than what God has provided.

Sin answers the call of misguided desires. Satan stands ready to aid in your wandering, but don't look to him to help or encourage you when your world falls apart. He will only condemn and ridicule you for your blundering.

Only God is loving enough to rescue one of His wandering flock. Have you strayed? If so, turn back to Jesus, and you will find Him waiting for you.

I reject the lies of the enemy. You are my Provider, God. I thank You that all I need is in You.

God Is Your Banner

SCRIPTURE READING: Psalm 37:1–9   KEY VERSE: Psalm 36:12

There the workers of iniquity have fallen;
They have been cast down and are not able to rise.

K ay Arthur asks,

Are there days in your life when you feel utterly defeated? Outnumbered, outflanked, and outgunned? Do you ever feel overwhelmed and overcome by yearnings of the flesh that run counter to God's Word and His desire and plan for you?

Where do you turn, Beloved? Where do you find the strength and will to stand fast and keep fighting the good fight? Where do you look for help when the enemy comes in like a flood?

Turn to Jehovah-nissi. Find your deliverance in "the Lord my Banner." Let your heart thrill at the victory that is ours in Him.

A banner in ancient times was an ensign or standard carried at the head of a military grouping. It became the rallying point in a time of war. Often it was a bare pole topped with a bright ornament that caught the light of the sun.

In times of battle, soldiers would look across the confusion and chaos of the battlefield for a glimpse of their king's banner. As long as the shining ensign was held high, they would fight with courage and confidence.

God is your Banner. He sees the war raging against you and is your eternal Source of hope and confidence. In times of stress and pressure, take courage. Look for God's standard moving out in front of you. The victory is yours as you trust Him.

You are my Banner, dear Lord. You are my Source of hope and confidence.
Give me courage in times of stress and pressure, knowing that Your stan-
dard moves in front of me into battle.

God with Us

SCRIPTURE READING: Romans 5:12–21   KEY VERSE: Romans 5:1

Therefore, having been justified by faith, we have peace with God through our Lord Jesus Christ.

One of the most instructive books on the Christian life is the book of Romans. The entire Bible fits together perfectly to form a complete message of truth concerning God and His will for mankind, yet Romans offers a direct look into the life of a believer.

The apostle Paul did not shrink back from such subjects as immorality. He was very forthright in telling us exactly how God views sin and how we should view our bodies.

We are the temples of the Holy Spirit. In the New Testament, Jerusalem was God's abode. The temple was there, and within its walls the Spirit of God dwelled. But the birth and death of Jesus Christ changed this. His very name, Immanuel, means "God with us, God with you."

When you accept Christ as your Savior, God comes to live within you. Your body becomes His temple, His abode, and an inner chamber. Understanding this and the significance involved will help you understand why it is so important for you to live free of sin.

In grace and love, God forgives sin. However, He wants you to continually seek to live a life of purity. When you yield to sin, you allow darkness to drift into His holy chamber, which is your heart. Accepting His forgiveness and grace brings restoration and fresh hope. However, the greater good is for you to remain pure before Him as you worship Him each day.

Father, I accept Your forgiveness and grace. Restore me and give me fresh hope. Help me to remain pure before You as I worship You each day.

Stop Sinning

SCRIPTURE READING: Galatians 6:7–10   KEY VERSE: Psalm 139:3

You comprehend my path and my lying down,
And are acquainted with all my ways.

Have you ever wondered if you can get away with sin? At some point, each of us has thought, *Well, I'll just do it; I know God will forgive me.* Or maybe our thought processes have gone like this: *No one will find out; it won't matter.*

The truth is, God knows much more than we like to think He does. Not only is He aware of our sin; He also knows the attitudes of our hearts and is familiar with all our ways. Even before we do something wrong, He knows all the details (Ps. 139:3).

Yet God who is rich in mercy promises to forgive and restore each person who admits his failure. This is the wonder of His grace. You don't have to worry if He will continue to love you. He has promised to love you with an eternal love.

Part of God's loving you is allowing you to face the consequences of your mistakes. God does not wash His hands of you. If you have fallen into sin and call out to Him, He responds with love, forgiveness, and hope.

After healing the disabled beggar, Jesus said, "Sin no more, lest a worse thing come upon you" (John 5:14). God is not waiting to rain down fire from heaven on those who disobey Him. However, He does expect you to heed His warning and turn from sin. Lay aside everything that would keep you entangled in darkness and separated from His love.

Dear Lord, help me lay aside all that would keep me entangled in sin and separated from Your love. Examine my heart. Reveal my secret sins.

The King of the Jungle

SCRIPTURE READING: Luke 8:1–15   KEY VERSE: Matthew 26:41

Watch and pray, lest you enter into temptation. The spirit indeed is willing, but the flesh is weak.

There is a reason that the lion is labeled "king of the jungle." It combines speed, power, and stealth that are difficult to overcome.

How does a lion attack? It uses whatever means necessary to bring down its prey. In certain situations, the lion needs speed to catch its kill. Sometimes it needs power in a monumental battle. Amazingly for a creature so large, the lion is expert at the element of surprise. It can sneak and bring down prey without warning. It then bites around the prey's throat, suffocating the life out of it.

The Bible says Satan is like a lion. He is expert at timing his temptations and attacks on us. He will sneak up on us and bring us down when we least expect it, and in areas we thought we had best fortified.

Yet we are not helpless in our confrontations with the enemy. Jesus gives us our ammunition when we're under assault. Consider His admonition to His sleepy disciples when He prayed in the Garden the night before His execution: "Watch and pray, lest you enter into temptation" (Matt. 26:41).

You are to be alert for the prowling lion. Keep watching. You are to know for a certainty that temptation will befall you, and you are to pray a God-centered prayer for His deliverance. The king of this world's jungle is no match for the King of kings.

Keep me from temptation, Lord. Keep me alert and watching. Deliver me from the snare of the enemy.

Training in Godliness

SCRIPTURE READING: 1 Timothy 6:1–12   KEY VERSE: 1 Timothy 4:7

Reject profane and old wives' fables, and exercise yourself toward godliness.

The athletes who run twenty-six-mile marathons usually have trained for years. So have those who run sixty-meter sprints. In more important confrontations—like those against temptations—are we to be any less prepared to run, to flee?

In *The Practice of Godliness*, Jerry Bridges writes,

> In urging Timothy to train himself in godliness in 1 Timothy 4:7, Paul borrowed a term from the realm of athletics. The verb which is variously translated in different versions of the Bible as "exercise," "discipline," or "train" originally referred to the training of young athletes . . .
>
> Paul said, "Train yourself to be godly." You and I are responsible to train ourselves. We are dependent upon God for his divine enablement, but we are responsible; we are not passive in this process. Our objective in this process is godliness—not proficiency in ministry—but God-centered devotion and Godlike character.
>
> Training in godliness requires commitment, the teaching ministry of the Holy Spirit through His Word, and practice on our part. Are we prepared to accept our responsibility and make that commitment? As we ponder that question, let us remember, "godliness has value for all things, holding promise—for both the present life and the life to come," and "godliness with contentment is great gain" (1 Tim. 4:8; 6:6).

Father, empower me with Your strength to train myself in godliness. I commit myself to walk in Your ways.

A Target for Temptation

SCRIPTURE READING: 2 Samuel 11:1–27   KEY VERSE: James 4:7

Submit to God. Resist the devil and he will flee from you.

Temptation has one goal: to render the believer ineffective in his walk with God. King David knew this, and for the greater part of his life he lived with the awareness of what sin could do to his relationship with God. However, Satan, who is the author of sin, never signals defeat. He seeks to cut inroads of temptation into your life, causing you to become unfaithful in your devotion to God.

That was what he did in David's life. In 2 Samuel, we learn that David should have been away with his army in battle. Instead, he remained at home. Had he become lazy? Proud? Self-sufficient? Bored? The Bible doesn't tell us exactly what was going on in David's heart, but we can surmise from what we are given that David was a target for Satan's temptation. And more than likely, he invited it.

Bathsheba knew what she was doing that night as she stepped into the cool pool of water within eyesight of the king's palace. That was the beginning of a desperate time for one of God's greatest servants. The plot of temptation was set, and David became a willing participant.

No matter how tempting the situation seems, nothing is worth risking your sweet fellowship with God and the love of family members. Say no to the tempter, and cry out to God for His strength and protection so that the enemy will be defeated in your life.

I am saying no to the tempter and yes to You today! Give me strength, Lord, to defeat the enemy in every area of my life.

Sin Does Not Fit

SCRIPTURE READING: Psalm 33:1–22   KEY VERSE: Romans 8:6

To be carnally minded is death, but to be spiritually minded is life and peace.

Paul cautioned us not to be ignorant of Satan's schemes. Peter issued a similar warning when he wrote, "Be sober, be vigilant; because your adversary the devil walks about like a roaring lion, seeking whom he may devour" (1 Peter 5:8).

Both men understood the nature of temptation and its effects on the believer. However, many, like spiritual lambs being led to slaughter, ignore God's warning concerning temptation and later end up wishing they had heeded His commands.

You have a choice. And as a believer, you are not overcome by the darkness of temptation. Jesus is your strong arm of protection. Proverbs tells us:

> These six things the LORD hates,
> Yes, seven are an abomination to Him:
> A proud look,
> A lying tongue,
> Hands that shed innocent blood,
> A heart that devises wicked plans,
> Feet that are swift in running to evil,
> A false witness who speaks lies,
> And one who sows discord among brethren. (Prov. 6:16–19)

One sure way to deal with temptation is keep the focus of your heart on His Word. The Word of God that Paul wrote about in Ephesians 6 is your greatest defense. It works only when you are willing to walk in the light of obedience and in Christ. Because you are a child of God, sin does not fit who you are in Christ.

Lord, I realize that sin does not fit who I am in You. Cleanse me from sin. Let me walk in the light of obedience to You and Your Word.

Running to the Father

SCRIPTURE READING: John 21:15–19   KEY VERSE: John 13:38

Jesus answered him, "Will you lay down your life for My sake? Most assuredly, I say to you, the rooster shall not crow till you have denied Me three times."

Peter spoke passionately to Jesus, "Lord, why can I not follow You now? I will lay down my life for Your sake"(John 13:37). The Lord's response left His disciple feeling grief stricken and out of control: "Will you lay down your life for My sake? Most assuredly, I say to you, the rooster shall not crow till you have denied Me three times" (John 13:38).

We know the story well: Peter ended up denying Jesus, not once but three times. It was the pinnacle of temptation: tempting you to deny Christ as your Lord and intimate Friend. Although nothing can keep you from the saving love of God, not even the vilest sin, entertaining thoughts of temptation certainly quenches His Spirit.

Turn a few pages farther in the book of John, and discover the goodness of God's mercy. The risen Lord was talking to Peter, and He made a point of encouraging and reinstating His wayward disciple (John 21:15–18). This is what Jesus does for you whenever you yield to temptation.

After Peter denied Christ, he remained with the others. He did not leave the stronghold of his spiritual environment. He was there in the Upper Room when Jesus appeared.

When you sin, do not run away from God. Instead, run toward Him. Seek His forgiveness and restoration. Accept His love and the fact that He has paid the price for your sins.

I run to You, Father. Forgive me. Restore me. Thank You for paying the price for my sins.

A Way of Escape

SCRIPTURE READING: Psalm 95:1–11   KEY VERSE: 1 Corinthians 10:13

No temptation has overtaken you except such as is common to man; but God is faithful, who will not allow you to be tempted beyond what you are able, but with the temptation will also make the way of escape, that you may be able to bear it.

For the past several days, we have been studying about temptation. As believers, we know that the victory is ours, and we are no longer under the powerful rule of sin. Jesus annihilated the final hold of sin over mankind. However, as we have said before, sin is a powerful enemy, and we must make a conscious decision to turn away from it and obey God.

If we fail to do this, we give the enemy room to build his power base of sin and deception in our lives. And while we may not be owned by the devil because of Christ's finished work on the cross, he can surely darken our lives and leave us feeling defeated and worthless.

You may ask, "How can I possibly live a victorious life with so many temptations facing me each day?" The apostle Paul offered this insight: "No temptation has overtaken you except such as is common to man; but God is faithful, who will not allow you to be tempted beyond what you are able, but with the temptation will also make the way of escape, that you may be able to bear it" (1 Cor. 10:13).

God always provides a way of escape from sin. If you fall, God does not want you to give up. Instead, you are to ask Him to forgive you and then continue in your walk with Him. This is the goodness of God's love for you: He never stops loving you.

> *Lord, I know that there is no temptation I experience that is not common to man. Thank You that You have provided a way for me to escape. Help me to take it.*

The Victory Is Won

SCRIPTURE READING: John 3:1–17   KEY VERSE: John 3:16

For God so loved the world that He gave His only begotten Son, that whoever believes in Him should not perish but have everlasting life.

One of the truly rewarding pursuits of Bible study is the exegesis, or detailed examination, of a word or a verse. Tracing biblical words to their original language can shed useful insight on the exact truth God wishes to share with us.

For example, the word *gospel* in its original Greek means "good news." But further examination of the word reveals another important truth. The Greek word for gospel is *evangelion*, from which we also get the word *evangelize*. But *evangelion*, before its New Testament rendering, was used most often as a reference to good news from the battlefield. A victory had been won when this word was used.

Guess what? The victory has been won! Jesus Christ, the Son of God, became a man, overcame temptation, died as an unblemished Lamb for your sins, rose from the dead on the third day, and ascended to heaven to make intercession for you with God the Father. The most famous Bible verse—John 3:16—is the gospel in a nutshell. It is one beautiful sentence revealing that victory is yours for the asking.

If you already are a child of God but have slipped or are in bondage to sin or a certain attitude, remember the good news from Luke and the other Gospels. Christ Himself emerged from the battlefield the absolute, undeniable, complete Victor!

You are the Victor, Lord, who makes it possible for me to live in victory. I reject the bondage of sin and embrace the truth of Your freedom.

The Great Liberator

SCRIPTURE READING: John 8:31–36   KEY VERSE: John 8:32

And you shall know the truth, and the truth shall make you free.

Jesus is life's Great Liberator, and one of the ways He rescues us is to free us from bondage to sin. If you are struggling with a particular sin, He will help you when you surrender and repent.

R. C. Sproul addressed the issue of sin:

> The reason we continue with these pockets of repeated sins is because we have a heartfelt desire to continue them, not because we have a heartfelt desire to stop them. I wonder how honest our commitment is to quit. There's a tendency for us to kid ourselves about this anytime we embrace a pet sin. We need to face the fact that we commit the sin because we want to do that sin more than we want to obey Christ at that moment. That doesn't mean that we have no desire to escape from it, but the level of our desire vacillates. It's easy to go on a diet after a banquet; it's hard to stay on a diet if you haven't eaten all day . . .
>
> I think what we have to do is first of all be honest about the fact that we really have a conflict of interest between what we want to do and what God wants us to do. I think we have to feed our souls with the Word of God so that we can get what God wants us to do clear in our mind and then build a strong desire to obey.

You find freedom in Christ when you surrender and lay aside the sin that besets you. Obedience is the threshold, and the Great Liberator knocks.

Father, I surrender my will and the sin that so easily besets me. Create within me a desire to live in obedience to You.

Our Fleshly Nature

SCRIPTURE READING: Proverbs 6:16–19   KEY VERSE: Galatians 5:17

For the flesh lusts against the Spirit, and the Spirit against the flesh; and these are contrary to one another, so that you do not do the things that you wish.

In Proverbs 6:16–19, the Lord lists six things He hates: a proud look, a lying tongue, hands that shed innocent blood, a heart that devises wicked plans, feet that are swift in running to evil, a false witness, and a person who sows discord. The seventh one He includes also as an abomination.

Each testifies to the fleshly nature that was ours before we came to know Jesus as Savior and Lord. Many times we don't know how to handle this side of our lives. Because we are believers, our sins have been forgiven. Still there are times when we return to our old way of thinking.

When this happens, go to God in prayer, and ask Him to speak His Word of truth to your mind and heart. By doing this, you can build discernment into your life. Godly wisdom does not come overnight. It must be cultivated. When the author of Proverbs wrote, "Feet that are swift in running to evil," he was writing about a lack of true spiritual discernment.

Esau sold his birthright to Jacob for a bowl of soup. He was spiritually shortsighted, and his feet rushed to evil. Here is an excellent rule to follow: do not make any decisions when you are too hungry, angry, lonely, or tired. When situations arise that demand immediate action, refuse to rush to satisfy your flesh. Allow God to control your appetite, and you will mature spiritually in every way.

Dear Lord, when situations arise that demand immediate action, grant me the strength to refuse to satisfy my flesh. Help me control my desires. I want to mature spiritually.

God Is Your Strength

SCRIPTURE READING: Mark 1:32–35   KEY VERSE: 2 Corinthians 11:3

I fear, lest somehow, as the serpent deceived Eve by his craftiness, so your minds may be corrupted from the simplicity that is in Christ.

Have you ever wondered why Peter was so quick to write a warning about Satan's tactics? He was so committed to telling us the straightforward truth because he knew what it felt like to face Satan's harshest trials.

Peter was the one who was tempted to deny Christ. He also was the one who allowed fear to enter his heart during a storm out on the Sea of Galilee. Both times, Peter underestimated the level of his faith and bypassed the fact that Satan was a powerful foe.

Peter's word to the early church was to count Satan as their deceiving adversary, one who would stop at nothing to disrupt and, if possible, destroy their faith in Christ. Peter used the word *resist* to describe the posture we are to assume when facing the enemy. This is a powerful position to take. We resist Satan's attacks by our belief in Christ.

Never enter into a talking or shouting match with the enemy. He will use that method to draw you away from your central focus—a focus that must be set firmly on Jesus Christ and His strength and ability.

You can do nothing in the spiritual realm apart from God. Therefore, when you battle the evil one, stay on your knees in prayer. Ask God to open your eyes to His faithfulness. Be encouraged. God is your victorious strength!

God, open my eyes to Your faithfulness. Help me recognize that You are my strength in the face of every temptation.

Living What You Believe

SCRIPTURE READING: Revelation 3:20–22   KEY VERSE: John 10:10

The thief does not come except to steal, and to kill, and to destroy. I have come that they may have life, and that they may have it more abundantly.

Peter followed the lead of James and instructed us to resist the enemy by standing firm in our faith. James's letter to the early church was written long before Peter's. In it, James addressed the persecuted Christians living outside Palestine.

The dispersion of Jewish believers came at the hands of the Roman government and was an attempt to disrupt the growing force of the New Testament church. Away from their homes and, in many cases, away from those they loved, Jewish believers faced all kinds of trials and temptations. Warren Wiersbe stated: "One of the major problems in the church was a failure on the part of many to live what they professed to believe."

Failing to live what we profess to believe is a major problem. It also is a major assault tactic of Satan. For the enemy to achieve his goal of discouraging the believer, he must first gain access to that person's life through sin. This is where he can easily catch us off guard if we are not in tune with the Spirit of God.

Jesus stands ready to fight for you. However, if you allow the enemy to gain access to your life through sin, you will suffer a sure defeat.

James instructed us to resist Satan's temptations. Use the name of Jesus Christ as your strong defense. Victory comes when you are eternally linked to the Savior.

Father, make me strong in the face of temptation. Deliver me from the muck and mire of the valleys of this world. I want to continually dwell spiritually on the mountaintop with You.

SEPTEMBER

Relationships with God and Others

MOUNTAIN: Mount of Beatitudes where Jesus taught

KEY VERSES: Matthew 5:1–10

And seeing the multitudes, He went up on a mountain, and when He was seated His disciples came to Him. Then He opened His mouth and taught them, saying:

"Blessed are the poor in spirit,
  For theirs is the kingdom of heaven.
Blessed are those who mourn,
  For they shall be comforted.
Blessed are the meek,
  For they shall inherit the earth.
Blessed are those who hunger and thirst for righteousness,
  For they shall be filled.
Blessed are the merciful,
  For they shall obtain mercy.
Blessed are the pure in heart,
  For they shall see God.
Blessed are the peacemakers,
  For they shall be called sons of God.
Blessed are those who are persecuted for righteousness' sake,
  For theirs is the kingdom of heaven."

Living Life to the Fullest

SCRIPTURE READING: 1 Thess. 5:1–14   KEY VERSE: 1 Thess. 5:5

You are all sons of light and sons of the day. We are not of the night nor of darkness.

What does living life to the fullest mean to you? Some may picture a life-long dream being fulfilled. Others may think of a comfortable retirement, while many more envision what they can achieve if given enough time. But if you really want to start living life to the fullest, begin with Jesus. He is the fulfillment of all your dreams. In Him, you will find the things you need the most—contentment, love, and friendship.

Living life to the fullest also involves your ability to encourage and support others emotionally through prayer. God commands us to love others. Without a godly love tucked away inside your heart, you cannot successfully encourage someone else. And all of us need encouragement. Let Jesus be the object of your affections; then you will find that loving even the unlovely will bring pleasure and encouragement to your heart.

When you encourage others from a position of unconditional love and acceptance, marvelous things can happen. God often uses His love to change and motivate hearts. Divisions may fade, differences may ease, and fears may subside. Where there once was disagreement, unity can prevail. And love—especially God's love—can change the way you view life. Evaluate your life. Are you living life to the fullest?

I want to live life to the fullest, Lord, and I know that will happen only as I experience Your love. Give me Your love—even for the unlovely.

The Struggle with Jealousy

SCRIPTURE READING: 1 Samuel 18:5–9 KEY VERSE: Song of Solomon 8:6

Set me as a seal upon your heart,
As a seal upon your arm;
For love is as strong as death,
Jealousy as cruel as the grave;
Its flames are flames of fire,
A most vehement flame.

Everything was going well for young David. Saul had given him a position of authority. He also had access to the king's household and often spent his evenings in the king's presence. Saul gave no indication of having any envy toward David. Yet both jealousy and envy were brewing within the king's heart. The only way jealousy can flourish is to have an acceptable atmosphere in which it feels at home and can grow.

In reality, jealousy is a symptom of a deeper problem. And while it needs to be dealt with swiftly, you also need to ask God to show you the root cause of any envy that has set up shop in your life. Usually, pride is the taproot of jealousy and envy as well as strife.

Saul was pleased with David's allegiance until one day when he returned from war and overheard the people shouting, "Saul has slain his thousands, and David his ten thousands" (1 Sam. 18:7). As a result of their cheers, Saul's need for acceptance evolved into an obnoxious jealousy that ruled his life until his death.

Only Christ can free you from the stronghold of pride and its cousins, jealousy and envy. If this is an area of concern in your life, be honest about it. Tell the Lord you want nothing to do with anything that keeps you from enjoying His fellowship. Pray that He will remove any hint of jealousy so that you may live free in Christ Jesus.

Dear Lord, please free me from pride, jealousy, and envy. I want to live free in You.

The Cycle of Jealousy

SCRIPTURE READING: 1 Samuel 18:10–16   KEY VERSE: Proverbs 6:34 (KJV)

For jealousy is the rage of a man; therefore he will not spare in the day of vengeance.

Jealousy is the emotion of displeasure with someone else's good fortune. For whatever reason—insecurity, selfishness, or pride—the person who is jealous of another person is entering into dangerous territory that has the potential to destroy everyone involved.

We learn in the book of 1 Samuel that David's great victory over Goliath led to Saul's bitter resentment of the young David. When women greeted their army and sang that Saul had slain his "thousands" and David had slain his "ten thousands," Saul was immediately enraged. David's accomplishments and rescue of an entire nation were buried under the weight that a jealous Saul ascribed to the people's well-intentioned words.

For many years thereafter, Saul was consumed with destroying David. He effectively made his monarchy lame duck by abandoning his promise and blessing. He chose to pursue a man who had done nothing but bring benefit to him and the nation of Israel.

Jealousy leads to irrational behavior. Suspicion was the first spoke in Saul's cycle of jealousy, which included his confusion, bitterness, fear, resentment, and anxiety. It all led to repeated irrational acts and broken relationships. Jealousy is nothing more than having a conflict with God over what He is doing in another person's life. It is best to focus on what God is doing in one's own life.

Father, help me focus on what You are doing in my life. Cleanse me from jealousy, bitterness, resentment, fear, and anxiety.

Focus on God

SCRIPTURE READING: Luke 10:38–42   KEY VERSE: Luke 10:42

But one thing is needed, and Mary has chosen that good part, which will not be taken away from her.

Martha had chosen to prepare the evening meal. No one forced her to do it. In fact, if we examined the situation, we would find that Martha really didn't mind the work. She loved receiving praise for her cooking.

Yet here's the scenario: Jesus is in the front room of the house talking to those gathered near Him. Martha is rushing around the cooking area in the back of the house. All is fine until she discovers her sister is missing. A quick check of the courtyard provides no clue of Mary's whereabouts. With her jaw set to reprove her sister, Martha storms by the doorway to the front room. Then she spots Mary sitting near the feet of Jesus. Envy and jealousy take control of Martha's heart: "Lord, do You not care that my sister has left me to serve alone? Therefore tell her to help me" (Luke 10:40).

All of us have fought feelings like these. Although God understands our weaknesses, jealousy is intolerable to Him. Why? For one, it proves that we are more interested in taking care of ourselves than in taking care of our love relationship with Him. Jesus told Martha, "Mary has chosen that good part, which will not be taken away from her."

Make every effort to rid your life of envy, strife, and jealousy. Let God bless you in the way He has chosen. Set the focus of your heart on Him, and rejoice that He greatly loves you.

Father, help me set the focus of my heart on You and rejoice in Your love today.

Solutions for Jealousy

SCRIPTURE READING: Psalm 84:1–12   KEY VERSE: 1 Peter 4:8

Above all things have fervent love for one another, for "love will cover a multitude of sins."

Christian counselor Don McMinn offers four solutions for jealousy:
1. Learn to receive and give God's love. "Love is not jealous" (1 Corinthians 13:4, NASB). Love is the divine antidote for jealousy because true love always wants the best for others. "Love covers a multitude of sins" (1 Peter 4:8).

2. Desire and pray for the welfare of others. "I pray that you may enjoy good health and that all may go well with you" (3 John 2). God's blessings are limitless; He will never run out, so by blessing others He is not limiting the degree to which He can bless us.

3. Do not covet; learn to be content. "The LORD gave and the LORD has taken away; Blessed be the name of the Lord" (Job 1:21). What we have and what others have is determined by the Lord, so we should refrain from being jealous of what others possess.

4. Establish confidence in who you are and what you do by living a holy life. Psalm 84:11 says, "For the LORD God is a sun and shield; the Lord bestows favor and honor; no good thing does He withhold from those whose walk is blameless." When we live blameless lives, we have confidence that God will lead us (sun), protect us (shield), honor us (bestows favor and honor), and meet all our needs (not withhold any good thing). This assurance should eliminate jealousy.

> *Dear heavenly Father, help me receive and give Your love. Give me a burden for the welfare of others. Let me learn to be content, and give me confidence in who I am in You.*

Godly Friendships

SCRIPTURE READING: Proverbs 27:6–10   KEY VERSE: Proverbs 18:24

A man who has friends must himself be friendly,
But there is a friend who sticks closer than a brother.

We need one another. More important, we need Jesus. However, the way we love the Lord exemplifies the way we love one another.

God created us for fellowship, and without it, something inside us dies. Fellowship with other believers is breath and life to Christians.

Therefore, if you want a deeper, more satisfying relationship with the Lord, learn to establish godly friendships with others who share your love for Jesus Christ. Don't be overly concerned with the depth of the relationship. Some people long for friendships and seek to build relationships that run deep and are emotionally binding. This can be constraining.

Instead, as you are beginning to work on your friendships with others, draw closer to the Lord. Ask Him to uncover any difficult areas of your personality that may block others from getting closer to you.

As you open your heart to the Lord in prayer, He will make more of Himself known to you. Love begins in the presence of God. Once you experience this unconditional love, you will find yourself wanting to share it with others, not just as an evangelistic tool but as a means of knowing and loving others who worship the Savior.

It is good to have friends from many walks of life. But let the pattern for your deeper relationships begin and end with a sincere love for Jesus Christ.

Lord, reveal to me any problems in my personality that may block others
from getting close to me. Let me experience Your unconditional love so I can
share it with others.

Heart Attack

SCRIPTURE READING: Ephesians 4:22–32   KEY VERSE: Ephesians 4:31

Let all bitterness, wrath, anger, clamor, and evil speaking be put away from you, with all malice.

In our health-conscious society, how we take care of our bodies is a concern. From warning labels on certain packages to fat content information on food products, a growing interest in understanding health issues is evident.

The things you consume play a large role in determining how well you are, but equally vital to your overall spiritual health is your understanding of the scriptural principles of forgiveness.

When you refuse to let go of a past hurt or you continue to nurse a grudge, you create a spot of hardness in your heart. Over time, as layers and layers of hardness accumulate, your heart becomes stiff and insensitive to the extent that you are almost incapable of giving or receiving love.

Such a scenario of bitterness is not far-fetched. The story is told of two sisters who in their youth spoke unkind words. They never resolved that point of conflict, and over the years, the problem was magnified. Only after a family member helped them work through the original difficulty were they able to set hostilities aside. They regretted the years lost to senseless anger.

You do not have to be a victim of this kind of "heart attack." Ephesians 4:31 tells us, "Let all bitterness, wrath . . . be put away from you." You can take advantage of the best preventive medicine, complete forgiveness.

Lord, I choose to put away bitterness and wrath. I choose to forgive all those who have hurt or wronged me. Heal my heart.

The Gift of Forgiveness

SCRIPTURE READING: Matthew 18:21–35   KEY VERSE: Luke 6:37

Judge not, and you shall not be judged. Condemn not, and you shall not be condemned. Forgive, and you will be forgiven.

That's it. I've had it. No more chances," the girl said in exasperation. For the umpteenth time, her good friend had done something that greatly annoyed her.

After she dealt with the situation, the conflict would not leave her mind. The issue of repeat offenses made her think about the time that Jesus explained to Peter what unlimited forgiveness really means. We can easily become weary of forgiving, but it is essential to our spiritual health.

Yet Jesus calls us to that kind of forgiveness. This girl shares the common feeling that there's a limit to human patience. She is right. There is a limit to your emotional resources when you do not rely on Jesus to do the job of forgiving. Peter thought he was being gracious by suggesting the number seven as the maximum. Then Jesus blew apart his limited thinking.

When Jesus died on the cross to pay for sin, He didn't pay only for a select few. He paid for all of them, in full—no limitations or reservations or exceptions. As you deal with personal relationships and people hurt you, sometimes repeatedly, you can draw on the unlimited account of His forgiveness.

You do not have to be concerned with protecting your rights and feelings because Jesus is in charge of taking care of you. You can never run out of love, the ingredient of forgiveness.

Thank You, Lord, for dying to pay for all sin. Help me draw on the limitless account of Your forgiveness as I deal with others.

Unconditional Forgiveness

SCRIPTURE READING: Matthew 6:1–15   KEY VERSE: Matthew 6:14

If you forgive men their trespasses, your heavenly Father will also forgive you.

In *The Weight of Glory*, C. S. Lewis writes,

> To forgive the incessant provocations of daily life—to keep on forgiving the bossy mother-in-law, the bullying husband, the nagging wife, the selfish daughter, the deceitful son—how can we do it?
>
> Only, I think, by remembering where we stand, by meaning our words when we say in our prayers each night "Forgive us our trespasses as we forgive those that trespass against us." We are offered forgiveness on no other terms. To refuse it is to refuse God's mercy for ourselves. There is no hint of exceptions and God means what He says.

Failing to forgive someone who offends you doesn't mean that you lose your own salvation, but your refusal to forgive discolors your experience of His grace. By not weeding out the roots of bitterness as they spring up, you will soon be controlled by the full-blown fruits of unforgiveness.

Have you ever seen a kudzu vine? One little tendril that takes root grows at an astonishing pace. If left to grow unchecked, the vines engulf trees and choke them off from the sunlight. Efforts to clean up the vines must be absolutely thorough because the tiniest piece of root left in the ground will start the process all over again.

Don't let the smallest grudge or insult have room to grow. Take it to the Lord immediately.

> *Father, I don't want to give any grudge or insult space to grow in my life. Teach me how to forgive others unconditionally.*

Resolving Disagreements

SCRIPTURE READING: Luke 17:1–4   KEY VERSE: Romans 12:19

Beloved, do not avenge yourselves, but rather give place to wrath; for it is written, "Vengeance is Mine, I will repay," says the Lord.

The two friends argued and then went their separate ways without reconciling their differences. That evening neither could sleep. The Bible instructs us to settle our differences before we part: "'Be angry, and do not sin': do not let the sun go down on your wrath, nor give place to the devil" (Eph. 4:26–27).

There are obvious reasons why God wants you to solve a disagreement quickly. For one, when you bring the right kind of closure to a hurtful matter, you free yourself and the other person emotionally and spiritually. Those who refuse to extend forgiveness are the losers. Nothing soothes a guilt-worn conscience like the forgiveness and love of God.

When we forgive others, we do what Jesus did for us. We also align our lives with His standard of obedience. Forgiveness is not always easy, but it is essential to emotional and physical health. God promises to deal personally with those who have harmed us (Rom. 12:19). However, many people refuse to wait on Him. They want vengeance, and they want it now.

If this is your attitude, ask God to remind you of how your life looked to Him before He saved you. Whether six or sixty, every one of us deserved death. Yet through the work of His wondrous grace and forgiveness, we were given eternal life.

I deserved death, Lord, but You forgave me and gave me life. Now give me the ability to extend Your love and forgiveness to others.

The Consequences of Words

SCRIPTURE READING: James 3:1–12   KEY VERSE: Matthew 12:37

For by your words you will be justified, and by your words you will be condemned.

The Bible has plenty to say about the words of the mouth:

In the multitude of words, sin is not lacking,
But he who restrains his lips is wise. (Prov. 10:19)

Pleasant words are like a honeycomb,
Sweetness to the soul and healthy to the bones. (Prov. 16:24)

These verses barely scratch the surface when it comes to addressing the subject of our speech. However, we can get a general feel that what we say has a powerful effect on our lives. James addressed this issue as he wrote about the tongue and the consequences of our words toward others (James 3:5–6).

We are communicators, and we are always in the process of communicating something, even in our sleep. Because we are created in God's image, and He is the greatest communicator, we have been entrusted with a tremendous ability. When we misuse our words, we go against an important principle of God—for the words of our mouths and the meditations of our hearts to be pleasing and acceptable to Him (Ps. 19:14).

God gave us speech to communicate with Him first and then with others. Ask the Lord to convict you each time you use your words in a way that could harm your fellowship with Him. Realize your communication with others also reflects the way you communicate with God.

Let the words of my mouth and the meditation of my heart be acceptable to You today, O God. Help me realize that my communication with others reflects the way I communicate with You.

Taking Charge

SCRIPTURE READING: 1 Timothy 1:1–12   KEY VERSE: 2 Timothy 1:7

God has not given us a spirit of fear, but of power and of love and of a sound mind.

She stood to the side of the lobby where she could watch him unobserved. He was an acquaintance from years ago, and she had spotted him coming through her office building. She wanted to speak and reintroduce herself, but something held her back.

Every time she wanted her feet to move, she felt rooted to the floor. Her mouth was going dry, and her hands began to tremble. Would he even remember her? Would he care? What if she looked silly? He might laugh, or he could be completely indifferent. No, she finally reasoned, I'm not going to bother.

Have you ever felt the fear of rejection or failure or embarrassment? You probably also know the longing of wishing you had taken a chance and risked being vulnerable. You do not want to let opportunities pass you by, but somehow you feel unable to change.

A key to victory over insecurity and social fear is remembering your identity in Christ. You are not a failure, even when you mess up. You are not ridiculous, even when you make silly mistakes. Paul wrote, "God has not given us a spirit of fear, but of power and of love and of a sound mind" (2 Tim. 1:7).

Stepping out and taking a chance is not an opportunity for pain; it's opening up your life in an area of weakness to allow God to demonstrate His strength (2 Cor. 12:9–10). Let the Lord absorb the risk.

God, You have not given me the spirit of fear. You have given me power, love, and a sound mind. Let me reach out to others today.

Fostering Friendships

SCRIPTURE READING: John 14:15–21   KEY VERSE: Proverbs 27:17

As iron sharpens iron,
So a man sharpens the countenance of his friend.

Many times, lonely people fall prey to the wrong kinds of friendships. When someone is hungry for companionship of any sort, he is less likely to be choosy in forming intimate friendships, and God calls His people to be selective.

From the earliest Old Testament times, when God guided the nation of Israel out of Egypt and into a land filled with strangers, He gave them specific instructions about how to treat the Canaanites, who were sometimes interested in forming alliances with Israel. Why? God knows the importance of avoiding close associations with those who do not have a relationship with Him.

In their book *Happiness Is a Choice*, Dr. Minirth and Dr. Meier explain,

> Select your friends very carefully, because you will become more and more like your friends whether you intend to or not! . . . You should have a few non-Christian friends as well, but if you are a committed Christian, you will want your most intimate friends to be committed Christians also.

> Don't overestimate your own spiritual strength. It is much easier than most Christians think for a non-Christian friend to bring a Christian down spiritually. In Proverbs 27:17, wise King Solomon wrote that "as iron sharpens iron, so a man sharpens the countenance of his friend."

Father, I want to be close to people who have a relationship with You. Help me foster genuine friendships with those who know and love You.

Controlling Anger

SCRIPTURE READING: James 1:19–27   KEY VERSE: Proverbs 16:32

He who is slow to anger is better than the mighty,
And he who rules his spirit than he who takes a city.

"Be angry, and do not sin" was Paul's carefully crafted, Spirit-inspired alert to the church at Ephesus. His admonition was delicately phrased for good reason. Constructively managed anger has no sinful connotations. You do not sin every time you fume or fuss. A flushed face or raised tone is not necessarily a willful sin.

However, anger crouches at sin's door. Mismanaged, it can be destructive to the offender and the offended. Suppressed, it can nurture bitterness, depression, and a stifling passiveness. Your best tactic in handling this powerful emotional current is to approach its expression with much caution.

The Bible says the believer should be slow to anger (Prov. 16:32; James 1:19). If you are constantly at a boiling point over even minor matters, then you probably have treaded into hazardous territory. Your anger should be short-lived. "Do not let the sun go down on your wrath," Paul said (Eph. 4:26). When angry feelings keep you awake at night, meet you in the shower in the morning, or race through your mind during the day, you are living on a ragged spiritual edge. God's peace and joy are fleeting.

If you blow up often, tell the Lord you want to change, and ask Him to bring your emotions under His control. If your temper short-circuited today, confess your sin now, and don't carry your grudge into tomorrow.

Keep me from mismanaged anger, Lord. Help me bring every emotion under Your control.

An Anger-Ridden Spirit

SCRIPTURE READING: 1 Samuel 25:2–38   KEY VERSE: Proverbs 29:8

Scoffers set a city aflame,
But wise men turn away wrath.

David was furious. He and his fatigued cadre of wilderness warriors had sought provisions from a rich businessman named Nabal, whose flock of sheep and herdsmen they had protected.

Nabal spurned David's request. David's response was quick and vivid. "Every man gird on his sword," he ordered his fighting men (1 Sam. 25:13). Only the intervention of Nabal's circumspect wife, Abigail, prevented David from murdering Nabal and his men.

You probably have never reached this level of hostility, but seething anger has no doubt caused you to consider irrational acts or erupt in speech you wish you could later retract. This illustration is marked with several takeaway principles.

First, it's not the fact that we are angry that matters; it's what you do with your anger that counts. Everybody gets angry. But does your anger remain as the impetus for future deeds and words? David's rage distorted his reasoning and prompted him to vengeful behavior.

Second, you can count on God to assuage your anger. If you take your hostile feelings to Christ, He will always prompt you to turn away from anger.

Third, it is better to trust God for the outcome than to take matters into your hands. If another wrongs you, leave the results to the Lord. Forgive as Christ has forgiven you, and you won't pay the price for an anger-ridden spirit.

Dear heavenly Father, help me trust in You rather than take matters into my own hands. Keep me from an anger-ridden spirit.

An Object of Bitterness

SCRIPTURE READING: Psalm 64:1–10   KEY VERSE: Psalm 69:4

Those who hate me without a cause
Are more than the hairs of my head;
They are mighty who would destroy me,
Being my enemies wrongfully;
Though I have stolen nothing,
I still must restore it.

What should you do when you find yourself the object of another's bitterness? For one, tell yourself the truth about the situation. Anytime you come under personal attack, recall God's personal love for you. Ask Him to encourage you through His Word.

All of us sooner or later will run into someone who is angry or bitter. Using more bitterness to confront the guilty party leads only to a combative situation. Listen to what the bitter person is saying. Bitterness and anger are usually offshoots of deep hurt. You may not be able to turn the bitterness around in someone else's life, but you can stop its continuation by asking God to help you understand why this person is the way he is.

Saying, "It seems that you are really upset. Can we talk about it?" may defuse the situation. Bitterness is much more involved than an act of quick anger. It is a stronghold and needs to be faced in an honest manner.

In Psalm 64, we read how one man prayed for God's deliverance from the attacks of an embittered enemy. When you find yourself the target of an acrid violation, pray for God's protection. Ask Him to give you wisdom in dealing with the other person as well as a healthy perspective on the entire matter. Your reaction to the assault is the most important issue with God. Therefore, be firm but loving in what you do and say.

Father, when I am the target of hostilities, give me the proper perspective in the face of adversity. Help me react firmly in love.

Burden Bearing

SCRIPTURE READING: 2 Corinthians 1:1–5   KEY VERSE: 2 Corinthians 1:5

As the sufferings of Christ abound in us, so our consolation also abounds through Christ.

When you see someone struggling with large packages, what is your first thought? Of course, you have the natural urge to give him a hand. You wouldn't just stand there empty-handed and watch him flounder around and drop things.

What happens, though, when you know someone who is hurting emotionally or struggling under a burden that isn't tangible? That's much more difficult to assess. You wonder whether the person even wants your help or whether it would be right for you to get involved.

The essence of burden bearing is not problem solving. You don't have to fix things for the other person; you simply need to come alongside him and show you care. That's true encouragement. In fact, the person may be more open to your words if he knows you are approaching him in love instead of correction.

"Blessed be the God and Father of our Lord Jesus Christ, the Father of mercies and God of all comfort, who comforts us in all our tribulation, that we may be able to comfort those who are in any trouble, with the comfort with which we ourselves are comforted by God" (2 Cor. 1:3–4).

When you see someone hurting, don't be afraid to offer comfort and compassion. The Lord will show you what to do from there.

Lord, help me reach out to others today to demonstrate comfort and compassion. Make me Your hands extended to a lost and hurting world.

Encouraging Others

SCRIPTURE READING: 2 Corinthians 1:6–11   KEY VERSE: Isaiah 40:1

"Comfort, yes, comfort My people!"
Says your God.

When we see a friend hurting or going through a difficult time, one of our first urges is to think of ways to help fix his situation. It's a natural response. If something's wrong, then there must be a solution. We're often surprised when the person isn't very open to our suggestions and seems to pull away from us.

Think about how you feel when you are down. Which would you rather experience—a warm hug and an expression of love or a discussion of solution alternatives? There is a time for both, but most people prefer a boost of encouragement. Sometimes a friend will come to you specifically for practical tips on how to work through a set of circumstances. If such is the case, don't turn down the request.

However, most of the time your friend will simply need your love and support. Often, God will bring someone into your life who can benefit from specific comfort that you have to offer. For example, if you have lost a loved one, you are better able to talk to someone experiencing deep grief.

"Blessed be the God and Father of our Lord Jesus Christ . . . who comforts us in all our tribulation that we may be able to comfort those who are in any trouble, with the comfort with which we ourselves are comforted by God" (2 Cor. 1:3–4). When you hurt, look for ways to share God's encouragement with others without trying to correct.

I praise You for Your comfort, Father. I receive it. Now help me share that encouragement with others in need.

Seasons of Relationship

SCRIPTURE READING: Galatians 6:1–5   KEY VERSE: Proverbs 27:17

As iron sharpens iron,
So a man sharpens the countenance of his friend.

In her book *Relationships,* Pamela Reeve shares insight on giving in the context of a long-term relationship:

> Commitment is the bond that keeps relationships intact through every storm that rolls over the horizon. There will be times when your friend isn't free to do what you want to do . . . Friends may become preoccupied with new interests or wrestle with heavy, emotionally-draining problems. They may not be functioning well physically. They may not be warm and responsive. Is that the time to abandon the friendship?
>
> Not if you've made a commitment! Your friend may need you more than ever before. "A friend loves at all times, and a brother is born for adversity" (Prov. 17:17). Why are you in the friendship to begin with? For what you can receive? For what you can get out of it to meet your own needs and stroke your own ego?
>
> No, following the example of our Lord, we enter into relationships to give and to bless. There are seasons in every relationship when one is called on to give disproportionately to the other.
>
> There may be years with a difficult elderly parent or a lifetime with an indifferent spouse. Here is where commitment is tested, and here is where you will encounter God's greatest blessings.

Teach me commitment, Lord—to You and to others. Help me not to abandon others when they are in need.

The Power of Encouragement

SCRIPTURE READING: Deuteronomy 3:23–8   KEY VERSE: Proverbs 12:25

Anxiety in the heart of man causes depression,
But a good word makes it glad.

Have you ever hesitated to speak words of encouragement because you weren't sure how they would be received? Being an encourager means reaching out even when you're not sure. You never know the impact you might have. In his book *The Power of Encouragement*, Dr. David Jeremiah explains,

I can be encouraged by what I hear. If I sense someone genuinely cares about me, that person's words can be powerful. As the adage goes, "Nobody cares how much you know until they know how much you care."

The Book of Proverbs speaks often about encouragement. Here's one example: "Anxious hearts are very heavy but a word of encouragement does wonders!" (Prov. 12:25, TLB). Have you ever been weighed down by anxiety when someone came along and spoke a good word which lifted your spirit?

During one of the deepest, darkest times in my life, a fellow pastor called me just to say "I want you to know I'm here if you need me. I want to pray with you." And he prayed with me on the phone. He called me every week for several weeks with a word of encouragement. He poured courage into my heart . . . Believe it or not, two or three sentences can turn a person's life around.

Father, give me words to speak to others that will encourage them in the difficult times of life. Pour Your love and compassion through me to them.

Friendship with Jesus

SCRIPTURE READING: Psalm 67:1–7   KEY VERSE: Isaiah 61:1

The Spirit of the Lord GOD is upon Me,
Because the LORD has anointed Me
To preach good tidings to the poor;
He has sent Me to heal the brokenhearted,
To proclaim liberty to the captives,
And the opening of the prison to those who are bound.

What is God like to you? Do you see Him as Someone who listens to your prayers with an open heart? Or do you imagine that He has His mind made up about your circumstance even before you come to Him?

Jesus had a reason for calling us His friends. He wanted to convey truth to us in such a way that we would accept and not reject the closeness of His love. A friend is someone you can call on any time of the day or night.

She listens patiently without judging the context of your words. She will even let you ramble, knowing you will settle down and come to a reasonable point of view. Friends weather the storms of life together. When life becomes rough and lonely, they hang tough.

Always give the Lord your adoration and devotion, but also be willing to give Him your love through fellowship. Make Him your very best Friend. It's okay to seek the counsel of other godly friends, but make a habit of going to Him first with your heartaches, troubles, and requests. Let Him speak the words of encouragement you so desperately need.

The God who listens as you pray wants you to know that He loves you completely. When you step into His presence, you enter into an inexhaustible pool of possibilities. It is His holy chamber, but it is also a place of loving friendship.

Take me into the holy chamber with You, Father. Let me rest in Your presence and have my vision renewed with limitless possibilities.

Discerning Godly Counsel

SCRIPTURE READING: 1 Kings 12:1–19   KEY VERSE: Proverbs 19:20

Listen to counsel and receive instruction,
That you may be wise in your latter days.

In this Scripture, King Rehoboam refused to listen to the godly advice of at least half his council. He chose, instead, to do what his younger advisors suggested, and the result was a rebellion that swept through the nation of Israel.

What causes a person to listen to ungodly advice? Crucial mistakes often come as a result of selfish ambitions. We weigh our options and choose the ones that appeal to our personal self-interest.

Leaders often surround themselves with people who will agree with their plans, even if those plans ultimately lead to destruction. This may sound unbelievable to some, but it happens. In fact, that was exactly what happened to Rehoboam.

Before he could go through the motions of his coronation as king, the people rebelled against his use of intimidation and misguided power. The Bible tells us, "Israel has been in rebellion against the house of David to this day" (1 Kings 12:19).

Make sure the counsel you receive is from God. Don't be quick to react to the words of others. Instead, spend time in prayer asking the Lord to confirm, guide, and provide the wisdom you need. Had the king listened to his godly advisors, the nation, at least for the time, would have remained united. Instead, Rehoboam's decision led to a costly mistake from which Israel never recovered.

Lord, give me the ability to discern godly counsel. Teach me to wait in prayer for You to confirm, guide, and provide the wisdom I need.

Responding to Criticism

SCRIPTURE READING: Proverbs 13:1–10   KEY VERSE: Proverbs 13:18

Poverty and shame will come to him who disdains correction,
But he who regards a rebuke will be honored.

Think back to the last time someone criticized you. Perhaps it came from family member, coworker, or friend. Perhaps it was totally unexpected and stung you bitterly. Perhaps even your reaction was unexpected in its harshness, pain, or grief.

As believers, we understand that we are not perfect. Sometimes God corrects us on His own. Sometimes He uses others. The criticism you received may have been accurate, and even if it was inaccurate, you can grow from the experience.

If you have had difficulty accepting criticism, ponder how you will react to such words in the future. God can use criticism or praise to mold you, but your attitudes toward both must be healthy.

When you are criticized, for the moment disregard whether it is valid. Disregard the temperament or tone of the critic. Instead, prepare yourself by thinking, *Could this be true?* And then respond in a most disarming fashion: "Thank you very much. I appreciate what you've said, and I'll consider it. Do you have any other suggestions on how I can improve?"

When you meet criticism with humility, you reveal your teachability. You won't need to change every time, but occasionally, you will receive valid criticism. A humble heart and receptive spirit can transform a potentially ugly, abrasive moment into lasting polish.

Give me a humble and teachable heart, dear Lord. Help me accept and respond to valid criticism in a positive way.

Eternal Friendship

SCRIPTURE READING: Luke 10:1–9   KEY VERSE: Proverbs 18:24

A man who has friends must himself be friendly,
But there is a friend who sticks closer than a brother.

Jesus did not send His disciples out alone. He sent them two by two. This is a strong indication that God intends for us to need the help and companionship of others. Ecclesiastes 4:9–10 tells us,

> Two are better than one
> Because they have a good return for their labor.
> For if they fall, one will lift up his companion.

Friendship softens us and makes us easier to live with. God uses the presence of friends to remind us of Himself. Often the avenue of blessing begins with a friend. But beyond our earth-bound friendships is the love of Christ, who is our dearest Friend. Through His Spirit, we receive the gift of His friendship.

The Holy Spirit instructs us in the ways of God, provides discernment, shouts a warning when we get off course, and provides a deep, residing sense of peace to all who have learned to rest in Christ. But the Spirit's greatest goal is to lead us into an intimate relationship with the Lord Jesus Christ.

Nothing comes close to the friendship you can have with God through the Holy Spirit. In the Greek language, He is our Comforter—the One who has been instructed to come alongside us whenever we are hurting, lonely, or fearful.

Jesus told His disciples, "I will never leave you." He meant it. The Holy Spirit is Christ living in you, your eternal source of friendship.

Lord, thank You for Your eternal friendship. I will never be alone. You are always with me.

Healing for Your Heart

SCRIPTURE READING: Psalm 37:1–40   KEY VERSE: Psalm 37:9

Evildoers shall be cut off;
But those who wait on the LORD,
They shall inherit the earth.

One subject that dominates many Christian counseling sessions is the subject of abuse. People seek help in working through the emotional agony that comes from being abused.

We now understand that abuse can be emotional, physical, or psychological. A controlling, domineering person can do as much damage as one who physically takes advantage of another person.

The devastation that follows abuse is a damaged personhood with undertows of low self-esteem, guilt, and shame. Abuse of any kind strikes at the core of who we are and, if not attended to, can put a thick covering over God's intended purpose for our lives. Those who have been abused often say they feel worthless, shameful, and purposeless. It is difficult to imagine why such pain happens. However, denying it does not remove or help the hurt.

Most of us know someone who has suffered due to the thoughtless actions of another. At times, healing may seem difficult. If you have been abused and continue to struggle emotionally and mentally, you may want to talk with your pastor or a trusted Christian friend. Ask him to listen and then to pray with you about what has happened in your life. While thoughts of revenge are a natural response, they cause only more heartache. God wants to set you free. Give Him your emotional pain, and He will bring healing to your heart.

Heavenly Father, take all my emotional baggage, and bring healing to my heart. Help me forgive my abuser. Set me free from the pain.

Born for Adversity

SCRIPTURE READING: Psalm 35:9–15   KEY VERSE: Proverbs 17:17

A friend loves at all times,
And a brother is born for adversity.

You've probably heard the homespun phrase that you never know who your real friends are until trouble comes. But perhaps you didn't realize that a biblical principle is behind the saying.

Today's verse states, "A friend loves at all times, and a brother is born for adversity." Maybe you've wondered who among your friends would love you at all times, not just when there are peace and plenty. But have you ever stopped to consider whether you are that kind of friend? Are you a brother or sister who was born for adversity?

One of life's most difficult challenges is to be a stalwart for a hurting friend, particularly if his trial involves potential wrongdoing or error on his part. Sometimes we are quicker to judge and condemn than to pray and be available to vicariously share a burden.

Take a moment to consider how you have reacted to the adversities of your friends throughout the years. Did you steer clear for a while until the situation settled? Did you cease relations altogether? Or did you put an arm around your struggling buddy and lend an ear, encouragement, and prayer?

Christ called His disciples friends. And when they hurt, He was there. Always. His example remains perfect today, and you'll never know what kind of real friend you are until their trouble comes.

Dear Lord, help me be a true friend to those in need, a strength to the weak,
a comfort to the hurting.

Responsibility and Forgiveness

SCRIPTURE READING: Luke 6:31–37   KEY VERSE: 1 Timothy 1:5

The purpose of the commandment is love from a pure heart, from a good conscience, and from sincere faith.

Being unforgiving and blaming others go hand in hand. In his book *Healing for Damaged Emotions,* David Seamands discusses responsibility and forgiveness:

> Facing responsibility and forgiving people are really two sides of the same coin. The reason some people have never been able to forgive is that if they forgave, the last rug would be pulled out from under them and they would have no one to blame. Facing responsibility and forgiving are almost the same action; in some instances you need to do them simultaneously. Jesus made it very plain that no healing occurs until there is deep forgiveness.

Some people fail to experience the joy of God's grace because a spirit of unforgiveness burdens them. False guilt, which means feeling guilty for something you did not do, is a joy killer. So is unforgiveness. If this is something you struggle with, ask a godly friend to help you see God's truth about your life. Be honest and willing to take responsibility for your feelings.

Another way you may fail to experience the freedom that God has planned for you is by refusing to forgive yourself for past sins. Allow the Lord to show you the way to complete healing. Once you do this, you won't be so quick to blame others because you will be too busy praising God and enjoying His goodness to get caught up in the blame game!

> *Dear Lord, You died not only for my sins, but also for my shame. If You carried it, I no longer need to carry it. Take it all—the guilt, the blame, the shame.*

Bearing Spiritual Fruit

SCRIPTURE READING: Galatians 5:22–25   KEY VERSE: John 15:5

I am the vine, you are the branches. He who abides in Me, and I in him, bears much fruit; for without Me you can do nothing.

Planning how to respond to a rival's torts and retorts is easy enough. We can pray and try to mentally prepare ourselves to be strong in our character and take the high road. But as Christians, we realize Satan wishes to bring us down. We all have experienced the difficulty in sticking to a preconceived formula when a relationship takes another bad turn.

Ephesians 6:12 tells us that our struggle is not against flesh and blood but against spiritual forces of wickedness in high places—against Satan's army. Don't take your rival's barbs personally, and don't respond in a way that assaults his personhood. Your real contention is with an element that you can't even see.

The strength to react in this manner is not self-generated. Instead, your capacity to respond properly to testy people in testy situations comes only from the Holy Spirit with whom you are indwelt. The power of Jesus can turn bitter water into sweet wine.

Notice that love, joy, peace, patience, kindness, goodness, faithfulness, gentleness, and self-control are fruit of the Spirit, spelled with a capital *S*. It is the Spirit of Jesus within you that will prompt right responses.

John 15:5 says that ensuring proper reactions is as natural as the agricultural process: all you must do is abide in the True Vine to bear the fruit of the Spirit.

Heavenly Father, help me abide in the Vine and bear the fruit of Your Spirit. Release your love, joy, peace, patience, kindness, goodness, faithfulness, gentleness, and self-control to flow through my life.

Responding to Rejection

SCRIPTURE READING: Colossians 1:18–22   KEY VERSE: John 1:22

Then they said to him, "Who are you, that we may give an answer
to those who sent us? What do you say about yourself?"

It is one of Satan's favorite traps to get a child of God to feel belittled by himself. Often, when people feel a gnawing sense of rejection, it comes not from an outside source such as criticism, but from within. Many people feel rejected because they've rejected themselves.

The root of these feelings could be one of many factors: something that happened in the past, an overbearing or apathetic parent, perceived physical flaws. These feelings also can manifest themselves for decades. Well into their adult years, people who feel rejection may practice perfectionism or be domineering or seek isolation.

If you are a believer, you are a child of God. If Satan buffets you with feelings of rejection or the notion that you do not measure up, let your Father answer him:

- John 1:12 declares, "But as many as received Him, to them He gave the right to become children of God, to those who believe in His name."
- John 3:16 tells you that God loves you so much that He sent His Son, Jesus, to die for your sins.
- In 1 John 3:1, you again learn the liberating truth that the only opinion that matters belongs to God.
- And you belong to Him too: "Behold what manner of love the Father has bestowed on us, that we should be called children of God!" (1 John 3:1).

I am Your child, Father—a child of the King. Help me realize it and act like
who I really am in You.

Unity of the Spirit

SCRIPTURE READING: Ephesians 4:1–16   KEY VERSE: Ephesians 4:15

But, speaking the truth in love, may grow up in all things into Him who is the head—Christ.

The structure and function of the human body are complex and endlessly fascinating. Even with all of the advances in modern biotechnology, scientists and doctors do not know everything about it. What they do understand, however, is that all of the body's organs and fluids work together in an intricate harmony.

When something goes wrong with one part, the entire body is affected in some way. All processes must be in good working order for the body to be healthy and growing. That is the way the body of Christ functions as well. We all work together and operate as one organic unit when we recognize our connectedness with Jesus as the Head.

Ephesians 4:15–16 explains this relationship: "But, speaking the truth in love, may grow up in all things into Him who is the head—Christ—from whom the whole body, joined and knit together by what every joint supplies, according to the effective working by which every part does its share, causes growth of the body for the edifying of itself in love."

If one part of the body is diseased or hurting, the entire body suffers. Trying to ignore the problems of one person is as futile and ultimately harmful as ignoring cancer and hoping it will just go away. Jesus wants us to come to Him to resolve difficulties and restore wounded members.

Dear heavenly Father, join me in vital union to Your spiritual body. Connect me by the Spirit to Your church.

OCTOBER

Revelation, Knowing God's Voice

MOUNTAIN: **Mount Horeb**

KEY VERSES: **1 Kings 19:11–18**

Then [God] said, "Go out, and stand on the mountain before the LORD." And behold, the LORD passed by, and a great and strong wind tore into the mountains and broke the rocks in pieces before the LORD, but the LORD was not in the wind; and after the wind an earthquake, but the LORD was not in the earthquake; and after the earthquake a fire, but the LORD was not in the fire; and after the fire a still small voice. So it was, when Elijah heard it, that he wrapped his face in his mantle and went out and stood in the entrance of the cave. Suddenly a voice came to him, and said, "What are you doing here, Elijah?" And he said, "I have been very zealous for the LORD God of hosts; because the children of Israel have forsaken Your covenant, torn down Your altars, and killed Your prophets with the sword. I alone am left; and they seek to take my life." Then the LORD said to him: "Go, return on your way to the Wilderness of Damascus; and when you arrive, anoint Hazael as king over Syria. Also you shall anoint Jehu the son of Nimshi as king over Israel. And Elisha the son of Shaphat of Abel Meholah you shall anoint as prophet in your place. It shall be that whoever escapes the sword of Hazael, Jehu will kill; and whoever escapes from the sword of Jehu, Elisha will kill. Yet I have reserved seven thousand in Israel, all whose knees have not bowed to Baal, and every mouth that has not kissed him."

On the Mountain with Jesus

SCRIPTURE READING: Mark 9:1–9   KEY VERSE: Matthew 17:5

While he was still speaking, behold, a bright cloud overshadowed them; and suddenly a voice came out of the cloud, saying, "This is My beloved Son, in whom I am well pleased. Hear Him!"

Peter, James, and John followed Jesus up the high mountain. They must have been mystified, knowing somehow it was a journey during which something important would happen.

Suddenly, Jesus was transformed before their eyes into a dazzling figure, "Shining, exceedingly white, like snow, such as no launderer on earth can whiten them" (Mark 9:3). And to add to their astonishment, Elijah and Moses appeared beside Jesus, talking with Him.

Peter's reaction was much as ours would probably be: "He did not know what to say, for they were greatly afraid" (Mark 9:6). He wanted to build the radiant figures tabernacles right there on the mountain, to preserve the beautiful moment and keep the vision before their eyes. But Jesus did not answer the request, and the heavenly spectacle was over almost as soon is it had begun. In fact, Jesus even told them not to speak about it until after He had risen from the dead.

When God gives you a special glimpse of His holiness—an intimate view of Himself— He doesn't let you remain in that place indefinitely. He wants you to come back down from the mountain and let His glory fill your heart as you go about the business of daily living. A deeper understanding of His greatness will give you encouragement and energy, and He wants His glory to shine forth from your life as you draw closer to Him.

Father, help me reflect in the valleys of everyday life what I receive in the mountaintop experiences with You.

The Will of God

SCRIPTURE READING: Romans 12:1–2   KEY VERSE: Micah 6:8

He has shown you, O man, what is good;
And what does the LORD require of you
But to do justly,
To love mercy,
And to walk humbly with your God?

What is God's will for your life? Does it include some detailed, elaborate plan with twists and turns and heroic acts? Chances are, it doesn't. The will of God is basically a reflection of the words written by the prophet Micah (Mic. 6:8).

The will of God is not that difficult to discover, though many fail to experience it. Their sights are set on what they believe God wants them to achieve. God's will for you and me is simply a matter of loving Him. He may call you to a certain profession, but this is not His ultimate goal. His goal in the life of a believer is one of intimate fellowship.

It is true that God has a plan for your life that corresponds with His will. When God thinks of you, He thinks thoughts of love and mercy, hope and goodness. You can spend a lifetime trying to achieve recognition and a sense of accomplishment, but when you die, the only things that will matter are your love for and obedience to God's Son.

When you surrender your will to God, He will make sure your life is in line with His perfect plan. The blessings that follow, and there are many, will only bring a sense of satisfaction to all that you do.

Lord, help me to act justly, love mercy, and walk humbly with You. I surrender my will to You. Bring my life into alignment with Your perfect plan.

God's Provision

SCRIPTURE READING: 2 Kings 6:8–23   KEY VERSE: Psalm 27:1

The LORD is my light and my salvation;
Whom shall I fear?
The LORD is the strength of my life;
Of whom shall I be afraid?

Do you remember looking through a microscope for the first time? Your eyes were opened to a teeming world of protozoan life. You had to look at the droplet in a new and different way to perceive another dimension of the physical world.

Elisha's servant had to learn to look at their circumstances in a new way. Things looked bad for them on the surface. The king of Syria and his men were angry with Elisha because they knew God told Elisha their attack strategies in advance; and of course, Elisha told their plans to the king of Israel.

It's no surprise that the Syrians wanted to do away with Elisha. So one night, the king of Syria sent horses and chariots and an army to surround the city where Elisha was staying. At first sight, Elisha's attendant went outside and saw the army circled to attack.

He ran to Elisha and cried, "Alas, my master! What shall we do?" But Elisha wasn't panicked. He said, "Do not fear, for those who are with us are more than those who are with them" (2 Kings 6:15–16). The attendant must have been mightily confused. The only people he saw were the ones with weapons pointed at them.

Then Elisha prayed for God to open his eyes, and the attendant saw an angelic host with horses and chariots of fire surrounding them. God had already arranged for their protection, but the attendant had to learn to see His provision.

Father, I thank You that You have already arranged for my protection.
Open my eyes to Your provision.

The Rewards of Waiting

SCRIPTURE READING: 1 Samuel 1:1–28   KEY VERSE: Psalm 27:14

Wait on the LORD;
Be of good courage,
And He shall strengthen your heart;
Wait, I say, on the LORD!

You've just finished gathering all the ingredients for baking, and you mix them together carefully in a large bowl. Then you pour the batter evenly in two round pans and slide them gently onto the oven rack. You set the timer and sit back for a while to enjoy the delicious smells coming from the kitchen.

Suppose that twenty minutes before the timer rings you decide you want to take the cake out of the oven anyway. It's only partially baked, with gooey spots everywhere, and obviously isn't fit for consumption.

Such a decision would be ridiculous, wouldn't it? Yet in an interesting way that scenario parallels what we do as believers when we try to outrun God's timing and take ourselves out of His preparation time too soon. We do not give Him time to reveal His purposes in the way He knows is best.

Hannah is an inspiration in the area of spiritual patience. She knew that God was the One in charge of whether she would conceive a child, and she took her sorrows and fears to Him daily. We don't know how long Hannah waited on the Lord. All the Bible says in 1 Samuel 1:7 is "year by year." What a wearying process, especially with the taunts of Peninnah.

God knows what you need. Don't give up and try to satisfy that need your own way. Wait on Him, and He will take care of you according to His goodness.

Heavenly Father, I thank You that I can rest in the assurance that You know exactly what I need.

Provision and Instruction

SCRIPTURE READING: 2 Timothy 3:14–17   KEY VERSE: Psalm 119:105

Your word is a lamp to my feet
And a light to my path.

Many people approach the subject of God's will with a good deal of fear and confusion. A certain air of mystery seems to surround it, as though finding His will is a lifelong hunt for a hidden and hard-to-find secret purpose.

It's true that God doesn't tell you everything about your entire life right now. You cannot possibly know all that He has in store for you. God is interested in your relationship with Him today, and along the way of day-by-day walking with Him, He unfolds your path according to the light of His Word (Ps. 119:105). He wants you to let Him lead.

In his book *Knowing and Doing the Will of God*, J. I. Packer explains,

> Scripture presents guidance as a covenant blessing promised to each of God's people in the form of instruction on how to live, both in broad policy terms and in making particular decisions.
>
> How does God guide? By instructing. How does he instruct? Partly by his shaping of our circumstances, and partly by his gift of wisdom to understand and digest the teaching of his word and to apply it to ourselves in our circumstances.
>
> So God's regular method of guidance is a combination of providential and instructional action . . . Wisdom will always be given if we are humble and docile enough to receive it.

Father, design my circumstances to lead me to the center of Your will. Give
me the wisdom to understand and digest the teaching of Your Word.

A Change of Plans

SCRIPTURE READING: 2 Corinthians 1:12–24   KEY VERSE: Psalm 31:3

For You are my rock and my fortress;
Therefore, for Your name's sake,
Lead me and guide me.

When a pilot flies a plane, he remains in touch with the tower at all times. The instruments on board the plane give him much information and help him make decisions, but he always makes choices within the context of the flight plan and instructions from the tower. There are even some critical moments when the pilot needs the tower to send him data for midcourse corrections.

At the beginning of his second letter to the Corinthians, Paul was explaining to them the reason for his midcourse alteration in plans. Some in the church thought that Paul had changed his plans to visit them based on human whim and felt that he was therefore unspiritual and unreliable.

Paul responded: "When I was planning this, did I do it lightly? Or the things I plan, do I plan according to the flesh? . . . But as God is faithful, our word to you was not Yes and No" (2 Cor. 1:17–18). Paul's itinerary was changed because God led him in another direction for a time, and Paul was obedient—even when it cost him his reputation in the eyes of certain suspicious church members.

Are you open to a change in plans if you sense God moving in another direction? Sometimes it's easy to confuse what you desire with what God wants. Ask Him to sort out the truth and help you become flexible and obedient.

Dear God, keep me open to a change in plans when I sense You moving in another direction. Don't let me confuse what I desire with Your plan for me.

Hearing Tests

SCRIPTURE READING: Ephesians 5:15–17   KEY VERSE: Psalm 19:12

Who can understand his errors?
Cleanse me from secret faults.

If you have been through a time in which you felt God was silent, you remember the disquiet you experienced in your inner being. Sometimes God chooses to withhold specific direction for a while. He wants you to wait on Him with a spirit of obedience and expectancy. However, it's always important to examine your heart because something there may block your ability to hear Him.

The influence of others might be getting in the way. If people close to you give you counsel, the temptation is strong to listen. They may be right. God may use them to direct you. But if they're wrong, then your ties of affection may actually bind you. It's so natural to want to please others that you may interpret that urge as trying to please the Lord.

A sin in your life may prevent good communication with the Lord. If you ask Him to reveal any problem areas, He certainly will. More than you can imagine, God wants you to be free of sin habits and the guilt that goes with them. He has already forgiven you in Christ, but you still need to confess and repent.

Finally, be sure to ask yourself, Do I really believe God wants to guide me? If you feel confused right now, maybe it's time for you to take these "hearing tests."

Dear Lord, don't let others influence me in decisions. Continually cleanse me
from sin so that the lines of communication will remain open between us.

Asking for Help

SCRIPTURE READING: Psalm 32:1–11   KEY VERSE: Psalm 32:8

I will instruct you and teach you in the way you should go;
I will guide you with My eye.

Are you secretly afraid to ask the Lord for guidance? Maybe you harbor the belief that what you need is not important enough to talk to God about, that somehow your request is too small. Catherine Marshall addresses this issue in her book *Adventures in Prayer*:

> A little child who has no shyness or hesitation about asking his parents for what he needs is unselfconsciously revealing his helplessness, along with a normal, right relationship with his father and mother.
>
> In the same way, asking immediately puts us into a right relationship to God. It is acting out of the fact that He is the Creator with the riches and resources we need; we are the creatures who need help. It's a cap-in-hand stance which we resist because it diminishes us—a certain amount of pride and self has to go for us to ask for help, whether of God or of another human being.
>
> Simple happenings uncover our pride and stubbornness about asking like the motorist who loses his way. Often we will go miles off our route, waste time trying one road after another, rather than stop and ask for the help we need. God insists that we ask, not because He needs to know our situation, but because we need the spiritual discipline of asking. Similarly, making our requests specific forces us to take a step forward in faith.

I step forward in faith, Lord. I bring my requests to You, believing that You will guide me in every circumstance of my life.

Straight Paths

SCRIPTURE READING: Proverbs 3:1–12   KEY VERSES: Proverbs 3:5–6

Trust in the LORD with all your heart,
And lean not on your own understanding;
In all your ways acknowledge Him,
And He shall direct your paths.

As we listen for God's still small voice to direct and guide us, we find Solomon's words in Proverbs 3 to be especially meaningful.

When we place our trust in the Lord, we essentially lay down our right to attempt what only God can do—determine the destiny of our lives. One of the reasons we struggle greatly at times is that we resist His intervention.

We brush aside His plan for our lives but not without consequence. In doing so, we often settle for second best. For many, it is easy to accept His love, protection, and salvation but difficult to submit to the conditions surrounding His eternal care.

Is there a war raging within you? Do you fight feelings of jealousy, anger, unforgiveness, and pride? These are the signatures of the flesh that are at constant war with God's principles and standards. They have nothing to do with the moving of His Spirit and everything to do with what keeps you from becoming all He desires.

The principles of God are timeless, and you never outgrow your need for them. Ask the Lord to open the eyes and ears of your heart so you may know His perfect will.

Help me trust and acknowledge You, Lord, rather than lean to my own understanding. Make my paths straight.

In the Presence of God

SCRIPTURE READING: Psalm 95:1–7   KEY VERSE: Isaiah 58:11

The LORD will guide you continually,
And satisfy your soul in drought,
And strengthen your bones;
You shall be like a watered garden,
And like a spring of water, whose waters do not fail.

You live in a fallen world. But as a believer in Christ, you do not have to operate with a fallen attitude. God's presence in you renews your mind. However, you must make a choice to seek God's guidance or go your own way. He has given you the Holy Spirit as His representative. And while the Spirit has many roles, one of the most energizing is His role as communicator of God's love, forgiveness, and truth.

When you speak to Christ in prayer, the Holy Spirit motivates you and encourages you by communicating God's mind and heart to yours. He enables you to think God's thoughts, live a godly life, and become the person you are called to be in Christ.

Many overlook God's will for their lives by thinking that He is not interested in them. The sad truth is that their minds and lives are too full of activity to allow entry by God. They rush from one mental dilemma to another, never realizing that God is standing by, calling to them. In the end, they wonder why God is not speaking, but He does, just as much as He did during Old and New Testament times.

Does God have your attention, or are you drawn away by other things? You can practice His presence anywhere. Know that when you commit yourself to a personal time of devotion, God will meet you there.

Dear Lord, thank You for the Holy Spirit who communicates Your love, forgiveness, and truth as I come into Your presence today.

A Way in the Wilderness

SCRIPTURE READING: Isaiah 43:18–19   KEY VERSE: Philippians 4:13

I can do all things through Christ who strengthens me.

It is amazing how God's still small voice can echo so loudly as soon as we step outside His plans for us. The restlessness we sometimes feel but can't figure out may be a sure sign God is working in our lives. "Behold, I will do a new thing," God promises in Isaiah. He doesn't say that He could or might do something. He says He will do it. So what hinders Him? Almost exclusively, we do.

God often sends frustration, a slight pressure, a restlessness to keep us from settling outside His will. We may think we know best about the most mundane of crossroads, but God has a unique way of showing us when we're wrong.

If you feel certain that you are right about a circumstance, honestly assess whether you have conferred with God enough to have reached your conclusion. Have you asked His opinion? Have you searched His Word? Have you asked His guidance?

If you are within God's will, His restlessness may fill you when you are about to step outside His will. If you already have stumbled, you will never have true peace until you have asked His forgiveness and guidance down even your most familiar paths. It boils down to a matter of trust. Do you trust an all-powerful God who loves you so much that He pledges to make roadways in the wilderness and rivers in the desert?

Father, I trust You to make a way in the wilderness of this world. Don't let me settle for anything less than Your perfect will.

Set Free to Take Risks

SCRIPTURE READING: Psalm 1:1–6   KEY VERSE: 1 John 4:18

There is no fear in love; but perfect love casts out fear, because fear involves torment. But he who fears has not been made perfect in love.

God enables us to do His will, and His presence, peace, power, and provision guarantee our achieving His end.

In *Telling Yourself the Truth*, author William Backus addresses the lack of confidence that paralyzes many Christians:

> The misbelief that it is stupid or sinful to make decisions which might turn out wrong is unfounded. We're told to be wise as serpents, harmless as doves. Wisdom does not mean acting in fear or cowardice.
>
> Perfect love casts out fear means to us that the love of God has wiped out the power of fear over our lives if we will use God's methods of conquering it. "Cast your fears [cares] on Me!" He explains. "Give them to Me! I know what to do with them." It is in this way we are set free to take risks.
>
> Then whether we succeed or fail is not our utmost concern. We are not enslaved by fear of negative results. We willingly allow ourselves possible failure, possible negative results. Painful fear and anxiety no longer play a dominant role in our lives.
>
> The Christian walking by the Spirit, in the will of God, can trust that outcomes of his actions in faith are totally in the hands of the Father. The truth for the Christian is that disaster, catastrophe, or utter defeat cannot occur. We have no business thinking in those terms!
>
> God never fails.

Here they are, Lord—all my fears, cares, and worries. I give them to You. Free me to take risks.

Seeking God's Will

SCRIPTURE READING: John 16:7–15   KEY VERSE: John 16:13

When He, the Spirit of truth, has come, He will guide you into all truth; for He will not speak on His own authority, but whatever He hears He will speak; and He will tell you things to come.

Former pastor Henry Blackaby is helping countless Christians answer their questions in seeking the will of God. In his popular book *Experiencing God*, Blackaby says we should not ask, "What is God's will for my life?" Rather, we should ask, "What is God's will?"

Right now God is working all around you and in your life. One of the greatest tragedies among God's people is that, while they have a deep longing to experience God, they are experiencing God day after day but do not know how to recognize Him.

Blackaby writes,

> The Holy Spirit and the Word of God will instruct you and help you know when and where God is working. Once you know where He is working, you will adjust your life to join Him where He is working.
>
> You will experience His accomplishing His activity through your life. When you enter this kind of intimate love relationship with God, you will know and do the will of God and experience Him in ways you have never known Him before. I cannot accomplish that goal in your life. Only God can bring you into that kind of relationship.

The relationship comes first. If you have received no clear direction about how to serve the Lord, perhaps it is time to deepen your fellowship with Jesus. The Christian life is a marathon that begins with a walk.

Dear heavenly Father, strengthen my relationship with You. I want to experience You in ways I have never known before.

Your Way or God's Way?

SCRIPTURE READING: Psalm 119:129–136   KEY VERSE: Psalm 27:11

Teach me Your way, O LORD,
And lead me in a smooth path, because of my enemies.

A father carefully explained the basics of safe driving to his newly licensed son. The boy ignored the message: "Dad, I already know how to drive. There's nothing you can really tell me." But a subsequent trip to the grocery store ended with a thud in the parking lot—the result of rear-ending a slow-moving vehicle.

We sometimes operate in the same stubborn manner. We make our plans, do it our way, and tag God onto the end. But since God's ways are higher—different and better—than ours, we do well to follow His plan of action.

How can you know God's ways when the path is unclear, the next step tentative at best? The best means to know God's way is to know His Word. God's Word expresses His will and character; and the better you know it, the more familiar you are with His ways.

Just as important is to be filled with the Holy Spirit, your Guide for rough ground and Teacher for perplexing circumstances. God is not reluctant to help you in time of need; you simply need to confess your helplessness and sincerely lean your weight on the Holy Spirit's ability.

Tell God you want to know His way in your situation. Then expect Him to show you. You won't be disappointed.

God, I want to know Your plan. Show me. Be my Guide through perplexing circumstances.

When God Doesn't Make Sense

SCRIPTURE READING: Hebrews 11:1–3   KEY VERSE: Psalm 25:20

Keep my soul, and deliver me;
Let me not be ashamed, for I put my trust in You.

If you have played the game blindman's bluff, then you know how it feels to be led when you cannot see where you are going.

With a blindfold around your eyes, you are forced to rely completely on your guide. If he says turn right and take three steps, you turn right and take three steps. Eventually, if you listen attentively and follow all the commands as given, you arrive safely at the destination. But suppose you choose to ignore the leader. He says turn right, and you swing left instead. Very likely, you are headed for a crash; you cannot see anything, yet you walk as though you can see the path clearly.

Have you ever felt blind in your circumstances? Are you struggling to understand what is going on in your life? Just a few months ago or even yesterday, you thought you knew where you were going. Then the unforeseen occurred—an illness, an accident, a death, an unwanted job change, a relationship gone sour.

Trying to work out the situation by yourself, selecting the path that seems best in your own eyes, can lead you away from close fellowship with your Savior and obscure the blessings that He gives you when you rest in His guidance. Trust the Lord to show the way.

When the unforeseen occurs, help me trust You, Lord. Don't let the trials of life obscure the pathway of Your will.

A Zeal for God

SCRIPTURE READING: Psalm 63:1–11   KEY VERSE: John 17:3

This is eternal life, that they may know You, the only true God, and Jesus Christ whom You have sent.

Jesus defined eternal life in John 17:3, our key verse today. Thus, while eternal life is certainly the possession of unending fellowship with Christ, the principal context is the quality of relationship with your Savior.

There is no substitute for a personal hunger to know Christ experientially. The God who sought you and saved you jealously desires to reveal Himself to you. But you must pursue Him.

"Everything is made to center upon the initial act of 'accepting' Christ (a term, incidentally, which is not found in the Bible) and we are not expected thereafter to crave any further revelation of God to our souls," A. W. Tozer wrote in *The Pursuit of God*.

> We have been snared in the coils of a spurious logic which insists that if we found Him we need no more seek Him.
>
> I want deliberately to encourage a mighty longing after God. The lack of it has brought us to our present low estate. The stiff and wooden quality about our religious lives is a result of our lack of holy desire. Complacency is a deadly foe of all spiritual growth. Acute desire must be present or there will be no manifestation of Christ to His people.

If your heart for God has dimmed, seek Him today. As Tozer announced, "He waits to be wanted."

Dear Lord, don't let my zeal for You grow dim. Don't let complacency hamper my spiritual growth. Manifest Yourself to me today in a new and deeper dimension.

How to Seek the Lord

Scripture reading: Isaiah 55:6–9   Key verse: Deuteronomy 4:29

But from there you will seek the Lord *your God, and you will find Him if you seek Him with all your heart and with all your soul.*

Here are some practical helps for seeking the Lord:
Seek God out of your need but be willing to accept His solution. Many of the psalms are the heart cries of God's people in deep distress. Their persecution, loneliness, anxiety, fears, and troubles have led them to a point of desperation. God often uses extremity to press you to Himself. You seek Him because you are in arduous straits.

Be careful not to seek the quick or easy way out of your dilemma. That would lessen your pain, but it may not be God's way of escape. Don't let the urgency of your need obscure God's wise and loving answer.

Seek counsel from others. Seeking God first and foremost is about knowing who He is. However, realize that He frequently reveals Himself through the counsel of others. When you seek God, you are receptive to the means He chooses to help and comfort you, including the loving touch of a friend, pastor, or counselor. Be alert to His leadership as you read Christian material and converse with other believers.

Try fasting as part of the seeking process. Fasting can be helpful on occasions, especially when your need is crucial. Skip a meal or two—or more as God directs—and you will find your focus on Christ even sharper. Fasting indicates you mean serious business with God.

> *Dear Lord, help me realize that extremity presses me closer to You. Help me not to seek an easy, quick way out of my problem. Don't let the urgency of my need obscure Your plan.*

Adjusting to God's Plan

SCRIPTURE READING: Matthew 4:18–20   KEY VERSE: Matthew 16:18

I also say to you that you are Peter, and on this rock I will build My church, and the gates of Hades shall not prevail against it.

There are plenty of examples of people who believe they should do one thing when God has another idea in mind. That was the case with the apostle Peter. When Jesus found him, he was totally engulfed by his work.

He believed that the Sea of Galilee was where he belonged. Yet Jesus knew differently. Peter was a hard worker, very committed, and loyal to those who worked alongside him. He also had a longing for the Messiah to come. Some scholars believe he was a Zealot—a member of a religious faction that was ready, if necessary, to physically fight for Israel's freedom from Roman rule.

However, Jesus' plan for Peter's life did not include overthrowing governments. It consisted of overthrowing hearts for the glory of God. It took Peter years to grasp that principle. After Jesus' death, he desperately tried to regain control by returning to his fishing boat and nets, but everything felt empty without Jesus. God did not allow Peter to fall back into his old way of life.

Jesus came to him and reminded him that he was Peter, the rock! With his heart and life—and with others who had similar hearts and lives—Jesus would establish His church on earth.

God has a plan for your life. It may be different from the one you envision. The key to great blessing is being willing to adjust your plan to God's will.

Father, Your plan may be different from the one I envision. Help me bring my plans into conformity with Your will.

Moving Forward in Faith

SCRIPTURE READING: 2 Chronicles 17:3–5   KEY VERSE: 1 Thessalonians 5:24

He who calls you is faithful, who also will do it.

Jehoshaphat had admonished Israel to return to the Lord, reminding a rebellious nation of the God who had freed it from bondage in Egypt and sustained it through much adversity. Then came the report that three tribes were mounting an attack on Israel.

Jehoshaphat's response was a godly example not only for Israel but also for us today. The king's first act was to immediately seek the Lord. By doing so, Jehoshaphat inherently demonstrated the knowledge that God is interested in all of man's problems and that nothing is bigger than God.

Becoming a Christian does not give you a free ride from the problems of life. When you encounter trouble, your first response always should be to seek the Lord. God will give you a solution to the problem in His timing. You may have to wait for His answer, and the wait may be long. He often uses such times to mold your character and to teach you principles He knows you lack. Sometimes, you may not be ready for His perfect answer, so He has to prepare you.

Finally, God's answer to your Christ-centered (not problem-centered) prayers usually requires an act of faith on your part. Sometimes—as with having a choir lead an army into battle—His plans won't immediately make sense. But they are perfect. "He who calls you is faithful, who also will do it" (1 Thess. 5:24).

I choose Your way, Lord—even when it doesn't make sense in the natural. Give me the strength to move forward in faith.

Waiting to Act

SCRIPTURE READING: Psalm 139:1–8   KEY VERSE: Psalm 55:22

Cast your burden on the LORD,
And He shall sustain you;
He shall never permit the righteous to be moved.

The toddler climbed to the top step of the plastic slide in the backyard and lifted one leg onto the top platform. With one leg on the top of the slide and the other on the top step, his undeveloped coordination left him trapped. He couldn't move either leg.

"Daaaaaddyyyyy!"

The toddler knew exactly what to do next. In his moment of complete helplessness, with fear setting in as he was stranded several feet above the ground, he called for his daddy. Watching nearby, the dad moved in to save the day. What child wouldn't immediately cry out to the nearest authority? What father wouldn't act quickly in such a situation?

When hit with a trial or when bad news comes our way, our most effective response is to immediately say, "Father." Not only does this immediately stunt the problem from growing into something that overwhelms us, but it reminds us of our rightful position as children of God.

Our Father says He will never leave us or forsake us. Armed with such a promise, we know that God is under His divine obligation to provide us guidance and direction. There will be many times when life will leave us stretched into an awkward position. We should always remember that our Father is watching nearby, ready to act when called.

Father, I thank You that You will never leave me or forsake me. Help me remember that You are always nearby, just waiting to act in my behalf when called upon to do so.

God's Warning System

SCRIPTURE READING: Deuteronomy 11:22–25   KEY VERSE: Deuteronomy 28:9

The LORD will establish you as a holy people to Himself, just as He has sworn to you, if you keep the commandments of the LORD your God and walk in His ways.

The young family had stepped outside the will of God several months earlier. They stopped attending church regularly, stopped tithing altogether, and gradually decreased in service as their interest in prayer and reading the Bible waned. Slowly, the husband started noticing changes.

Things seemed to wear out more easily, including their bodies. Colds and infections were more frequent. So were trips to the mechanic as the cars continued to have nagging problems. The couple's investments lagged, even lost ground, as the rest of the economy boomed. Trying to fill the void, they began making unwise financial decisions that further increased their problems, and their marriage started to strain under the duress. Finally, the young couple realized what went wrong: they were leaving out God.

If there is sustained, habitual sin in our lives, it will affect God's response to our prayers. If He continued to answer all of our prayers despite our sinful conduct, He in effect would be condoning our actions, and a holy God cannot sanction sin. One of the ways God gets our attention is by withholding blessings when there is sin in our lives.

We should always consider it God's gracious gift, a warning system He has put in place to steer us back within His will.

Dear Lord, thank You for Your warning system that steers me back into Your will. Help me to listen and respond in obedience.

Setting Goals by Faith

SCRIPTURE READING: Romans 8:28–30   KEY VERSE: Jeremiah 29:11

I know the thoughts that I think toward you, says the LORD, thoughts of peace and not of evil, to give you a future and a hope.

God reminds us that He has a plan for our lives (Jer. 29:11). This is an important word of encouragement. But often we worry what His plan is and how we can achieve it. While goals are very important because they help to set a positive tone for our lives, they should never take the place of true love and devotion to the Savior.

Establish your goals with God in mind. In Romans 8:28–30, the Lord underscores the fact that He truly has His eye on our lives. Every detail is woven together so that the outcome will be beautiful.

Sorrows, heartaches, and failures play an important part in your life, as do the times when you achieve great accomplishments. Set your goals and live by faith in God. Trust Him to guide you as you dream of good things for the future. Be sure each goal you set is something He would approve. Prayer is vital to goal setting.

When you pray, ask the Lord to make you sensitive to His desires for your future. If you find yourself doing something that is not in keeping with His plan for your life, abandon it immediately.

Be encouraged! God will never leave you without direction and hope. Seek Him, and He will guide you. Remember, some goals take a long time to achieve. But the Captain of your soul is a God of love, who has wonderful blessings in store for you!

Heavenly Father, I praise You for the blessings You have in store for me!

God is Talking

SCRIPTURE READING: Psalm 138:1–8   KEY VERSE: Isaiah 49:1

Listen, O coastlands, to Me,
And take heed, you peoples from afar!

If you've ever wondered whether God still talks to people, allow Him to use today's verse to give an answer: God calls for people to listen and take heed (Isa. 49:1). God wants people to listen. Therefore, He must be talking.

Although God was speaking primarily to the nation of Israel in Psalm 138, you can be sure that His voice still guides, confirms, disciplines, and assures His children. Generally, there are four reasons He speaks.

Reasons: (1) God desires to have fellowship with us, His most precious creation, and loves us just as much as He loved the saints of the Bible; (2) God knows that we need clear direction in a difficult world; (3) God realizes we need comfort and assurance just as much as did Abraham, Moses, Peter, Paul, and others; and, (4) God wants us to get to know Him.

But how do we know when God is speaking to us? Today, He uses four primary ways to share His heart with ours.

Methods: God speaks (1) through His Word, the foremost tool He uses to impart His truth; (2) through the Holy Spirit, who witnesses to our spirits; (3) through other believers who are walking in His Spirit; and (4) through circumstances He providentially arranges. It may be a still small voice, but it resounds loudly because of whose voice it is.

> **Dear Lord, speak to me today through Your Word, Your Spirit, other believers, and the circumstances of my life.**

Hearing and Doing

SCRIPTURE READING: James 1:22–25   KEY VERSE: Romans 9:26

It shall come to pass in the place where it was said to them,
"You are not My people,"
There they shall be called sons of the living God.

How you enter church each week will have a great impact on how you exit it. The reference here is to attitude and intention, not to whether you look or act just right.

James told us to be doers and not just hearers of the Word. The only way to be a doer is to be an intense hearer. We must know what to do and how to go about it before we can be doers. It is imperative that we walk into church services having resolved that we will intently, actively listen to the preaching of the Word of God.

Pray for God to prepare your heart for what He wants you to hear from your pastor. Take notes. Pray during the message. Say something like, "Lord, what are You trying to teach me here?" If there is a particular point that God continually is impressing upon your spirit, ask Him, "Father, what am I missing? Reveal what You would have me learn. How can I absorb what I am hearing and apply it to my life?"

Comprehending God's Word will help you become a doer of God's Word. This is the truth behind Romans 8:29, in which God would have us to be conformed to the image of His Son. You must comprehend to be conformed, and you must be conformed to effectively communicate in speech and deed the Word of God.

Make me an intense hearer, Lord, so I can be an obedient doer. Conform me
to the image of Your Son, so I can effectively communicate Your Word in
speech and deed.

A Restless Spirit

SCRIPTURE READING: Esther 6:1–7:10   KEY VERSE: Esther 6:1

That night the king could not sleep. So one was commanded to bring the book of the records of the chronicles; and they were read before the king.

The night before King Ahasuerus's edict to destroy all Jews was to be executed by Haman, the king could not sleep. Eventually, he called for the book of records to be read to him. In those records was an account of where Esther's uncle, Mordecai, had reported an assassination plot on the king's life. The record reminded the king that Mordecai, a Jew, had saved his life.

In the end, Mordecai and the nation of Israel were saved because God put a stop to Haman's wicked plan. Haman, not Mordecai or the Jews, was the one executed. How did all of this come about? God gave King Ahasuerus a restless spirit. He could not sleep, so he began searching for answers to what was troubling him.

One of the ways God gets your attention is to give you a restless spirit. Often, in those times when "something is just not right," God wants you to stop and wait on a word from Him. Inevitably, when you ignore the static in your spirit and continue on your own path, you will only worsen what could have been a much less troublesome situation.

Do you feel that you're continually striving without really getting anywhere? Do you keep winding up at the same spiritual spot? God will bring you back to that starting point until you agree that His direction will be yours. Then come rest and peace.

Thank You for a restless spirit, Lord, which directs me to Your perfect will. Use it to bring me into conformity to Your will.

Strength to Obey

SCRIPTURE READING: 1 Samuel 3:1–10   KEY VERSE: 1 Samuel 3:10

The LORD came and stood and called as at other times, "Samuel! Samuel!" And Samuel answered, "Speak, for Your servant hears."

God uses a variety of methods to get our attention. Sometimes He'll give us a restless spirit. At other times He can get our attention through a word from a fellow believer, through tragedy, through unanswered prayer, through disappointment, and through financial difficulty, among other ways.

Whatever method God chooses to bring you within His will is perfect and is born of His love. He can see not only your present but also your future. He has plans for you and will keep you in precise accordance with those plans if you obey Him.

When you cease traveling on the path He has chosen for you, God has to get your attention. He may use one method today, another next week, another next year. Yet He always acts out of love and never out of whim, anger, or vindication. Your response, then, should be to examine every single area and circumstance of your life and ask the Lord to clarify what He is trying to show you and how He wants you to proceed.

God got Samuel's attention through someone else, his mentor, Eli. When finally Samuel understood who was calling him, he told God that he was "listening." This particular Hebrew word means "to hear with a view to obeying." Samuel answered with clear intentions to obey, though he had no idea what God would say next. May his response be your model.

Lord, when I hear Your voice, give me the strength to obey, even if I have no idea what comes next.

The Real Thing

SCRIPTURE READING: John 14:1–17   KEY VERSE: Psalm 25:5

Lead me in Your truth and teach me,
For You are the God of my salvation;
On You I wait all the day.

The most potent hearing aid known to man is the Holy Bible. It is the standard of truth against which you can test every message that comes your way.

Making a decision on an issue important to you can be extremely difficult. Sometimes it may seem as if you are hearing two or more voices, all of which make seemingly good points but also tug you in different directions. In these times you must learn to discern the voice of God.

You can apply several principles to what you're hearing to gauge whether it is of God, but the most basic is whether the message conflicts with Scripture. God won't tell you to do something that counters what He already has recorded for all mankind.

Therefore, the best way to know God's voice is to get to know Him. Spend time in His Word and soak in His truths. You must know God's Word before you can differentiate God's instructions from the messages that Satan or your flesh is sending you.

Do you know how investigators are trained to recognize counterfeit money? They don't spend all of their time trying to keep up with the latest technological advances in creating false money. Instead, they first and foremost diligently study the original, the real thing. Then, held against the standard, the fake stuff stands out.

I want to know You better, Lord—and in so doing, learn to walk in Your will and Your ways.

Your View of God

SCRIPTURE READING: Psalm 31:1–24   KEY VERSE: Psalm 31:23

Oh, love the LORD, all you His saints!
For the LORD preserves the faithful,
And fully repays the proud person.

What you hear from your heavenly Father will be affected by your attitude. Your relationship with God also will be impacted for better or worse by how you view God Himself. What is your understanding of this loving God, our blessed Creator, Sustainer, and Redeemer?

There is a revealing exercise you can conduct to monitor how properly you view God. Draw a line down the middle of a sheet of paper. Use the left-hand side for one list of descriptions and the right-hand side for another.

On the left side, write (1) "a loving Father," and on the right side, write "demanding." In the same manner, record the following phrases on opposite sides of the line: (2) an intimate Friend; distant; (3) a patient Teacher; intolerant and critical; (4) a gentle Guide; rigid and strict; (5) an understanding Counselor; insensitive; (6) a generous Provider; reluctant and stingy; (7) a faithful Supporter; inconsistent.

Now, which god do you serve? The God of the Bible is the One you have characterized with the descriptions on the left-hand side of your page. There is no shadow of turning in your heavenly Father, and He did not create you for a relationship with Him only to become demanding, distant, intolerant, critical, rigid, strict, insensitive, reluctant, stingy, and inconsistent.

Father, thank You for Your love, patience, and understanding. You are my
Provider, Supporter, and intimate Friend. I rejoice in You today!

The Quiet Time

SCRIPTURE READING: Psalm 62:1–12   KEY VERSE: Psalm 62:5

My soul, wait silently for God alone,
For my expectation is from Him.

You may be waiting for God to answer your prayers, but are you listening? There is a reason our daily devotion and prayer time is called quiet time; we are supposed to be still and quiet before Him. It is easiest to hear a still small voice when all is silent. Yet in the hustle and bustle of a workaday world it is easy to fall into a rut of simply reporting requests to God and walking away without taking the time to be quiet and listen.

Patrick Morley comments on the problem:

> Our quiet times often become yet another perfunctory duty of the Christian life, another activity to verify our Christianity to ourselves. When this happens, the quiet time has become secularized. We cannot apply worldly methods to spiritual needs.
>
> We are too busy. The suffocating pace of secular society subtly strangles our personal devotions. We must come apart to meet with the Lord. But, it seems we can barely function without the dull drone of a radio or a television in the background.
>
> Some of us have forgotten why we take time, and with Whom we spend it. Instead of thinking of devotions in terms of what we want from God, perhaps some of us need to reevaluate. Let us go and meet with God and humbly quiet ourselves before the throne of His grace. Leave the religious party horns and hats to others.

Help me be quiet in Your presence, Lord, then speak to me with a still small voice.

Praying for God's Will

SCRIPTURE READING: Colossians 1:9–14   KEY VERSE: Psalm 68:28

Your God has commanded your strength;
Strengthen, O God, what You have done for us.

The most powerful act anyone can perform is to pray for someone. Of course, the power is not in the praying, but in the release God gives in His perfect answer to our prayers. Paul provided an example of one of the most effective prayers we could utter. He prayed for the Colossian church:

- to be filled with the knowledge of God's will. What a wonderful gesture to ask God to make clear for family members or friends the precise, exact decisions He wishes them to make in every circumstance.
- to walk in a manner worthy of the Lord. This means asking that someone's life will have weight—will count eternally and not temporally.
- to bear fruit in every good work. We should pray for loved ones to remain so Christ-centered that He through them determines their conversation, conduct, and character.
- to increase in the knowledge of God. Can there be a more precious request than that of wanting someone to grow ever closer to our heavenly Father?
- to be strengthened and sustained with the power of God. Within an evil world system, we need the supernatural power of God to help us bear up under the strain.
- to give thanks for having qualified as saints of God. There is nothing for which we should be more appreciative.

Father, today I pray for those I love—that they will be filled with the knowledge of Your will and walk in a manner worthy of You. Let them bear fruit in every good work and be strengthened and sustained by Your power.

Your Unmet Needs

SCRIPTURE READING: Job 23:1–12   KEY VERSE: Job 13:15

Though He slay me, yet will I trust Him.
Even so, I will defend my own ways before Him.

While waiting on God's answer for your unmet needs, you may want to question yourself. Examine your heart. Do your best to objectively consider your motives and to separate desires from needs. In short, contemplate your attitude.

What you hear from God will be affected by the manner in which you ask Him to talk to you. In other words, if you are a proud, egotistical, self-sufficient, rebellious, or indifferent person, your communication with God is hampered.

However, if in approaching God to attend to your unmet needs you are submissive, trusting, and grateful, your petitions will be pleasing in God's sight. He will answer your prayers in His perfect timing and in His perfect way, but your attitude and faith are catalysts.

Being submissive means agreeing in advance that whatever God decides or asks, you will say, "Yes, Father." Being trusting means telling God in genuine faith that you know He will never lead you in the wrong direction. You believe what He says is best. Being grateful means that whatever your present circumstance or future answer from God, you're thankful and secure in the truth that He has your best interests at heart and never will leave or forsake you. In good and bad, thank Him for all He has done, is doing, and will do for you.

> *Lord, I am so thankful that You have my best interests at heart, both in the present and in the future. I thank You for all You have done, are doing, and will do for me.*

NOVEMBER

THEME

Adversity

MOUNTAIN: Mt. Horeb

KEY VERSES: Joshua 14:6–14

Then the children of Judah came to Joshua in Gilgal. And Caleb the son of Jephunneh the Kenizzite said to him: "You know the word which the LORD said to Moses the man of God concerning you and me in Kadesh Barnea. I was forty years old when Moses the servant of the LORD sent me from Kadesh Barnea to spy out the land, and I brought back word to him as it was in my heart. Nevertheless my brethren who went up with me made the heart of the people melt, but I wholly followed the LORD my God. So Moses swore on that day, saying, 'Surely the land where your foot has trodden shall be your inheritance and your children's forever, because you have wholly followed the LORD my God.' And now, behold, the LORD has kept me alive, as He said, these forty-five years, ever since the LORD spoke this word to Moses while Israel wandered in the wilderness; and now, here I am this day, eighty-five years old. As yet I am as strong this day as on the day that Moses sent me; just as my strength was then, so now is my strength for war, both for going out and for coming in. Now therefore, give me this mountain of which the LORD spoke in that day; for you heard in that day how the Anakim were there, and that the cities were great and fortified. It may be that the LORD will be with me, and I shall be able to drive them out as the LORD said." And Joshua blessed him, and gave Hebron to Caleb the son of Jephunneh as an inheritance. Hebron therefore became the inheritance of Caleb the son of Jephunneh the Kenizzite to this day, because he wholly followed the LORD God of Israel.

Marching into Battle

SCRIPTURE READING: 1 Samuel 17:1–11, 22–51   KEY VERSE: 1 Samuel 17:45

David said to the Philistine, "You come to me with a sword, with a spear, and with a javelin. But I come to you in the name of the LORD of hosts, the God of the armies of Israel, whom you have defied."

When David stepped onto the battlefield to face Goliath, he was immediately thrust into what appeared to be an impossible situation.

It was in the times David spent alone in the wilderness tending his father's sheep that God built a tenacious spirit within him. During those years, he learned to trust God with his entire life. When danger approached, he cried out to the Lord and was saved.

David loved the Lord, and the bond between them grew. He could pour his heart out to Him in prayer and not feel silly or unaccepted. Over time, the relationship developed into a deep commitment and respect for God.

When David heard the taunts of the Philistines and saw the arrogance of Goliath, he was incensed. How could anyone oppose the armies of God and live? With five smooth stones and a slingshot David faced his adversary, "You come to me with a sword, with a spear, and with a javelin. But I come to you in the name of the LORD of hosts, the God of the armies of Israel."

Here's a formula that works when facing difficulties: make sure your life is right with God, ask forgiveness for any known sin, and pray for God's wisdom and guidance. Then you can go into battle with the confidence of David, knowing that you are marching off not in your own strength but in the strength of almighty God.

Dear heavenly Father, give me Your wisdom and guidance so I can advance into the battles of life with full assurance of Your abiding presence.

Through Troubled Waters

SCRIPTURE READING: Psalm 18:1–6   KEY VERSE: Isaiah 43:2

When you pass through the waters, I will be with you;
And through the rivers, they shall not overflow you.
When you walk through the fire, you shall not be burned,
Nor shall the flame scorch you.

At six weeks of age, Fanny Crosby lost her eyesight. The tragedy came at the hands of a man claiming to be a physician. Her entire life was spent in physical darkness because of his mistreatment, and yet she lived in the eternal light of God's blessed hope.

She could have become bitter and angry, but she didn't. Instead, biographers have written that in reality her blindness did not slow her down. In her youth she played with other children, participated in sports, and traveled. Good-natured humor was a vital part of her life. Laughter filled her household. Most of us remember her deep affection for Christ through the many songs she wrote.

At one point when questioned about the incident that altered her life, she answered, "Although it may have been a blunder on the physician's part, it was no mistake on God's. I verily believe it was His intention that I should live my days in physical darkness, so as to be better prepared to sing His praises and incite others so to do. I could not have written thousands of hymns."

You may be facing troubled times and wonder if you will ever be happy again. No matter what has happened, God is able to take the trial and turn it into a blessing. Nothing is too formidable for Him. When you pass through troubled waters, He will be with you (Isa. 43:2).

You will be with me, no matter what I face today. Thank You, Lord!

In the Face of Despair

SCRIPTURE READING: Psalm 143:1–12   KEY VERSE: Psalm 143:8

> *Cause me to hear Your lovingkindness in the morning,*
> *For in You do I trust;*
> *Cause me to know the way in which I should walk,*
> *For I lift up my soul to You.*

When despair overtook David's life, he discovered the sure remedy; his attention needed to be redirected to the Lord. He felt his spirit failing within him, and in hurt and humility, he cried out to God: "Cause me to hear Your lovingkindness in the morning" (Ps. 143:8).

Emotional and spiritual upheaval has a way of fragmenting the mind, sending your thoughts reeling in a thousand different directions as you try to quickly bring order to confusion. It's not easy to respond calmly, and sometimes carrying on with daily chores may seem an intolerable burden.

The Lord understands the way your heart and mind work. He designed you to be sensitive to your surroundings and to interact with other people, so it's no surprise to Him when a shock to your system causes disturbance.

That is why He gives these specific directions for responding to trials: "Therefore gird up the loins of your mind, be sober, and rest your hope fully upon the grace that is to be brought to you at the revelation of Jesus Christ" (1 Peter 1:13).

Getting the right view of His love-filled plan for your life is the way to push through the numbness of spirit and despair that often accompanies severe circumstances. You can then say with David: "Revive me, O LORD, for Your name's sake! . . . Bring my soul out of trouble" (Ps. 143:11).

For Your name's sake, O Lord, revive me, and bring my soul out of trouble.

The Fires of Affliction

SCRIPTURE READING: Psalm 77:1–20   KEY VERSE: Hebrews 12:1

We also, since we are surrounded by so great a cloud of witnesses, let us lay aside every weight, and the sin which so easily ensnares us, and let us run with endurance the race that is set before us.

During her life, Mrs. Charles Spurgeon faced many difficult trials. The following is an excerpt from a devotional she wrote:

At the close of a dark and gloomy day, I lay resting on my couch . . . and though all was bright within my cozy room, some of the external darkness seemed to have entered into my soul and obscured its spiritual vision . . . In sorrow of heart I asked, "Why does my Lord thus deal with His child? Why does He so often send sharp and bitter pain to visit me? . . ."

For a while silence reigned in the little room, broken only by the crackling of the oak log burning in the fireplace. Suddenly I heard a sweet, soft sound, a clear, musical note, like the tender trill of a robin . . . plaintive notes, so sweet, so melodious, yet mysterious . . . Suddenly I realized it came from the log on the fire! The fire was letting loose the imprisoned music from the old oak's innermost heart.

Perchance it had garnered up this song in the days when all was well . . . and the soft sunlight flecked its tender leaves with gold. "Ah," I thought, "when the fire of affliction draws songs of praise from us, then indeed we are purified, and our God is glorified." Perhaps some of us are like this old oak log, cold, hard, insensible; we should give forth no melodious sounds, were it not for the fire which kindles around us, and releases notes of trust and love in Him.

Heavenly Father, when I am being tried in the fires of affliction, help me to praise You. Give me a song in the night.

The Difficulties of Life

SCRIPTURE READING: Psalm 57:1–11   KEY VERSES: Romans 8:26–28

Likewise the Spirit also helps in our weaknesses. For we do not know what we should pray for as we ought, but the Spirit Himself makes intercession for us with groanings which cannot be uttered. Now He who searches the hearts knows what the mind of the Spirit is, because He makes intercession for the saints according to the will of God. And we know that all things work together for good to those who love God, to those who are the called according to His purpose.

The question of God's allowing pain and suffering has plagued man's heart since the beginning of time: If God is a good God, why does He allow bad things to happen? God always has a purpose for allowing the difficulties of life:

Spiritual cleansing. Nothing exposes sin like pain and suffering. If there is something in your life that needs His forgiveness, go to Him immediately; then ask Him to restore the sweetness of the fellowship you once shared.

Companionship. God is not the author of evil, but He uses it to bring you into a closer relationship with Himself. Any sin in your life needs to be removed because it blocks the flow of God's love.

Conformity. C. S. Lewis once commented: "Prayer does not change God; it changes us." Adversity purifies your motives and strips away the dross in your life so that you reflect His love to others with an even greater brilliance.

Conviction. After Christ's death, the disciples had to hold fast to what they believed concerning God's Son. In the end, the adversity they faced led to an increased joy that came through the reality of living in harmony with the Holy Spirit.

Comfort. When God becomes your only Source of comfort in times of trials, you will experience an inner peace like nothing you have felt before.

> *Dear Lord, thank You for the supernatural purposes that You are accomplishing in me through the difficulties of life. Strip away the dross in my life so that I can reflect Your love to others with an even greater brilliance.*

The Storms of Life

SCRIPTURE READING: 1 Peter 5:9–11   KEY VERSE: 2 Timothy 2:12

If we endure,
  We shall also reign with Him.
If we deny Him,
  He also will deny us.

Seventeenth-century theologian François Fénelon stated:

> We have much trouble convincing ourselves of the kindness with which God crushes those he loves with crosses. Why take pleasure, we say, in making us suffer? Would he not know how to make us good without making us miserable? Yes, doubtless, God could do so, because nothing is impossible for him . . .
>
> But God, who could have saved us without crosses, has not wished to do so . . . what we see clearly, is that we cannot become entirely good except as we become humble, disinterested, detached from ourselves, in order to relate everything to God without any turning back upon ourselves . . .
>
> God never makes trouble for us except in spite of himself, so to speak. His father's heart does not try to desolate us. But he cuts to the quick to cure the ulcer of our heart. He has to take from us what we love too dearly, what we love in the wrong way and without discretion, what we love to the prejudice of his love.

There can be only one goal for the life of the believer, and that is to "love the LORD your God with all your heart, with all your soul, and with all your strength" (Deut. 6:5). When trials come, know that God's presence surrounds you. There is a purpose for every storm; therefore, pray for the strength to be found faithful.

Lord, thank You for Your presence, which surrounds me in the midst of the storm. Help me realize that each gale of life has purpose. Give me the strength to be found faithful.

Sufficient Provision

SCRIPTURE READING: Matthew 14:22–34   KEY VERSE: Matthew 14:31

*Immediately Jesus stretched out His hand and caught him, and said
to him, "O you of little faith, why did you doubt?"*

The storm the disciples encountered in the Scripture was tenacious. Even
though several of them were seasoned fishermen, they thought they were
about to die. And if that wasn't enough, they looked out over the raging sea and
saw what appeared to be a ghost walking toward them.

How many times have you found yourself in a frightening situation and
seen things differently from what they actually were? When you are fighting
fear and anxiety, it is easy to be carried away by your emotions.

Jesus sent His disciples on before Him across the Sea of Galilee for a purpose. He knew the storm was coming. He also knew how they would respond
to the thundering skies. They trusted Him as their Teacher; now they were
going to learn about His lordship. Their faith had to be tested, and nothing
tries faith like trouble and difficulty.

When we feel stretched to the limit and have no place to go, Jesus wants us
instinctively to run to Him. However, instead of crying out to God, the disciples vainly struggled with oars and sails. They were captivated by fear and did
not recognize Jesus even when He crossed over the waves of the sea to save
them.

No matter what you face, you can trust Jesus to be your peace amid the
storm. When you lay aside your human efforts, you will find His provision infinitely sufficient and true.

*You are my peace, O God. You are my provision. You are sufficient for every
need today.*

Nothing Is Wasted

SCRIPTURE READING: John 11:1–45   KEY VERSES: John 11:25–26

Jesus said to her, "I am the resurrection and the life. He who believes in Me, though he may die, he shall live. And whoever lives and believes in Me shall never die. Do you believe this?"

By the time Jesus reached Bethany, Mary and Martha were overwhelmed by the reality of their brother's death. Jesus loved Lazarus, too, and He was not ashamed to display His sorrow. God is sensitive to our needs and doesn't hesitate to weep with us when we hurt.

He also had a greater plan in mind for the sisters and all who were present. He used this tragedy to point others to Himself. Jesus told those who had gathered at the tomb: "I am the resurrection and the life. He who believes in Me, though he may die, he shall live. And whoever lives and believes in Me shall never die . . . Did I not say to you that if you would believe, you would see the glory of God?" (John 11:25–26, 40).

You may wonder why a certain tragedy had to happen, but you need never doubt the goodness of God's sovereign will. He sees the beginning and the end of your life, and only He can transform your tragedies into something of lasting value.

In Jesus Christ, Mary and Martha found the hope of eternal life. Author and speaker Elisabeth Elliot says nothing is a waste with God. He takes everything, even the slightest detail, and works it all together for our good. No matter what you are facing, the Lord has a plan in mind for the future. Tell Him of your doubts, fears, and inadequacies, and He will strengthen and encourage you.

How I thank You, Father, that nothing is wasted in Your divine economy. You take everything and work it together for my good.

The Way of Adversity

SCRIPTURE READING: 2 Corinthians 12:7–10   KEY VERSE: Romans 8:18

I consider that the sufferings of this present time are not worthy to be compared with the glory which shall be revealed in us.

The way of greatness is also the way of adversity. Anyone wishing to be used greatly of God will face suffering at some point in his lifetime. Suffering is not something that can be counterfeited or manifested to lift one up to a higher spiritual level.

It is a gift that God gives to everyone who longs for a deeper relationship with Him. In times of trial we learn to release self-sufficiency and seek God's help.

If suffering has found you and you are weary under its load, turn to today's passage in 2 Corinthians written by the apostle Paul. See within the text the hidden anguish and secret pleading of prayers offered by a man of God who was facing a great physical difficulty. Recall also the fact that opposition waited for him in almost every town he preached.

God has a purpose for your suffering. It is in the difficulties of life that He sharpens you for service and sands away the dross of your life. Because of his elite Jewish background and abiding fellowship with God, Paul fought the temptation to become prideful. God in His mercy allowed Satan to humble His servant through physical suffering, to keep him from exalting himself.

How great is the Father's love? Too great to allow you to drift away from His abiding care. In trial and heartache, open your eyes to His nail-scarred hands.

Father, in the midst of my trials and heartaches, let me see the imprint of Your nail-scarred hands at work in my life.

An Eternal Perspective

SCRIPTURE READING: 2 Corinthians 4:1–18   KEY VERSES: 2 Corinthians 4:16–18

We do not lose heart. Even though our outward man is perishing, yet the inward man is being renewed day by day. For our light affliction, which is but for a moment, is working for us a far more exceeding and eternal weight of glory, while we do not look at the things which are seen, but at the things which are not seen. For the things which are seen are temporary, but the things which are not seen are eternal.

In the book *Shadow of the Almighty: The Life and Testament of Jim Elliot,* Elisabeth Elliot writes of the last time she saw her husband alive:

> Jim slung the carrying net across his forehead, and started for the front door. As he put his hand on the brass handle I almost said aloud: "Do you realize you may never open that door again?"
>
> He swung it open, followed me out and slammed it, striding down the bamboo trail in his usual firm, determined gait. As we reached the strip, the plane was circling to land, and it was only a matter of minutes before Jim kissed me, hopped in beside the pilot, and disappeared over the river. On Sunday, January 8, 1956, the men for whom Jim Elliot had prayed for six years killed him and his four companions.

Jim Elliot's life was one of total commitment to Jesus Christ. He owned few things of worldly value; however, his was a life of eternal treasure. At the age of twenty-two, he wrote, "He is no fool who gives what he cannot keep to gain what he cannot lose."

He saw life from a different angle. His goal was to be remembered not as someone who had done a great work but as one who exemplified total love of and devotion to his Savior. Because of his devotion to his Savior, his martyrdom at age twenty-eight remains an inspiration to all who would dare to live and die by the cross of Jesus Christ.

O God, give me an eternal perspective. I want to live and die by the cross of Your Son, Jesus Christ.

A Higher Purpose

SCRIPTURE READING: Job 42:1–6   KEY VERSES: Hebrews 4:14–16

Seeing then that we have a great High Priest who has passed through the heavens, Jesus the Son of God, let us hold fast our confession. For we do not have a High Priest who cannot sympathize with our weaknesses, but was in all points tempted as we are, yet without sin. Let us therefore come boldly to the throne of grace, that we may obtain mercy and find grace to help in time of need.

Mary Slessor was the daughter of a devout Christian mother and an alcoholic father. Her early years in the mid-1800s were devoted to survival in the slums of Dundee, Scotland. She was beaten frequently by her father and often thrown out of the house.

Yet in this cruel injustice, Mary gained a steadfast spirit, one that God used mightily in the years to come. She came to know Christ at the age of twenty-eight and soon after left for missionary training.

Chronic illness and loneliness brought her to the point of despair, but God gave her strength to answer His call. "Christ sent me to preach the Gospel," she said, "He will look after the results." In Africa, she chose to identify with the people to whom she witnessed by eating and sleeping on dirt floors of huts.

As a result of her earlier life, Mary was able to handle the most threatening situations. Her missionary efforts accounted for the rescue of countless twins, babies who were viewed as being children of the devil. She quickly earned the title "Ma Slessor" by the Okoyong tribe.

Adversity molded her for a higher service. Whatever you are facing, give it to Jesus, and allow Him to make something beautiful out of your life. Trust Him for the outcome and all the moments in between.

Lord, take the adversities of my life, and use them to mold me for a higher purpose. Take all that is ugly, and make something beautiful from it.

The Dedication of Your Life

SCRIPTURE READING: Psalm 138:1–8   KEY VERSE: Galatians 6:9

Let us not grow weary while doing good, for in due season we shall reap if we do not lose heart.

Julian of Norwich (1343–1413) lived through plagues, poverty, and war. But a serious illness brought her into a new awareness of God's personal love. In *I Promise You a Crown*, a compilation of her writings by David Hazard, she writes,

> It had come to me that nothing can keep us from knowing the joy of heaven while we remain under the cross—that is, in humble obedience to God no matter what is sent to us. . . . I will tell you what faith showed me in its light. In my struggle, I saw the terror that lies in forsaking the power of the cross. For in making our soul submit, as Jesus submitted, we are remade into the image of Christ. This will never happen if we seek only earthly blessings. When I understood this, I did not want to look up, as if I had already achieved a place in heaven among the blessed. I knew that to do so would make my soul proud and arrogant in itself. And so I made my choice.
>
> And I can tell you this: I would rather have remained in my terrible pain until the Day of Judgment than to try to come into heaven by any other means than the Way of Jesus. The light of faith had shown me He had bound this bundle of suffering to me. And faith showed me He would unbind me when suffering had done the work of His will in perfecting me.

Let the dedication of your life be set on pleasing Jesus above all else.

Dear heavenly Father, I rededicate my life to You today—to serve Your purposes, fulfill Your plans, and please You above all else.

The Comfort of God

SCRIPTURE READING: Psalm 23:1–6   KEY VERSE: Isaiah 41:10

Fear not, for I am with you;
Be not dismayed, for I am your God.
I will strengthen you,
Yes, I will help you,
I will uphold you with My righteous right hand.

As Catherine Marshall turned to leave the room where her husband, Peter, had died, a portion of the Twenty-third Psalm came to mind, "Surely, goodness and mercy shall follow you all the days of your life." Those were words she had come to love and claim throughout the years. Now she felt it was God's personal pledge to her.

She wrote,

> During the funeral preparations and all the myriad decisions to be made, it was as though I were taken over and managed. In addition, a sort of protective shield was placed over my emotions. Somehow for those days I was lifted into a higher realm . . .
>
> Then about eight days after Peter's death, suddenly that higher realm in which I had been so lovingly enveloped was gone, and I plummeted to earth to stand again on feet of clay in the valley where salt tears and loneliness and the fear of coping alone with the problems of everyday life are all too real . . .
>
> There is another side to God's comfort for His ways are never man's ways. It is not the feather-cushion kind or pat on the cheek . . . It does not tiptoe into the chamber of grief with its shuttered windows: it marches in. There is steel at its backbone. It is a bugle call for reinforcements . . . God comforts us with strength by adding resources. His way is not to whittle down the problem but to build up our ability to cope with it.

I praise You for Your comfort, Lord, which consoles me in times of need.
Thank You for giving me the ability to face every adversity in Your strength.

Hope to Continue

SCRIPTURE READING: Psalm 62:1–12   KEY VERSE: Psalm 62:8

Trust in Him at all times, you people;
Pour out your heart before Him;
God is a refuge for us.

For several days now, we have talked about pain and suffering. Some of the examples have brought profound thoughts of devotion for our Savior. But ask yourself, Is my affection the kind that remains intact, even when the answer to my prayers is not what I expected?

In *Candles in the Dark*, Amy Carmichael wrote,

> I once wrote that God always answers us in the deeps, not in the shallows of our prayers. Hasn't it been so with you?
>
> One of the hardest things in our prayer life is to accept with joy and not with grief the answers to our deepest prayers. At least I have found it so. It was a long time before I discovered that whatever came was the answer.
>
> I had expected something so different that I did not recognize it when it came. And He doesn't explain. He trusts us not to be offended; that's all.

Sometimes God reveals at least a portion of His will to you. Other times He doesn't. In periods of adversity, this can be unsettling. But God requires you to go on in faith, even when adversity closes in all around you. In accepting His will, you find lasting joy. Does this mean you are never to feel sorrow or be burdened by stress? No. God weeps with you, and through the life of His Son, He gives you hope to continue. At times, this may simply mean to be still under His restful care.

Lord, when adversity closes in around me, help me continue to advance in faith. I know that in accepting Your will, I will find the hope to continue.

Call Out to God

SCRIPTURE READING: Mark 6:45–52   KEY VERSE: Mark 6:50

They all saw Him and were troubled. But immediately He talked with them and said to them, "Be of good cheer! It is I; do not be afraid."

The disciples frantically wrestled with oars and sails as the little fishing boat became engulfed by the sea's angry waves. How did they get into this mess? The answer: Jesus had sent them there. What a sobering thought. God leads us along ways that at times seem very dark and lonely.

Suffering pushes the limits of our ability to cope. The sudden death of a loved one brings shock. The news of a mate's unfaithfulness leaves us numb. Our hearts seek comfort; our minds feel as though they will crush under the pressure. And we find ourselves crying out in anguish, even when we know that all He wants from us is an act of faith.

Jesus came to the disciples amid the storm. He didn't come when the waves were calm, before the wind picked up its pace. He came when it appeared that all hope was lost during the fourth watch of the night. From their point of view disaster was unavoidable.

When Jesus approached the boat that night on Galilee, His first words were words of hope: "Be of good cheer! It is I; do not be afraid." God had a deeper principle in mind for the disciples to learn; He is Lord over all things. Nothing, not even death, can overpower Him.

Regardless of your past or your present circumstances, God is with you. Never be afraid to call out to your sovereign Savior. He has His eye on you, and He will bring you into a safe harbor.

Savior, I call out to You today! Be with me and bring me into a safe harbor.

Strength in Weakness

SCRIPTURE READING: Job 23:8–10   KEY VERSE: Psalm 66:12

You have caused men to ride over our heads;
We went through fire and through water;
But You brought us out to rich fulfillment.

He knew he was a poor speaker. He always got so nervous standing up before a crowd that his voice quivered, his face flushed red, and he could barely remember what to say. When his manager asked him to give a product demonstration to some potential clients, he was less than thrilled. He was too embarrassed to decline the opportunity, and everyone was counting on him.

The night before his talk, he knelt beside his desk chair to pray and give the problem to God: "Dear Lord, You know that I am weak in this area. Like Moses, I don't even want to try to speak before important people, but I'm trusting You for the strength and ability. Father, show Your power tomorrow through me. Give me the words. Fill me with Your calm and peace, and guide my every syllable. In Jesus' name, amen."

The next morning when he began the presentation, he could feel the Lord answering his prayer. He spoke slowly and distinctly, and his voice didn't shake once. After it was over, a colleague gave him a slap on the back in approval. The man replied, "Hey, it wasn't me—God handled this one."

That is the truth of 2 Corinthians 12:10 in action: "Therefore I take pleasure in infirmities, in reproaches, in needs, in persecutions, in distresses, for Christ's sake. For when I am weak, then I am strong."

Dear Lord, in my weaknesses today, demonstrate Your strength. Help me remember that when I am weak, You are strong.

Picking Up the Pieces

SCRIPTURE READING: Lamentations 3:18–58   KEY VERSE: Lamentations 3:57

You drew near on the day I called on You,
And said, "Do not fear!"

Barbara Johnson has experienced intense levels of maternal pain. After her oldest son was killed in Vietnam, she and her husband unpacked his duffel bag, crying, and shared memories of his growing-up years. In her last letter to him, she reminded him of Jesus' love, and that no matter what happened, he would be safe with the Lord. The letter was still in his wallet, wrinkled and blurred with water from the rice paddy where he fell.

She tells about this moment of grief in her book *Pack Up Your Gloomies in a Great Big Box:*

> My letter had arrived the very morning of the ambush in which Steve had been killed. Sitting there in that bedroom surrounded by Steve's smelly Marine gear, I was reminded of Jeremiah's words in Lamentations.
>
> We, too, had been afflicted and filled with bitter herbs. Our teeth had been broken on the gravel of grief. We had been trampled in the dust. Prosperity seemed like a forgotten word, and our souls were downcast.
>
> But as I re-read the letter Steve had taken with him into his final battle, I realized that, despite all the pain, we still had an endless hope and with it endless joy. The Lord's great love and compassion fail not. Truly, they are new every morning. Great is His faithfulness. Steve was our deposit in heaven. We could pick up the pieces of our lives and move on.

O Lord, sometimes when tragedies strike, I feel like giving up. Help me to pick up the pieces of my life and move on in faith.

A Twofold Objective

SCRIPTURE READING: Philippians 4:5–13   KEY VERSE: Psalm 30:5

His anger is but for a moment,
His favor is for life;
Weeping may endure for a night,
But joy comes in the morning.

When things are going your way, it's easy to attribute the circumstances to the Lord. It is much more difficult to utter praise when you have suffered hurt or injustice.

Jerry Bridges addresses this inner conflict in his book *Trusting God*:

> Well known theologian J. I. Packer defines providence as, "The unceasing activity of the Creator, whereby, in overflowing bounty and goodwill, He upholds His creatures in ordered existence, guides and governs all events, circumstances, and free acts of angels and men, and directs everything to its appointed goal, for His own glory."
>
> Clearly there is no concept of stop-and-go, part-time governance on God's part in this definition . . . Nothing, not even the smallest virus, escapes His care and control. But note also, the twofold objective of God's providence: His own glory and the good of His people. These two objectives are never antithetical; they are always in harmony with each other. God never pursues His glory at the expense of the good of His people, nor does He ever seek our good at the expense of His glory.
>
> What comfort and encouragement this should be to us. If we are going to learn to trust God in adversity, we must believe that just as certainly as God will allow nothing to subvert His glory, so He will allow nothing to spoil the good He is working out in us and for us.

Reveal Your glory through me, Father. I know that nothing will spoil the good You are working in and through me.

Trusting Through Tragedies

SCRIPTURE READING: Psalm 139:7–12   KEY VERSE: Psalm 139:17

> *How precious also are Your thoughts to me, O God!*
> *How great is the sum of them!*

Anne Bradstreet, the greatest female poet of colonial America, was a busy wife and mother as one of the early settlers. Yet in the middle of unrelenting duty and hardships, she poured out the passions of her heart in poetry that is admired today for its rich simplicity.

On the night of July 10, 1666, she was awakened by terrible cries in the night—"Fire! Fire!" After she and her family made their way to safety, she stood outside and watched the fast-moving flames consume everything they owned. The next morning she picked over the smoking ruins, finding the remains of old keepsakes, chests, the family table. She was brokenhearted and wept as she thought of the joys that were gone.

In her poem "Upon the Burning of Our House," notice the conclusion she reaches as she works through the pain of traumatic loss:

> And did thy wealth on earth abide?
> Didst fix thy hope on mold'ring dust? . . .
> Thou hast an house on high erect,
> Framed by that mighty Architect . . .
> There's wealth enough, I need no more;
> Farewell, my pelf, farewell my store.
> The world no longer let me love;
> My hope and treasure lies above.

Anne understood that God was taking care of her and her family, regardless of how much they had or did not have. She also knew that He would provide for their future. Do you have the peace of trusting Him through your tragedies?

Father, help me trust You in bad times as well as good. Give me a faith that shines brightest in the darkest hours.

A Purpose for Pain

SCRIPTURE READING: Ephesians 3:14–21   KEY VERSE: Psalm 71:20

You, who have shown me great and severe troubles,
Shall revive me again,
And bring me up again from the depths of the earth.

The book *A Prisoner and Yet Free* details the time Corrie ten Boom spent in the concentration camps of World War Two. She described solitary confinement:

> A solitary cell awaited me. I was pushed inside and the door closed after me. I was alone. Everything was empty and gray. In the other cell there had been at least the colors of my cell mates' dresses. Here there was nothing, only an emptiness, a cold gray void . . .
>
> I threw myself down on the mattress, pulled the filthy cover over me, and shut my eyes. The storm howled, and every now and then a gust of wind shook the door so violently it seemed as if someone were beating against it from the outside . . . "Oh, please, not this loneliness. Oh Savior, take away this anxiety, this desolation . . . Take me into your arms and comfort me," I prayed. And peace stole into my heart. The weird noises still surrounded me, but I fell quietly asleep.

The deepest possible adversity was Corrie's. "It was dark in my cell," she wrote, "but I talked with my Savior. Never before had fellowship with Him been so close. It was a joy I hoped would continue unchanged. I was a prisoner, and yet . . . how free!"

Because of Corrie's life, thousands have come to know Jesus as their personal Savior. Let Him take the painfulness of your life and make it a shining light of hope to someone today.

Dear heavenly Father, please take the painfulness of my life and use it for Your purposes—reaching out through me to a lost and hurting world.

God Is at Work

SCRIPTURE READING: Psalm 107:1–21   KEY VERSES: Philippians 2:7–8

But made Himself of no reputation, taking the form of a bondservant, and coming in the likeness of men. And being found in appearance as a man, He humbled Himself and became obedient to the point of death, even the death of the cross.

In his book *Making Sense Out of Suffering*, Peter Kreeft asserts:

> The most oft-repeated teaching of Jesus is the paradox that the poor are rich, the weak are strong, the lowly are exalted. It is the point of the Beatitudes, of the Sermon on the Mount, of most of his parables; it is illustrated by his whole life, by the incarnation, the kenosis, the emptying. "He emptied himself, taking the form of a servant, being born in the likeness of men. And being found in human form He humbled himself and became obedient unto death, even death on a cross" (Philippians 2:7–8).
>
> This is the radical counter to the wisdom of our age, of any age. The fundamental dictum of nearly all modern psychologists is to love ourselves, to accept ourselves as we are, to feel good about ourselves. When we obey this wisdom of the world, God has two choices. He can either let us stay in that state and run the risk of becoming contented, respectable, self-righteous Pharisees; or else he can mercifully slap us out of it with a dose of suffering, frustration, and discontent with ourselves, and thus move us on to a new state . . .
>
> Only when we are dissatisfied, only when we are weak, only when we are failures in ourselves, can God come in.

Adversity is God's choice tool in molding you into a person of tremendous potential. In difficult times, He is at work.

You are at work in me, O Lord. I can rejoice in that today despite the circumstances of my life. I praise You!

God in Your Boat

SCRIPTURE READING: Romans 5:1–5   KEY VERSE: Isaiah 51:12

I, even I, am He who comforts you.
Who are you that you should be afraid
Of a man who will die,
And of the son of a man who will be made like grass?

There is no escaping it. Trouble comes at some point to everyone, but there also is a victory in suffering that cannot be overlooked. Joni Eareckson Tada explains, "I believe those who suffer the greatest on earth have the greatest confidence of sharing in His highest glory. This is a wonderful inspiration to those who are hurting. Amy Carmichael wrote something I will never forget: 'We will have all of eternity to celebrate the victories, but only a few hours before sunset in which to win them.'"

Some of our greatest triumphs come as a result of being willing to weather the storms of life. When we commit ourselves to trusting Jesus regardless of the outcome, God's power is released in mighty ways. The disciples did not forget what it was like to face the gale-force winds of the Sea of Galilee. Neither did they forget the power of the hush that came as a result of Christ's command to the wind and the sea.

The faith they gained in troubled times could not be imitated or duplicated. It became a part of their personal testimony to a great and wondrous God. Jesus saves those who place their trust in Him.

Are you facing something much greater than your ability to handle? Turn your fear and sorrow over to Jesus. Allow Him to take your hurt and disappointment. When He is in your boat, there is no need to worry.

Father, I turn every fear and sorrow over to You today. Take my hurt and disappointment. I know there is no need to worry because You are in my boat!

Working Together for Good

SCRIPTURE READING: Hebrews 11:23–29   KEY VERSE: Hebrews 6:19

This hope we have as an anchor of the soul, both sure and steadfast, and which enters the Presence behind the veil.

Oswald Chambers wrote, "Suffering either makes fiends of us or it makes saints of us; it depends entirely on our relationship towards God."

Most Christians deny having anger toward God when trouble comes. But their irritation shows when they are quick to recall how He is in control of all things. A mere nod from Him is enough to stop any form of trial or persecution.

When heartache or disappointment comes, try dropping to your knees in humble prayer. Searching for a way out only magnifies the problem. God is your heavenly Counselor. You can go to Him anytime, and He will give you strength and a new perspective. You also can ask Him to show you why He allowed the hurt to touch your life. He had rather you come to Him than run from Him, as Adam did in the Garden of Eden.

In some cases it is wise to talk your feelings out with someone who understands what you are experiencing. In most cases this is healthy. However, make sure the person you talk with is someone who loves the Lord and wants His best for your life. Confidentiality is a sign of true trust. End your conversation in prayer, asking God to take your hurt and frustration and bring something good out of them.

Romans 8:28 is much more than a time-worn cliché. If we allow Him the opportunity, God will work everything together for our good and His glory.

Dear Lord, please take my hurt and frustration and bring something good out of them. Give me a new perspective on my circumstances and renewed strength to face the challenges ahead.

Don't Let Him Pass By

SCRIPTURE READING: Matthew 8:1–3 KEY VERSE: Psalm 3:4

I cried to the LORD with my voice,
And He heard me from His holy hill. Selah

Read the description of this scene: "When He had come down from the mountain, great multitudes followed Him. And behold, a leper came and worshiped Him, saying, 'Lord, if You are willing, You can make me clean.' Then Jesus put out His hand and touched him saying, 'I am willing; be cleansed.' Immediately his leprosy was cleansed" (Matt. 8:1–3).

Jesus wants us to see Him as our only Source of help in every situation. Although the multitudes pressed in on Him, compassion rose up from within Him at the sight of the approaching man with leprosy who was deeply despised by others.

Leprosy was a curse. All who associated with people having leprosy were considered ceremonially unclean as well. Yet the man dared to venture into the city in hopes of talking to Jesus. When Christ came near, the man immediately knelt before Him. It was a demonstration of his adoration of God. Next he told Jesus: "If You are willing, You can make me clean." They were words of tremendous faith spoken by a man who did not doubt God's ability but feared that somehow he might be overlooked.

Some who read these words have suffered for a long time. Jesus can heal your infirmity. He may choose to do so completely, or He may change the circumstances so that you can find peace and rest in your suffering. Don't let the Savior pass by; step forward in worship and allow Him to work in your life.

Don't pass me by, Lord. Work in my life as I humbly bow in worship before You.

Comforting Others

SCRIPTURE READING: 2 Corinthians 1:3–11   KEY VERSE: 2 Corinthians 1:5

As the sufferings of Christ abound in us, so our consolation also abounds through Christ.

The apostle Paul wrote to a church that had just gone through a difficult time of discipline. He reminded them that since they had corrected the problem, they needed to turn and comfort one another, just as God comforted them.

It is true; the believers knowingly allowed sin to come into their fellowship. However, once it was dealt with, they needed to give the entire matter to God. Dwelling on sin, wishing we could go back and erase what happened in the past, and carrying guilt that God never intended for us to bear weary us spiritually, emotionally, and physically.

"Put it behind you and comfort those who have turned away from sin" was the basis of Paul's opening words. God is able to forgive, cleanse, and restore those who have yielded to temptation. They don't need our reminder of failure; they need our understanding and godly love.

Paul wrote, "God of all comfort, who comforts us in all our tribulation, that we may be able to comfort those who are in any trouble, with the comfort with which we ourselves are comforted by God" (2 Cor. 1:3–4). The message is clear—once we were trapped in sin. But it was God's holy intent to forgive us, and it should be our goal to do the same for others. Therefore, open your heart, and allow Him to use you to soothe a hurting soul.

Thank You for deliverance, Lord. I praise You for setting me free. Work through me to comfort others.

Speak to My Heart

SCRIPTURE READING: Psalm 46:1–3   KEY VERSE: Psalm 54:7

He has delivered me out of all trouble;
And my eye has seen its desire upon my enemies.

Children have an uncanny ability to show the emotional side of disappointment when it comes. Their eyes fill with tears as the lower lip protrudes and quivers. Many of us as grown-ups have felt this same way. We have a certain expectation in mind, and suddenly, something happens to change everything. Although we may try to hide our hurt, deep inside we are struggling.

God knows when we face disappointment of any kind. He knows the painfulness that accompanies rejection as well as the feeling of isolation in lonely times. He sees our hurts and has every intention of taking care of our needs.

However, He wants us to learn to come to Him first instead of trying to solve things on our own. The old saying "God helps those who help themselves" is completely unfounded in Scripture. The truth is, God wants us to stop striving and start relying on Him for even the smallest details.

When things don't go your way, you need to immediately talk to Him about it. He works through each situation to make you sensitive to His will. His purpose for delaying or altering an answer to prayer could be to teach you more about His faithfulness. However, if you are not in close fellowship with Him because of sin in your life, the adversity could be His way of getting your attention. Regardless, if you will ask Him to speak to your heart, He will.

Father, help me submit to Your plan, even when I am disappointed. Make me sensitive to Your will, and help me respond in obedience. Speak to my heart.

An Eternal Light of Hope

SCRIPTURE READING: Daniel 3:16–18   KEY VERSE: Romans 8:39

Nor height nor depth, nor any other created thing, shall be able to separate us from the love of God which is in Christ Jesus our Lord.

A. B. Simpson spoke of trials:

> I once heard a simple man say something that I have never forgotten: "When God tests you, it is a good time for you to test Him by putting His promises to the proof, and claiming from Him just as much as your trials have rendered necessary."
>
> There are two ways of getting out of a trial. One is to simply try to get rid of the trial, and be thankful when it is over. The other is to recognize the trial as a challenge from God to claim a larger blessing than we have ever had, and to hail it with delight as an opportunity of obtaining a larger measure of Divine grace. Thus even the adversary becomes an auxiliary, and the things that seem to be against us turn out to be for the furtherance of our way. Surely this is to be more than conquerors through Him who loved us (Romans 8:39).

Daniel never planned to be tossed into the lions' den. Shadrach, Meshach, and Abed-Nego didn't expect to see the inside of the fiery furnace. Joseph had no idea when he showed his coat of many colors to his brothers that they would sell him to Egyptian bondsmen. Life contains many difficult twists and turns. But God customarily takes hopeless situations and turns them around for His glory and our good.

You always can trust the fact that God is your Eternal Light. Look to Him for hope, and He will bring encouragement to your heart.

O God, You are my Eternal Light. I look to You today for hope and encouragement.

The Fragrance God Loves

SCRIPTURE READING: Matthew 6:25–34   KEY VERSE: Matthew 6:33

Seek first the kingdom of God and His righteousness, and all these things shall be added to you.

Adversity can be handled one of two ways. Either you can deal with it on your own, or you can allow God to carry your burden for you. The first requires human strength and effort, which are rarely sufficient in handling grievous trials. Heartache erodes human ability.

The wiser course of action is to allow God to handle your adversity. This requires faith, an action that is far from passive. In *The Cross of Christ*, John Stott writes, "Faith is the eye that looks to Christ, the hand that lays hold of him, the mouth that drinks the water of life."

In Matthew 6:25–34, Jesus exhorted His followers to lay aside their feelings of anxiety and fear and trust Him for their every need. God's ability to provide goes beyond our greatest imagination. He is the God who has the ability to calm every storm. When you have a need, He is there. Let Him be your help.

In *Streams in the Desert*, Mrs. Charles Cowman painted this word picture:

> Sometimes God sends severe blasts of trial upon His children to develop their graces. Just as torches burn most brightly when swung to and fro; just as the juniper plant smells sweetest when flung into the flames; so the richest qualities of a Christian often come out under the north wind of suffering and adversity. Bruised hearts often emit the fragrance that God loveth to smell.

Father, please let my hurting, bruised heart emit the fragrance that is pleasing to You.

A Hidden Blessing

SCRIPTURE READING: Psalm 18:29–33   KEY VERSE: Habakkuk 3:19

The LORD God is my strength;
He will make my feet like deer's feet,
And He will make me walk on my high hills.

Nothing has the ability to strip away human pretense and false humility like adversity. It has a way of revealing who we really are, what we are made of, and how we view life. Not only that, but adversity also reveals our view of God and our ability to trust Him in difficult situations.

It brings to the surface hidden emotions such as fear, low self-esteem, and jealousy. It is likewise efficient in illuminating our strengths. If the adversity comes as the result of a personal attack or betrayal, it shows whether we are willing to forgive those who have betrayed us.

Most important, adversity is a gauge of our level of faith. If we trust God in the small trials, then when the winds of adversity howl, we are much more likely to stand in faith rather than retreat in weakness. This principle was magnified in the life of the apostle Paul. Several times, he mentioned the hardships he endured. Recalling past trials gave Paul an opportunity to honor God for His faithfulness.

Within every problem or sorrow is a hidden blessing as well as an opportunity for a lesson of faith. Paul's "thorn in the flesh" kept him humble and focused on the sufficiency of Christ. If adversity has besieged your life, ask God to show you the blessing He has for you and the lesson He wants you to learn.

Lord, keep me focused on Your sufficiency as I face the challenges of life today. Reveal the lessons You want me to learn. Help me claim the hidden blessings You have reserved for me.

The School of Sorrows

SCRIPTURE READING: Genesis 50:18–21   KEY VERSE: Genesis 41:52

The name of the second he called Ephraim: "For God has caused me to be fruitful in the land of my affliction."

In *Streams in the Desert*, Mrs. Charles Cowman commented:

The hardest ingredient in suffering is often time. A short, sharp pang is easily borne, but when a sorrow drags its weary way through long, monotonous years, and day after day returns with the same dull routine of hopeless agony, the heart loses its strength, and without the grace of God, is sure to sink into the very sullenness of despair. Joseph's was a long trial, and God often has to burn His lessons into the depths of our being by the fires of protracted pain. "He shall sit as a refiner and purifier of silver," but He knows how long, and like a true goldsmith He stops the fires the moment He sees His image in the glowing metal.

We may not see now the outcome of the beautiful plan which God is hiding in the shadow of His hand; it yet may be long concealed; but faith may be sure that He is sitting on the throne, calmly waiting the hour when, with adoring rapture, we shall say, "All things have worked together for good." Like Joseph, let us be more careful to learn all the lessons in the school of sorrow so that we are anxious for the hour of deliverance . . .

God is educating us for the future, for higher service and nobler blessings . . . Don't steal tomorrow out of God's hands. Give God time to speak to you and reveal His will. He is never too late; learn to wait.

Heavenly Father, teach me to wait. Let me learn the lessons You have for me in the school of sorrow.

DECEMBER

Hope and Promise

MOUNTAIN: Mountain of the Ascension—Olivet

KEY VERSES:

Matthew 28:16–17

Then the eleven disciples went away into Galilee, to the mountain which Jesus had appointed for them. When they saw Him, they worshiped Him; but some doubted.

Acts 1:7–11

And He said to them, "It is not for you to know times or seasons which the Father has put in His own authority. But you shall receive power when the Holy Spirit has come upon you; and you shall be witnesses to Me in Jerusalem, and in all Judea and Samaria, and to the end of the earth." Now when He had spoken these things, while they watched, He was taken up, and a cloud received Him out of their sight. And while they looked steadfastly toward heaven as He went up, behold, two men stood by them in white apparel, who also said, "Men of Galilee, why do you stand gazing up into heaven? This same Jesus, who was taken up from you into heaven, will so come in like manner as you saw Him go into heaven."

A Bright Beginning

SCRIPTURE READING: Acts 1:1–14   KEY VERSE: Acts 1:8

You shall receive power when the Holy Spirit has come upon you; and you shall be witnesses to Me in Jerusalem, and in all Judea and Samaria, and to the end of the earth.

The Crucifixion left the disciples stunned and bewildered. When they were sure all hope was gone, Jesus came to them. All that He had told them was true! He was with them again, only this time it was even better. Then came the day that He returned to heaven.

The Bible tells us that the group gathered at Christ's ascension stood gazing into heaven. Do you wonder what they were thinking? Whatever it was, God knew they needed immediate direction and hope.

Two angels appeared and spoke to them, "Men of Galilee, why do you stand gazing up into heaven? This same Jesus, who was taken up from you into heaven, will so come in like manner as you saw Him go into heaven" (Acts 1:11).

As they dispersed and went back to their homes, Jesus' last words filled their thoughts: "You shall be witnesses to Me in Jerusalem, and in all Judea and Samaria, and to the end of the earth" (Acts 1:8).

They had heard the words of Christ and understood His desire, yet it took angels from heaven to move the disciples to the next step.

Don't let the disappointments of this world discourage you. What you see as an ending, God sees as a bright and glorious beginning. Therefore, as you go, share His love and hope with everyone.

Dear heavenly Father, I thank You for endings that are really new beginnings. Help me move on by faith to take the next step.

A Message of Hope

SCRIPTURE READING: Philippians 1:19–24   KEY VERSE: Philippians 1:20

According to my earnest expectation and hope that in nothing I shall be ashamed, but with all boldness, as always, so now also Christ will be magnified in my body, whether by life or by death.

Upon entering a city, Paul immediately went into the local temple, synagogue, or meeting place to present the gospel message to the Jews. However, his words were often met with anger and rejection. But God did not allow Paul to suffer disgrace.

He had given the Jewish people a promise: He would send Messiah to them for their redemption. Over the years their hearts had hardened. In piety they worshiped God but refused His offer of redemption. Going through the motions of worship cannot save anyone.

Israel missed God's greatest gift of love when they rejected the Lord Jesus Christ. The years they spent in suffering were meant to draw them closer to God. Yet even this bitter fate did not move them to heartfelt worship.

When you live above the hardness of your circumstances as Paul did, God will protect and keep you. He will also preserve the message of hope He has commanded you to take to a lost and dying world. Don't let others' criticism keep you from obeying God. When you feel discouraged, go to Him. Ask Him to plant Scripture in your heart, so you may experience His hope in desperate times.

Dear Lord, plant Your Word in my heart, so I can experience Your hope in desperate times. Use me for Your purposes.

The Hope of His Return

SCRIPTURE READING: Matthew 25:1–13   KEY VERSE: Luke 21:36

Watch therefore, and pray always that you may be counted worthy to escape all these things that will come to pass, and to stand before the Son of Man.

Books about dying and life after death regularly make the best-seller list. Major periodicals, even media specials, examine the possibility of an afterlife and how we should handle it. Such concern, however, is not unusual. From the earliest empires to today's high-tech world, people have pondered questions about life after death.

Outside God's analysis, everything else is only guesswork. While many devise theories concerning future events, there is only one source of truth—the Word of God—and we turn to its authority when it comes to eschatology.

In God's Word we find that Jesus instructs us to watch, pray, and prepare for His return (Matt. 25:1–13). No one knows the hour or the day, but we do know that it will happen just as He has said.

Paul did not want these believers to feel uninformed or to "sorrow as others who have no hope" (1 Thess. 4:13–17). Rather, because of Christ's death and resurrection, he wanted them to look forward to being with Jesus one day soon.

We have this same sure hope today. Those who know God's Son as their Savior shall always be with the Lord. You rest in this fact: Jesus will return for you. The world cannot offer the peace that this one truth brings.

Lord, thank You for the hope of Your soon return. I look forward to the day that I will be with You forever.

God's Delay

SCRIPTURE READING: 2 Peter 3:9–13   KEY VERSE: 1 Corinthians 16:13

Watch, stand fast in the faith, be brave, be strong.

The rapture of the church, the second coming of Christ, and the judgment seat of Christ have long been subjects of much debate among Christians. Varying thoughts about when the church will be raptured abound.

However, you can trust this fact: Jesus will do exactly what He promised. He will return for you. It is easy to see how misconstrued theologies often obscure the impact of God's will for our lives.

Immediately following Paul's clarification of the rapture to the Thessalonian church is an exhortation for them to return to faithful, vibrant, sober living. The Thessalonians had been focused on the rapture and were worried that they might have missed it. Many of them had stopped working. In essence, Paul wrote to tell them to go back to work—to be watchful and not lazy.

Paul was not the only apostle to encounter this type of error concerning future events. Peter dealt with false teaching and realized the deadly threat it presented to the young church. In his second letter, Peter admonished his readers to be diligent in their faith and to remember that God is not slow in keeping His promise (2 Peter 3:9).

Warren Wiersbe observed, "God's 'delay' is actually an indication that He has a plan for this world and that He is working His plan." Remain watchful and prayerful in all you do.

> *Lord, help me remain watchful and prayerful as I await Your return. Help me live faithfully, vibrantly, and soberly while I wait.*

The Rapture

SCRIPTURE READING: 1 Cor. 15:50–57   KEY VERSES: 1 Cor. 15:1–2

Moreover, brethren, I declare to you the gospel which I preached to you, which also you received and in which you stand, by which also you are saved, if you hold fast that word which I preached to you— unless you believed in vain.

No one knows the actual date of Christ's return; only God knows that for sure. Not even the most renowned theologians know when Christ will return to earth. There are theories. Some Christian scholars even try to set dates. But none of this is God's goal in telling us to watch for His Son's return. Throughout history, God has faithfully given promises to mankind so that as His plan of redemption unfolds, man can have something of lasting hope to cling to.

The end result of the rapture is to bring the saints of God into a place of eternal fellowship and worship with the Father. There is no way to adequately describe the hope this future event offers to the heart of every believer who ponders its truth. One day soon, we will see Jesus face-to-face.

However, for now, the words of Christ call us to action: "Take heed; keep on the alert." How are you watching for Christ's return? In waiting, refuse to become complacent but remain alert. God is using this interlude in time to ready His church for this glorious event. Satan is busy gathering his forces for the final day.

Therefore, guard your heart. Tell others of the hope that is to come. Avail yourself to God, and keep one eye lifted toward the eastern sky because one day very soon He will return for you.

Prepare me for Your return, dear Lord. Don't let me become complacent. Help me remain alert.

A Refuge and Rock

SCRIPTURE READING: Psalm 18:1–6   KEY VERSE: Proverbs 23:19

Hear, my son, and be wise;
And guide your heart in the way.

K ing David often used words such as *refuge* and *rock* to explain his relationship with God. For him, God was a refuge—a place where he could go anytime to find encouragement and understanding.

Encouragement and hope are crucial to our well-being, especially when we
deal with the pressures of this world. Before we know it, we can become
drained mentally and physically and wonder, from whence comes our help?
(Ps. 121:1). The psalmist continued,

My help comes from the LORD,
Who made heaven and earth.
He will not allow your foot to be moved;
He who keeps you will not slumber. (vv. 2–3)

If your hope is in anything other than Jesus Christ, it is temporal hope and
will not last because our world changes daily. It is passing away.

People come and go. Disappointments can leave us floundering and wondering how we ever got into such positions. But God is tenacious in His affections toward us.

Nothing is too small for you to bring to Him in prayer. He has the answer
you seek to every question. Solving problems on your own leads only to more
frustration and wrong decisions.

Lord, I thank You that You have the answer to all my questions, the provi-
sion for all my needs. You are my refuge and rock.

Things to Come

SCRIPTURE READING: Revelation 1:1–3   KEY VERSE: Revelation 1:8

"I am the Alpha and the Omega, the Beginning and the End," says
the Lord, "who is and who was and who is to come, the Almighty."

Maybe the book of Revelation is one of those books you've avoided. You tried, but you felt bogged down in mysterious symbolism or frightening visions of coming devastation. Many Christians admit they do not understand its applicability to their lives.

The apostle John, who was exiled on the island of Patmos in the first century A.D. during the reign of the Roman emperor Domitian, received a vision from an angel of the Lord. From the start, John was emphatic about the relevance and value of every word: "Blessed is he who reads and those who hear words of this prophecy, and keep those things which are written in it; for the time is near" (Rev. 1:3).

Why is it so important to understand the end time and the events that will culminate in Christ's return to earth? Why isn't it enough to trust the Lord with the outcome and not worry about the specifics? Jesus wants you to have the whole story. When you understand the magnitude and scope of His plan for all mankind, you gain a realistic perception of your important place in the grand scheme of redemption.

God wants you to be prepared for the things to come, and He doesn't want you to worry about the upheaval of this age. He is in perfect control. Be sure to take time to tell others of the love and forgiveness of Jesus Christ.

Dear heavenly Father, thank You for Your plan of redemption that includes
me. Prepare me for the things to come. Give me hope for the future.

His Mighty Arms

SCRIPTURE READING: Revelation 1:19–20   KEY VERSE: Revelation 1:17

When I saw Him, I fell at His feet as dead. But He laid His right hand on me, saying to me, "Do not be afraid; I am the First and the Last."

John wasn't accustomed to seeing Jesus as he did in the overpowering, apocalyptic vision of Revelation.

His memory stretched back to a time when he had walked and talked with the Lord. During Jesus' ministry on earth, His human appearance was absolutely ordinary. He interacted with people, listening to them and talking with them about the Father.

Imagine how stunned John was when Jesus appeared to him on the isle of Patmos. The Bible tells us that Christ's head and His hair were white like white wool, like snow; and "His eyes like a flame of fire . . . He had in His right hand seven stars, out of His mouth went a sharp two-edged sword" (Rev. 1:14, 16).

Not surprisingly, John reacted in the same way he did at the Transfiguration—he fell down, overcome with terror. But in His unchanging mercy and tenderness, Jesus comforted John with the same reassurance: "He laid His right hand on me, saying to me, 'Do not be afraid'" (Rev. 1:17).

Jesus' intent is never to terrify or exercise tyrannical authority. He came to save and forgive you. His goal is to bring eternal comfort, hope, and restoration to your heart. He chooses to display His awe-inspiring majesty to demonstrate His true godhood and ability to save. This is the Jesus who welcomes you into His almighty arms.

Lord, thank You for the gifts of Your eternal comfort, hope, and restoration. I lean upon Your mighty arms today.

Take It to the Cross

SCRIPTURE READING: Revelation 6:1–17   KEY VERSE: Revelation 6:17

For the great day of His wrath has come, and who is able to stand?

In 1498, artist Albrecht Durer created his masterpiece woodcutting called *The Four Horsemen of the Apocalypse*, a rendering of the horsemen described in Revelation 6. One look at this vivid picture, with the wild-eyed riders wielding swords and trampling people underfoot, conveys a sense of the horror and swiftness of God's coming judgment on those who reject Jesus as their Savior.

These horsemen are not figments of the apostle John's imagination, but the very real agents of destruction who will arrive during the seven-year period of the Tribulation. Each represents a set of events not described in detail in this passage, yet they are actual beings whom God will send on a deadly mission.

Terrible as they will be, not everyone will fear the horsemen. Many will remain unrepentant. Instead of falling on their faces, crying out for mercy, these rebellious people will seek the futile option of escape—the same choice many make today when confronted with the truth about Jesus.

God does not reveal events in order to threaten or intimidate. He simply wants you to heed His warning while there is still time. Today, ask Him to reveal to you anything that is standing in the way of your having a whole-hearted devotion toward Him. Whatever He shows you, take it to the Cross, and receive His forgiveness and mercy.

Father, please reveal to me anything that is standing in the way of my wholehearted devotion toward You. I want to take it to Your cross and receive Your forgiveness and mercy.

Praise Him for the Future

SCRIPTURE READING: Matthew 24:3–25   KEY VERSE: Matthew 24:25

See, I have told you beforehand.

During a quiet moment alone with the disciples, someone asked Jesus, "What will be the sign of Your coming?" (Matt. 24:3). Christ's answer was meant for us as much as it was for the disciples.

He told His followers of the coming of a Great Tribulation, one that will usher in the end of things as we know them. It will be a time when Satan has great advantage over the earth. People will turn from God, and many will refuse to believe in His Son as the Savior of the world.

There are different interpretations of the end times. However, one thing is sure: Christ will return for His church. He will gather to Himself those who believe in Him, and together they will reign in the kingdom of God.

Jesus' words were meant to be encouraging and not a point of argument. He wanted His followers to be prepared for the future. In telling them about the end times, He sought to provide insight, warning of the things to come, and comfort in the fact that He would always be near them.

God warns us not to be slothful in our devotion to Him, but to live holy and pure lives. He comforts us when we hurt so we will not become discouraged.

There has never been, nor will there be, a time when God is not aware of your needs. When you think about the future, praise Him for His soon and sure return.

Heavenly Father, I praise You for the insight, warning of things to come, and comfort for the future that Your Word gives me. I praise You for Your soon and sure return.

An Invitation to Life

SCRIPTURE READING: Psalm 103:1–8   KEY VERSE: Revelation 9:20

The rest of mankind, who were not killed by these plagues, did not repent of the works of their hands, that they should not worship demons, and idols of gold, silver, brass, stone, and wood, which can neither see nor hear nor walk.

Some people have great difficulty reconciling the truth that a God who shows great mercy is the same God who allows incomprehensible destruction. To make sense of these events, we must understand the character and nature of God. He is absolutely loving. He sent His Son, Jesus Christ, to die on the cross as payment for the sins that doom every one of us to death. Jesus is the embodiment of love and mercy.

When we reject God's love, He respects our choice and allows us to experience the consequences that come as a result of going against the sovereign God of the universe. However, until He comes again as reigning King and sovereign Judge, Jesus is committed to offering His salvation to a lost and dying world. He knocks at the door of every heart.

The judgments of the Tribulation period are in keeping with this purpose. It seems hard to imagine that any human being could remain unmoved by these tragedies, but notice the response that comes from those who do escape death during this dark hour: "The rest of mankind, who were not killed by these plagues, did not repent of the works of their hands" (Rev. 9:20).

No one wants to face such terrors, and that is why responding to Jesus' invitation of eternal life is a matter for the present. Reward and blessing await those who accept Him as their Savior.

Thank You for the invitation to eternal life, Lord. I accept, knowing I can face the future with joyful anticipation.

A Role Reversal

SCRIPTURE READING: Luke 16:19–31   KEY VERSE: Hebrews 9:27

As it is appointed for men to die once, but after this the judgment.

What a role reversal! The poor man who once begged bread beside the rich man's table is with God forever, and the rich man is in perpetual torment in Hades. It's quite a stark image.

Jesus wasn't emphasizing the difference between rich and poor, however. He was calling attention to the decisions they made in life. The rich man was so caught up in his wealth that he had no concern for his spiritual well-being. Even the presence of the poor man at his gate was not enough to stir his conscience and move him to compassion.

The verse that is the most gripping in this whole sad scene is the one in which the rich man cried out to Father Abraham for relief. Abraham replied, "And besides all this, between us and you there is a great gulf fixed, so that those who want to pass from here to you cannot, nor can these from there pass to us" (Luke 16:26).

In other words, there were no more chances. The rich man's place in Hades was permanent and unchanging. His chance to make a decision to seek God was when he was still alive, and he turned a deaf ear. Part of his torture was living with eternal regret.

Are you putting off thinking about God until a better time? That "better time" might not come. Jesus is waiting to hear from you right now—don't put off the decision any longer. Ask Him to come into your heart.

Dear Lord Jesus, come into my heart. Prepare me for eternity. Give me hope for the future.

The Unchanging Promises

SCRIPTURE READING: 1 John 4:1–6   KEY VERSE: 1 John 2:22

Who is a liar but he who denies that Jesus is the Christ? He is antichrist who denies the Father and the Son.

The Antichrist will be a very real person someday. He will enter as a peacemaker and exit as Satan in human form, banished to eternal torment by Jesus Christ. You can be certain that the victory Jesus secured almost two thousand years ago will extend to eternity.

The subject of the Antichrist sometimes scares Christians into less-threatening areas of study. But because you have accepted Christ as Savior, you are assured you will never endure the atrocities of the Antichrist's reign during the Tribulation period. Jesus will have raptured you home before the Antichrist assumes power for seven years.

Yet today there exists the spirit of antichrist—that is, all things anti-Christian (1 John 2:18). As you sometimes strain to happily exist in an evil world system, remember the work and counsel of your Lord and Savior. Jesus promises that all authority has been given Him in heaven and earth and that He is with you always, even to the end of the age (Matt. 28:18–20).

Fortified with the unchanging promises of Jesus, you can remain steadfast in your faith, unbending and uncompromising in the face of temptation, oppression, and adversity. In a quickly dying world, live for Jesus. Be excited by the assurance that during the wicked reign of the Antichrist, you will be looking down on him.

O Lord, I praise You for Your unchanging promises. Help me remain steadfast in my faith, unbending and uncompromising in the face of temptation, oppression, and adversity.

The White Throne Judgment

SCRIPTURE READING: Revelation 20:11–15   KEY VERSE: Matthew 25:41

Then He will also say to those on the left hand, "Depart from Me, you cursed, into the everlasting fire prepared for the devil and his angels."

At the White Throne of Judgment, those who have rejected Jesus Christ will stand before God and be judged for their sins. This judgment is not to be confused with the believers' judgment where God rewards those who have placed their trust in Christ.

Warren Wiersbe stated,

> Hell is a witness to the righteous character of God. He must judge sin. Hell is also a witness to man's responsibility, the fact that he is not a robot or a helpless victim, but a creature able to make choices. God does not "send people to hell"; they send themselves by rejecting the Savior (Matthew 25:41; John 3:16–21). Hell is also a witness to the awfulness of sin. If we once saw sin as God sees it, we would understand why a place such as hell exists.
>
> In the light of Calvary, no lost sinner can condemn God for casting him into hell. God has provided a way of escape, patiently waiting for sinners to repent. He will not lower His standards or alter His requirements. He has ordained that faith in His Son is the only way of salvation . . .
>
> At the White Throne, there will be a Judge but no jury, a prosecution but no defense, a sentence but no appeal. No one will be able to defend himself or accuse God of unrighteousness. What an awesome scene it will be!

However, you can be saved right now. By placing your trust in Jesus Christ, hell will no longer be your future destiny.

Heavenly Father, I praise You for the security that comes from knowing my future destiny. Thank You for Your gift of salvation.

Our Eternal Home

SCRIPTURE READING: 2 Corinthians 5:1–9   KEY VERSE: 2 Corinthians 5:1

For we know that if our earthly house, this tent, is destroyed, we have a building from God, a house not made with hands, eternal in the heavens.

There is something special about home. Built on God's wisdom, it is a refuge from the storm, a greenhouse for maturity and growth, a haven of unconditional love. During special seasons, such as Thanksgiving and Christmas, home is a magnet, attracting adults back to their childhood roots with warm simplicity.

That is what makes heaven so wonderful. It is not just a place of pearly gates, golden streets, and angelic hosts. It is more than tearless perfection, sheer ecstasy, and freedom from all want. It is home—blissful, sweet, unending, eternal, blessed home.

At last we can end our earthly pilgrimage, lay down our burdens and pain, kick off our shoes of suffering, and rest forever in our eternal abode. Even now our hearts yearn for home. Home is where the heart is, and the man who has given his life to Jesus has transferred the deed of his heart to Christ. He is our Owner, and He is preparing a place for us in heaven that we can finally call home.

Enjoy your present home and its delights now. But remember, your dream home is in heaven, awaiting those who have built their lives on the foundation of Christ's death, burial, and resurrection.

Lord, Thank You for Your promise of an eternal home.

Evaluation and Reward

SCRIPTURE READING: Romans 7:18–25 KEY VERSE: Genesis 18:25

Far be it from You to do such a thing as this, to slay the righteous with the wicked, so that the righteous should be as the wicked; far be it from You! Shall not the Judge of all the earth do right?

Concerning the judgment of God, theologian Henry Thiessen explains,

> The whole philosophy of the future judgments rests upon the sovereign right of God to punish disobedience and the personal right of the individual to plead his case in court. Though God is sovereign, as judge of all the earth, he will do right (Genesis 18:25). He will do this not in order to submit to an external law, but as the expression of his own character.
>
> The individual will have the opportunity to show why he acted as he did and to know the reasons for his sentence. These are fundamental factors in every righteous government. Insofar as human governments follow this order, they are imitating God's methods of government.

God's judgment always fits the crime. He never responds to sin out of His character. His first desire is to save you so that you might enjoy His fellowship for eternity.

In Revelation 16, the judgment of God is poured out on the earth because man has chosen another way—a way opposed to God. In Romans 7:24, Paul asked, "Who will deliver me from this body of death?" The answer: only the Lord Jesus Christ (Rom. 7:25)!

Judgment for the believer is a time of evaluation and reward, but for the nonbeliever it is the beginning of eternal death.

Lord, I praise You for the future You have planned for me—eternal life in Your presence. Help me live today with that hope in mind.

The Ultimate Victory

SCRIPTURE READING: Revelation 19:1–8   KEY VERSE: John 16:33

*These things I have spoken to you, that in Me you may have peace.
In the world you will have tribulation; but be of good cheer, I have
overcome the world.*

Jesus Christ has been ascribed many fitting names. He is the Lamb of God, sacrificed for our sins. But He also is the Lion of Judah, and someday in one cataclysmic moment His power will roar in immeasurable volume.

In one instant at his second Coming, Jesus will return to earth not as a gentle, nurturing Savior but as victorious Judge, Ruler, King, and Lord. He will destroy the evil world system propagated by the Antichrist and will bind Satan and cast him into hell. It is an absolute done deal!

Those who have aligned themselves with Christ through the ages, meaning those who have accepted Him as Savior, are assured victory. After the Tribulation period, the raptured church will return with Jesus and live on a new earth for one thousand years before joining Jesus in heaven for eternity.

If it all seems overwhelming, focus on the one constant: Jesus. Allow Him to be your Guide through earth and eternity.

Make the assurance of His ultimate victory a motivation to serve Him while you remain in this world. Think of one person you can tell about Jesus today. Now imagine how indescribably rewarding it would be to meet that person in heaven and realize God used you to help get him there. All of your praise and honor is due the Lord.

Heavenly Father, please use me today to tell others about You. Help me direct others to Your Son, Jesus Christ.

God's Guarantee

SCRIPTURE READING: **Revelation 21:1–7**   KEY VERSE: **Hebrews 11:3**

By faith we understand that the worlds were framed by the word of God, so that the things which are seen were not made of things which are visible.

Have you ever known the frustration of canceled hotel reservations? Sometimes even the "guaranteed late arrival" system isn't foolproof. You hustle through two airports, fumble with bags all the way, grab a rental car, drive through unfamiliar territory, and finally make it to the hotel, only to hear the clerk say, "I'm sorry, but no rooms are available."

When Jesus told His disciples about His impending departure, He gave them special assurance for the future: "In My Father's house are many mansions; if it were not so, I would have told you. I go to prepare a place for you" (John 14:2). This promise was not for the disciples only; it is for everyone who accepts Jesus as Savior and trusts Him for salvation.

Your name is written in the Lamb's Book of Life, and it cannot be erased (Rev. 21:27). Your reservation in heaven can never be changed, and the place Jesus is making ready is custom-made just for you. In fact, you are supposed to consider heaven your real home; earth is a mere way station.

Hebrews 11:13 notes that the heroes of faith regarded themselves as "strangers and pilgrims on the earth" because they were so focused on the end of their temporary journey here. You have God's guarantee: no mansion on earth can compare to the eternal home waiting for you.

Dear Father, thank You for the guarantee of a place reserved for me for eternity. I'm on my way!

Our Heavenly Home

SCRIPTURE READING: Revelation 22:6–21   KEY VERSE: 1 Corinthians 2:9

As it is written: "Eye has not seen, nor ear heard,
Nor have entered into the heart of man
The things which God has prepared for those who love Him."

In *The Pilgrim's Progress*, a spiritual allegory written in the mid-1670s, the characters Christian and Hopeful finally get a glimpse of their heavenly home. Here is John Bunyan's vision of what they saw when they arrived:

Now they went along together toward the gate. Though the Celestial City stood on a great high hill, the pilgrims went up the hill with perfect ease because of the two heavenly ones leading them by the arms . . . They ascended through the regions of the air, joyously conversing as they went . . . Their conversation was about the glory of the place, which the shining ones termed inexpressible . . .

When they drew near the gate, they were met by a company of the heavenly host . . . The heavenly host gave a joyous hallelujah, saying, "Blessed are those who are invited to the wedding supper of the Lamb!" There also came out several of the king's trumpeters to welcome the pilgrims with heavenly music. Then they walked on together to the gate.

When they came to the gate leading to the City they saw written over it in letters of gold: "Blessed are they that do His commandments, that they may have the right to the tree of life, and may go through the gates into the city."

Human words are inadequate to describe the matchless joy God has for you now and in future times.

O Lord, I am looking forward to what You have planned for me in the future. Thank You for the joys that lay ahead.

The Glory to Come

SCRIPTURE READING: Revelation 22:1–5   KEY VERSE: John 14:27

Peace I leave with you, My peace I give to you; not as the world gives do I give to you. Let not your heart be troubled, neither let it be afraid.

You may not consider yourself to have a very active imagination, and fantasy stories may hold little attraction for you. But the scene unfolded in this passage of Revelation is no fairy tale. Heaven, a place of such wonder and beauty, may be beyond your immediate comprehension, but it is as real as the chair you are sitting in right now.

Every detail is worth savoring, even though this picture is only a shadow of what you will experience. There will no longer be the loneliness that comes from darkness, the curse of sin, tears shed, pain felt, or the anxiety of fear. Jesus will be your Light and secure comfort. He will wipe away every tear and end all anxious thoughts.

Heaven is the absolute, unending presence of almighty God: "There shall be no night there. They need no lamp nor light of the sun, the Lord God gives them light. And they shall reign forever and ever" (Rev. 22:5).

It may not seem relevant to dwell on the glory to come, but you need this hope to keep your perspective. When you have "heavenly vision," then heartache, disappointments, and difficulties assume their place—under the light and authority of an eternal Lord who lives in the lives of those who believe in Him through the power of the Holy Spirit. Be at peace today because He is with you.

You are with me today. I am at peace. Thank You, Father.

True Contentment

SCRIPTURE READING: John 4:3–18   KEY VERSES: John 4:13–14

Jesus answered and said to her, "Whoever drinks of this water will thirst again, but whoever drinks of the water that I shall give him will never thirst. But the water that I shall give him will become in him a fountain of water springing up into everlasting life."

In talking to the woman at the well, Jesus spoke of life-giving water. The water of the world can never satisfy the God-shaped void that is in the heart of each lost person. However, there is an even starker reality: even after we become believers, the things of the world cannot bring true, lasting contentment. No matter how much money we have, we are never satisfied apart from Jesus Christ.

He waters your heart with His unfailing hope. He fills you with His blessed presence so that you do not fear as the world fears. He comforts you in times of sorrow and holds you close when disappointment and rejection strike. He is your ever-present Savior and Lord.

God does not want you to live a life that feels empty and unrewarding. When you feel either of these, you may end up taking great risks with the hopes that something along the way will fill the void inside. The woman at the well had tried in vain to find true happiness. Yet nothing worked before she met the Savior.

Today, Jesus stands waiting to touch your life with fresh hope. Drink of Him, and be blessed by His unconditional love for you.

Dear Lord, thank You for Your unfailing hope that waters my heart. Thank You for Your presence that alleviates my fears. Thank You for Your comfort in times of sorrow.

An Assured Destiny

SCRIPTURE READING: Revelation 9:11–21   KEY VERSE: Revelation 9:11

They had as king over them the angel of the bottomless pit, whose name in Hebrew is Abaddon, but in Greek he has the name Apollyon.

William Bradbury's song, "The Solid Rock," underscores the faith and hope we have in Jesus Christ:

> My hope is built on nothing less than Jesus' blood and righteousness;
> I dare not trust the sweetest frame, but wholly lean on Jesus' name.
> When darkness veils his lovely face, I rest on his unchanging grace;
> In every high and stormy gale, my anchor holds within the veil.
> When he shall come with trumpet sound, O may I then in him be found.
> Dressed in his righteousness alone, faultless to stand before the throne.
> On Christ, the solid rock, I stand;
> All other ground is sinking sand,
> All other ground is sinking sand.

Our world is one of turmoil and grief. And if we're not careful, we will begin to wonder whether God has forgotten His promises to us, but He never does. He knows us perfectly and is preparing us for that glorious day when He will return and gather us unto Himself.

The other part of His return is His triumph over the Beast and the False Prophet (Rev. 19). Revelation makes it clear that the victory belongs to Jesus Christ, and we should never be discouraged by the sorrows of the world.

The surest place to be found is in the care of God's Son. He is not only your future hope; He is also your present help in every situation. He is your solid Rock.

O God, You are not only my future hope—You are my present help in every situation. I praise You that because of this, I can walk in victory today.

Satan's Last Fling

SCRIPTURE READING: Revelation 20:1–10   KEY VERSE: Revelation 20:10

The devil, who deceived them, was cast into the lake of fire and brimstone where the beast and the false prophet are. And they will be tormented day and night forever and ever.

Satan began his war on mankind in the Garden of Eden when he convinced Eve not to trust God. He works to pervert God's truth at every opportunity, even though he knows his doom is coming. God said,

> I will put enmity
> Between you and the woman,
> And between your seed and her Seed;
> He shall bruise your head,
> And you shall bruise His heel.

God was telling Satan that even though He would allow him to be free for a time, working on his foul plots, one day his head would be crushed by the ultimate Seed of the woman, the Messiah, Jesus Christ.

Years later, the apostle John received a more complete picture of Satan's future in a special, revelatory vision from God: "He [an angel] laid hold of the dragon, that serpent of old, who is the Devil and Satan, and bound him for a thousand years; and he cast him into the bottomless pit, and shut him up, and set a seal on him . . . till the thousand years were finished. But after these things he must be released for a little while" (Rev. 20:2–3). After the short time of release, Satan will be cast for eternity into the lake of fire.

The comfort for you as a believer is that Satan's power is limited. God determines how long he will be allowed to continue his evil. Your hope is in the Messiah who defeated him once and for all at the cross.

Lord, I am so thankful that these difficult times will not be forever. You have limited Satan's power, and I will be victorious in the end.

The Exalted Lord of Revelation

SCRIPTURE READING: Revelation 5:1–14   KEY VERSE: John 1:29

The next day John saw Jesus coming toward him, and said, "Behold! The Lamb of God who takes away the sin of the world!"

Lambs were significant for the people of Israel. When they fled Egypt, they put the blood of lambs on their doorframes as a sign of belonging to God (Ex. 12). They had to kill a perfect lamb as a sacrifice for certain sins.

Sheep were stock animals, common, somewhat dirty, and not known for their intelligence. Many must have reacted with surprise when John the Baptist said to Jesus, "Behold! The Lamb of God who takes away the sin of the world!" (John 1:29). He did not look like a lamb, and few understood at that point that Jesus Himself would die as a sacrifice for sin.

Revelation 5 describes an even more amazing picture of the Lamb: "And I [the apostle John] looked, and behold, in the midst of the throne and of the four living creatures, and in the midst of the elders, stood a Lamb as though it had been slain, having seven horns and seven eyes, which are the seven Spirits of God sent out into all the earth" (v. 6).

This image is beyond our human understanding; it is full of awe-inspiring power and mystery and might. The Lamb who died is now glorified, reigning over all His creation as its true Master. Christ the Lamb is to be worshiped and revered. It is no wonder that hosts of angels praise Him saying,

> Worthy is the Lamb who was slain
> To receive power and riches and wisdom,
> And strength and honor and glory and blessing! (Rev. 5:12)

You are worthy, O Lord, to receive power, riches, wisdom, strength, honor, glory and blessing!

The Greatest Gift

Therefore the Lord Himself will give you a sign: Behold, the virgin shall conceive and bear a Son, and shall call His name Immanuel.

Many parents know the feeling of wanting to buy just the right Christmas gifts for their children. It can seem almost an obligation, especially if there has been some sort of promise, expressed or implied.

Parents can get into a quandary if they can't deliver the precise gifts, and many times they compromise and buy something similar in hopes of appeasement. Actually, the entire exercise can be a lesson in how the world has skewed the real message of Christmas.

Part of the real message of Christmas is about promising a gift. But God made the promise and, in His infinite love delivered His Son, Jesus Christ. Consider today's Bible verse, and then turn to Isaiah 9:6–7. Also read Micah 5:2.

These are just a few of the dozens of Old Testament prophecies foretelling that God would send His Son to earth. In other places, such as Psalm 22 and Isaiah 53, the Old Testament details how God's Son would die on the cross for our sins. God kept His promise in the birth of Jesus, who fulfilled every prophecy to the letter.

The prophecies in Isaiah and Micah occurred seven hundred years before Jesus was born. Through His honored promises, we can know that, two thousand years after the birth of Jesus, God is faithful. After all, He gave us the greatest Gift ever.

Dear heavenly Father, I pause on this special day to give You thanks for Your greatest Gift—Your Son, Jesus Christ.

The Rapture of the Church

SCRIPTURE READING: 1 Thessalonians 4:13–17   KEY VERSE: Romans 1:4

And declared to be the Son of God with power according to the Spirit of holiness, by the resurrection from the dead.

Books about life after death regularly make the bestsellers' list. Major periodicals, even media specials, examine the possibility of an afterlife and how we should handle it.

Such concern, however, is not unusual. From the earliest empires to today's high tech world, questions about death and dying have been pondered by critical thinkers and common man.

However, the analysis and conclusions of each generation are only guesswork apart from the one authoritative element—the death, burial, and resurrection of God's Son. Christ, who was God during his ministry on earth, demonstrated His absolute deity and power over death when He rose from the dead (Romans 1:4).

In his letter to the Thessalonian church, Paul emphasized the importance of Christ's resurrection. He did not want them to be uninformed or to grieve, as do the rest who have no hope (1 Thessalonians 4:13).

Rather, because of Christ's death and resurrection (verse 14), they could look forward to being with Christ forever and seeing their loved ones who had died in Christ (verses 17–18).

It is the same sure hope we have today. Those who know Christ shall always be with the Lord (verse 17). This is a fact in which you can find extravagant comfort. The world has no counter offer.

Father, thank You for the comfort that comes from knowing I will see You and my loved ones. I praise You for this eternal hope.

Come, Lord Jesus

SCRIPTURE READING: 1 Thessalonians 5:4–8   KEY VERSE: Revelation 22:20

He who testifies to these things says, "Surely I am coming quickly."
Amen. Even so, come, Lord Jesus!

The rapture of the church, the second coming of Christ, the judgment seat of Christ—these and other doctrines of things to come often are the subject of much debate among Christians.

However, the variant theologies developed around these future events often obscure the impact of God's will for our lives in the here and now. Immediately following Paul's clarification of the rapture to the Thessalonican church is an exhortation to faithful, vibrant, sober living for the daily routine (1 Thessalonians 5:5–8).

When Peter discussed a new material order for the universe at Christ's second coming, he couched it with this plea: "What manner of persons ought you to be in holy conduct and godliness?" (2 Peter 3:11).

This is the crux of all revelation concerning the return of Christ. Since we have such a tremendous destiny, what a difference it should make in our behavior, motivation, and priorities.

Why should we place such a significant value on the accumulation of things if we can take nothing with us into Christ's presence? Since His return is imminent, refuse to set any goals without relying on His input.

The return of Christ is a sure fact. He is coming back for His church. Are there changes you should make so that your heart's cry may honestly be, "Come, Lord Jesus" (Rev. 22:20).

Come, Lord Jesus! That is my heart's cry today.

Waiting for His Return

SCRIPTURE READING: Luke 12:37–48   KEY VERSE: Luke 12:40

Therefore you also be ready, for the Son of Man is coming at an hour you do not expect.

The second coming of Jesus Christ is fact. However, as for the actual date of His return, only God knows that for sure. Not even the most renowned theologians know when Christ will return to earth.

There are theories. Some even try to set dates. But none of this is God's goal in telling us to watch for His Son's return. Throughout history, God has faithfully given promises to mankind so that as His plan of redemption unfolds, there is something of lasting hope to cling to.

The end result of the rapture is to bring the saints of God into a place of eternal fellowship and worship with the Father. There is no way to adequately describe the hope this future event offers to the heart of every believer who ponders its truth. One day soon we will see Him face to face.

However, for now, the words of Christ call us to action. "Take heed, keep on the alert." How are you watching for Christ's return? In your waiting, refuse to become complacent but remain alert. While God is using this interlude in time to ready His church for this glorious event, Satan is busy gathering his forces for the final day.

Therefore, guard your heart. Tell others of the hope that is to come. Avail yourself to God and keep one eye lifted toward the eastern sky, because one day very soon He will return for you.

Dear Lord, keep me alert. Make me ready for Your return. Help me keep my spiritual eyes on the eastern sky.

Using Today for His Glory

SCRIPTURE READING: 2 Timothy 2:1–7   KEY VERSE: 2 Timothy 2:15

Be diligent to present yourself approved to God, a worker who does not need to be ashamed, rightly dividing the word of truth.

Most of us have heard a grandparent or older person talk of the second coming of Christ. The sense of longing conveyed in his voice reminds us of the deep desire that God has placed within each believer to finally one day behold His perfect love and glory. Yet now we are called to wait, not as forgotten men and women, but as commissioned soldiers (2 Tim. 2:3–4) with one purpose, and that is to tell as many people as possible of His unconditional love and forgiveness.

This is what the apostle Paul instructed Timothy to do: "Be diligent to present yourself approved to God, a worker who does not need to be ashamed" (2 Tim. 2:15). Because of the violence of his society, no one was more aware of the persecution of the saints than Paul. Nor was there a man more attuned to the probability of discouragement.

When our hearts and minds are set on God's call and what we can do to accomplish it, we are less likely to get caught up in the hopelessness of our sin-riddled society. Paul's eyes were eternally focused. He had a sure hope planted within his heart—Jesus Christ would return.

While you wait for the Lord's return, make it your goal to tell as many as possible of the Savior's love and care. The rapture may come tomorrow, but as a believer you are given today to use for His glory.

Father, let me use today for Your glory. Show me the work You would have me do, then equip me to accomplish it.

The Reality of the Resurrection

SCRIPTURE READING: John 11:21–26   KEY VERSE: Hebrews 2:14

Inasmuch then as the children have partaken of flesh and blood, He Himself likewise shared in the same, that through death He might destroy him who had the power of death, that is, the devil.

The duke of Wellington once remarked that "man must be a coward or a liar who could boast of never having felt a fear of death."

Samuel Johnson, the British essayist, commented that "no rational man can die without uneasy apprehension."

While the prospect of death can create emotional conflict even for Christians (death is still our enemy, though a defeated one), the sure hope of the Resurrection settles our souls.

"Jesus Christ is able to set free even those who all their lives have been 'held in slavery by their fear of death,'" writes John Stott in *The Cross of Christ*.

This is because by his own death he has "destroyed" (deprived of power) "him who holds the power of death—that is, the devil" (Hebrews 2:14).

Christ had died for our sins and taken them away. With great disdain, therefore, Paul likens death to a scorpion whose sting has been drawn, and to a military conqueror whose power has been broken. Now that we are forgiven, death can harm us no longer.

So the apostle shouts defiantly: "Where, Oh death, is your victory? Where, Oh death, is your sting?" There is of course no reply.

Until Christ returns, we must face the physical and emotional pain of death. Yet our perplexity and fear can be displaced by the reality of the Resurrection, when death was overthrown.

Father, when I face the physical and emotional pain of separation from loved ones, help me realize that death is overshadowed by the reality of the Resurrection.

The Good News About Death

SCRIPTURE READING: 2 Corinthians 5:1–9   KEY VERSE: Acts 2:28

You have made known to me the ways of life;
You will make me full of joy in Your presence.

Christianity is the only religion in the world that has the final word on death. While other belief systems hypothesize about death, leading to such mysterious offerings as reincarnation, Christianity alone presents a clear and compelling portrait that is defined in the death and resurrection life of Jesus Christ.

Lawrence Richards writes,

> In view of the varied and terrible meanings that Scripture ascribes to death, it would be wrong to think of Jesus's death as a mere biological event. When the Bible teaches that Jesus suffered and tasted death (Hebrews 2:8), a full experience of all that death involves is implied . . . Death is the direct result of sin. And the fact of death testifies to the overwhelming importance of a personal, obedient relationship to God.
>
> The dying Christian has the calm assurance that biological ending is nothing but a new beginning. When our earthly tent is destroyed, we go to be with the Lord "so that what is mortal may be swallowed up by life" (2 Corinthians 5:4).

Jesus Christ, the Son of God, died for our sins and rose again from the dead. His resurrection is a historical fact, verified by the testimony of the Scriptures. It was impossible for death to reign over Him (Acts 2:28).

The last word about death is good news for Christians.

O Lord, thank You for taking the fear of death from me. I praise You that when my earthly tent is destroyed, I will be in Your presence.

About the Author

D r. Charles Stanley is pastor of the 14,000-member First Baptist Church in Atlanta, Georgia. He is well known through his *In Touch* radio and television ministry to thousands internationally and is the author of many books, including *On Holy Ground, Our Unmet Needs, Enter His Gates, The Source of My Strength, The Reason for My Hope, How to Listen to God,* and *How to Handle Adversity.*

Dr. Stanley received his bachelor of arts degree from the University of Richmond, his bachelor of divinity degree from Southwestern Theological Seminary, and his master's and doctor's degrees from Luther Rice Seminary. He has twice been elected president of the Southern Baptist Convention.

Other Best-Selling Books by Charles Stanley

Enter His Gates

Spiritual gates are much like the gates of a city. They are vital to your well-being as a Christian and, if not maintained, leave you open to attack by the enemy. *Enter His Gates* is a daily devotional that encourages you to build or strengthen a different spiritual gate each month.

0-7852-7546-0 • Hardcover • 400 pages • Devotional

In Touch with God

This unique gift book is filled with inspirational Scriptures as well as thoughts and prayers from Dr. Stanley. It will help you know God's heart on a variety of topics, including forgiveness, relationships, Spirit-filled living, Christian character, and God's plan for your life.

0-7852-7117-1 • Printed Hardcover • 208 pages • Gift/Devotional

On Holy Ground

This daily devotional contains a year's worth of spiritual adventures. Dr. Stanley uses the journeys of Paul, Ezra, Elijah, Abraham, and other heroes of the Bible and his own valuable insights to encourage you to step out in faith and allow God to lead you to new places.

0-7852-7662-9 • Hardcover • 400 pages • Devotional

The Power of the Cross

Using inspirational Scriptures as well as personal insights and heartfelt prayers, Charles Stanley encourages you to see the transforming power of the Resurrection for salvation, victory over temptation, healing of emotional pain, and restoration with the heavenly Father.

0-7852-7065-6 • Printed Hardcover • 208 pages • Gift/Devotional

The Reason for My Hope

Dr. Stanley shares his personal struggles to remain focused on Christ and keep hope alive in the middle of difficult circumstances. In his warm and insightful style, he reveals the promises and resources God provides His children, identifying nine key reasons for all believers to have unshakable hope.

0-8407-7765-5 • Hardcover • 256 pages • Christian Living